eKNOW 2022

The Fourteenth International Conference on Information, Process, and Knowledge Management

June 26th – 30th, 2022

Porto, Portugal

eKNOW 2022 Editors

Eric J.H.J. Mantelaers, Zuyd University of Applied Sciences, Sittard, the Netherlands

Samia Aitouche, Laboratory of Automation and Manufacturing (LAP), University Batna 2, Algeria

Printed from e-media with permission by:

Curran Associates, Inc.
57 Morehouse Lane
Red Hook, NY 12571

Some format issues inherent in the e-media version may also appear in this print version.

International Academy, Research, and Industry Association (IARIA)
412 Derby Way
Wilmington, DE 19810

Phone: (408) 893-6407
Fax: (408) 527-6351

petre@iaria.org

Additional copies of this publication are available from:

Curran Associates, Inc.
57 Morehouse Lane
Red Hook, NY 12571 USA
Phone: 845-758-0400
Fax: 845-758-2633
Email: curran@proceedings.com
Web: www.proceedings.com

Table of Contents

eKNOW 2022

Forward

The Fourteenth International Conference on Information, Process, and Knowledge Management (eKNOW 2022) was held in Porto, Portugal, June 26 - 30, 2022. The event was driven by the complexity of the current systems, the diversity of the data, and the challenges for mental representation and understanding of environmental structure and behavior.

Capturing, representing, and manipulating knowledge was and still is a fascinating and extremely useful challenge from both theoretical and practical perspective. Using validated knowledge for information and process management and for decision support mechanisms raised a series of questions the eKNOW 2022 conference was aimed at.

eKNOW 2022 provided a forum where researchers were able to present recent research results and new research problems and directions related to them. The topics covered aspects from knowledge fundamentals to more specialized topics such as process analysis and modeling, management systems, semantics processing and ontology.

We take this opportunity to thank all the members of the eKNOW 2022 Technical Program Committee as well as the numerous reviewers. The creation of such a broad and high-quality conference program would not have been possible without their involvement. We also kindly thank all the authors who dedicated much of their time and efforts to contribute to the eKNOW 2022. We truly believe that, thanks to all these efforts, the final conference program consists of top quality contributions.

This event could also not have been a reality without the support of many individuals, organizations, and sponsors. We are grateful to the members of the eKNOW 2022 organizing committee for their help in handling the logistics and for their work to make this professional meeting a success.

We hope that eKNOW 2022 was a successful international forum for the exchange of ideas and results between academia and industry and for the promotion of progress in knowledge management research. We also hope that Porto provided a pleasant environment during the conference and everyone saved some time for exploring this beautiful city

eKNOW 2022 Chairs

eKNOW Steering Committee
Susan Gauch, University of Arkansas, USA
Martijn Zoet, Zuyd University of Applied Science, The Nederland
Samia Aitouche, Laboratory of Automation and Manufacturing (LAP), University Batna 2, Algeria
Eric J.H.J. Mantelaers, Zuyd University of Applied Sciences, Sittard, the Netherlands

eKNOW 2022 Publicity Chair
Laura Garcia, Universitat Politècnica de València (UPV), Spain
José Miguel Jiménez, Universitat Politecnica de Valencia, Spain

eKNOW 2022

COMMITTEE

eKNOW Steering Committee

Susan Gauch, University of Arkansas, USA
Martijn Zoet, Zuyd University of Applied Science, The Nederland
Samia Aitouche, Laboratory of Automation and Manufacturing (LAP), University Batna 2, Algeria
Eric J.H.J. Mantelaers, Zuyd University of Applied Sciences, Sittard, the Netherlands

eKNOW 2022 Publicity Chair

Laura Garcia, Universitat Politècnica de València (UPV), Spain
José Miguel Jiménez, Universitat Politecnica de Valencia, Spain

eKNOW 2022 Technical Program Committee

Giuseppe A. Di Lucca, University of Sannio | RCOST (Research Center on Software Technology), Italy
Rocío Abascal Mena, Universidad Autónoma Metropolitana - Cuajimalpa, Mexico City, Mexico
Raoua Abdelkhalek, LARODEC | Institut Supérieur de Gestion de Tunis | Université de Tunis, Tunisia
Marie-Hélène Abel, Sorbonne universités - Université de technologie de Compiègne, France
Awais Adnan, Institute of Management Sciences Peshawar, Pakistan
Nitin Agarwal, University of Arkansas at Little Rock, USA
Maroi Agrebi, Université Polytechnique Hauts-de-France, France
Joyce Aguiar, Center for Psychology at University of Porto (CPUP), Portugal
Abdullah Fathi Ahmed, University Paderborn, Germany
Samia Aitouche, University Batna 2, Algeria
Arnulfo Alanis, Instituto Tecnológico de Tijuana | Tecnológico Nacional de México, Mexico
Abdulwahab Alazeb, University of Arkansas, USA
Mohammed Alqahtani, University of Arkansas, USA
Mohammad T. Alshammari, University of Hail, Saudi Arabia
Bráulio Alturas, Instituto Universitário de Lisboa (ISCTE-IUL) | ISTAR-Iscte (University Institute of Lisbon), Portugal
Gil Ad Ariely, Lauder School of Government, Diplomacy and Strategy - Interdisciplinary Center Herzliya (IDC), Israel
Mohamed Anis Bach Tobji, ESEN – University of Manouba | LARODEC Laboratory – ISG of Tunis, Tunisia
Mário Antunes, Polytechnic of Leiria, Portugal
Jorge Manuel Azevedo Santos, Universidade de Évora, Portugal
Michal Baczynski, University of Silesia in Katowice, Poland
Zbigniew Banaszak, Koszalin University of Technology, Poland
Basel Bani-Ismail, Oman College of Management and Technology, Oman
Dusan Barac, University of Belgrade, Serbia
Peter Bellström, Karlstad University, Sweden
Hajer Ben Othman, National school of computer science - University of Manouba, Tunisia
Asmaa Benghabrit, Moulay Ismaïl University, Meknès, Morocco
José Alberto Benítez Andrades, University of León, Spain
Julita Bermejo-Alonso, Universidad Isabel I, Spain

Carlos Bobed, University of Zaragoza, Spain
Zorica Bogdanovic, University of Belgrade, Serbia
Gregory Bourguin, LISIC | Université Littoral Côte d'Opale(ULCO), France
Loris Bozzato, FBK-Irst | Fondazione Bruno Kessler, Trento, Italy
Bénédicte Bucher, University Gustave Eiffel | ENS | IGN | LaSTIG, France
Ozgu Can, Ege University, Turkey
Qiushi Cao, Swansea University, UK
Lorenzo Capra, State University of Milano, Italy
Massimiliano Caramia, University of Rome "Tor Vergata", Italy
Vítor Carvalho, 2Ai-EST-IPCA / Algoritmi Research Center - Minho University, Portugal
Dickson K.W. Chiu, The University of Hong Kong, Hong Kong
Ritesh Chugh, Central Queensland University, Australia
Anacleto Correia, Naval Academy, Portugal
Miguel Couceiro, University of Lorraine | CNRS | Inria Nancy G.E. | Loria, France
Juan Pablo D'Amato, Universidad Nacional del Centro de la PRov (UNCPBA) / CONICET, Argentina
Anca Daniela Ionita, University Politehnica of Bucharest, Romania
Gustavo de Assis Costa, Federal Institute of Education, Science and Technology of Goiás, Brazil / LIAAD - INESC TEC, Portugal
Joaquim De Moura, University of A Coruña, Spain
Andrea De Salve, University of Palermo, Italy
Cláudio de Souza Baptista, University of Campina Grande, Brazil
Sylvie Despres, Université Sorbonne Paris Nord, France
Vasiliki Diamantopoulou, University of the Aegean, Greece
Mihaela Dinsoreanu, Technical University of Cluj-Napoca, Romania
Tomasz Dudek, Maritime University of Szczecin, Poland
Tygran Dzhuguryan, Maritime University of Szczecin, Poland
Tome Eftimov, Jožef Stefan Institute, Ljubljana, Slovenia / Stanford University, Palo Alto, USA
Kemele M. Endris, L3S Research Center, Hannover, Germany
Fairouz Fakhfakh, Universiy of Sfax, Tunisia
Lamine Faty, Université Assane Seck de Ziguinchor, Senegal
Amélia Ferreira da Silva, Centre for Organizational and Social Studies of Porto Polytechnic, Portugal
Joan Francesc Fondevila, Universitat de Girona / Universitat Pompeu Fabra, Spain
Igor Garcia Ballhausen Sampaio, Instituto de Computação (UFF), Brazil
Susan Gauch, University of Arkansas, USA
Dipesh Gautam, Institute for Intelligent Systems (IIS) | The University of Memphis, USA
Alfonso González Briones, University of Salamanca, Spain
Malika Grim-Yefsah, University Gustave Eiffel | ENSG (Ecole Nationale des sciences géographique - Géomatique), France
Markus Grube, VOQUZ IT Solutions GmbH, Germany
Teresa Guarda, Universidad Estatal Peninsula Santa Elena - UPSE / Universidad de las Fuerzas Armadas – ESPE / ALGORITMI Research Centre | ESPE | UPSE, Ecuador
Michael Guckert, Technische Hochschule Mittelhessen, Germany
Carolina Guerini, Cattaneo University Castellanza (Varese) / Sda Bocconi, Milan, Italy
Barbara Guidi, University of Pisa, Italy
Gunadi Gunadi, Gajayana University, Malang, Indonesia
Juncal Gutiérrez-Artacho, Universidad de Granada, Spain
Mounira Harzallah, LS2N | University of Nantes, France
Stijn Hoppenbrouwers, HAN University of Applied Sciences, Arnhem / Radboud University, Nijmegen,

Netherlands
Marjan Hosseinia, University of Houston, USA
Farah Jemili, Higher Institute of Computer Science and Telecom (ISITCOM) | University of Sousse, Tunisia
Richard Jiang, Lancaster University, UK
Maria José Sousa, ISCTE-Instituto Universitário de Lisboa, Portugal
Maria José Angélico Gonçalves, P.Porto/ ISCAP / CEOS.PP, Portugal
Katerina Kabassi, Ionian University, Greece
Yasushi Kambayashi, Nippon Institute of Technology, Japan
Jean Robert Kala Kamdjoug, Catholic University of Central Africa, Cameroon
Dimitris Kanellopoulos, University of Patras, Greece
Michael Kaufmann, Hochschule Luzern, Switzerland
Ron Kenett, Samuel Neaman Institute for National Policy Research - Technion, Israel
Noureddine Kerzazi, ENSIAS Mohamed V University in Rabat, Morocco
Sandi Kirkham, Staffordshire University, UK
Wilfried Kirschenmann, Aldwin by ANEO, France
Agnieszka Konys, West Pomeranian University of Technology in Szczecin, Poland
Christian Kop, Alpen-Adria-Universität Klagenfurt | Institute for Applied Informatics, Austria
Jarosław Korpysa, University of Szczecin, Poland
Olivera Kotevska, Oak Ridge National Laboratory (ORNL), Tennessee, USA
Milton Labanda-Jaramillo, Universidad Nacional de Loja, Ecuador
Birger Lantow, The University of Rostock, Germany
Chaya Liebeskind, Jerusalem College of Technology - Lev Academic Center, Israel
Erick López Ornelas, Universidad Autónoma Metropolitana, Mexico
Pierre Maillot, INRIA, France
Paulo Maio, ISEP - School of Engineering of Polytechnic of Porto, Portugal
Carlos Alberto Malcher Bastos, Universidade Federal Fluminense, Brazil
Federica Mandreoli, Universita' di Modena e ReggioEmilia, Italy
Eric Mantelaers, RSM Netherlands / Maastricht University / Zuyd University of Applied Sciences / Open University, Netherlands
Elaine C. Marcial, Universidade de Brasília, Brazil
Nádia Junqueira Martarelli Fróes, São Carlos School of Engineering - University of São Paulo, Brazil
Claudia Martínez Araneda, Universidad Católica de la Santísima Concepción (UCSC), Chile
Yobani Martínez Ramírez, Universidad Autónoma de Sinaloa, Mexico
Michele Melchiori, Università degli Studi di Brescia, Italy
Fernando Moreira, Universidade Portucalense, Portugal
Vincenzo Moscato, University of Naples "Federico II", Italy
Tathagata Mukherjee, The University of Alabama in Huntsville, USA
Mirna Muñoz, CIMAT, Mexico
Phivos Mylonas, Ionian University, Greece
Susana Nascimento, NOVA University of Lisboa, Portugal
Samer Nofal, German Jordanian University, Jordan
Issam Nouaouri, LGI2A | Université d'Artois, France
Vilem Novak, University of Ostrava - Institute for Research and Applications of Fuzzy Modeling, Czech Republic
Roy Oberhauser, Aalen University, Germany
Daniel O'Leary, University of Southern California, USA
Eva Oliveira, 2Ai Polytechnic Institute of Cávado and Ave, Barcelos, Portugal
Wiesław Paja, University of Rzeszów, Poland

João Paulo Costa, University of Coimbra, Portugal
Jean-Éric Pelet, EMLV and SKEMA Business Schools, France
Rúben Pereira, ISCTE, Portugal
Adriano Peron, University of Napoli "Federico II", Italy
António Miguel Pesqueira, Bavarian Nordic, Denmark
Sylvain Piechowiak, Université Polytechnique Hauts-de-France, France
Salviano Pinto Soares, University of Trás-os-Montes and Alto Douro (UTAD), Portugal
Rodica Potolea, Technical University of Cluj-Napoca, Romania
Adam Przybylek, Gdansk University of Technology, Poland
Saqib Qamar, Huazhong University of Science and Technology (HUST), China
Paulo Quaresma, University of Évora, Portugal
Lukasz Radlinski, West Pomeranian University of Technology in Szczecin, Poland
Arsénio Reis, Universidade de Trás-os-Montes e Alto Douro, Portugal
Simona Riurean, University of Petrosani, Romania
Irene Rivera-Trigueros, University of Granada, Spain
Mário Rodrigues, University of Aveiro, Portugal
Alberto Rossi, Huawei, Italy
Polina Rozenshtein, Aalto University, Helsinki, Finland
Inès Saad, Amiens Business School & University Picardie Jules Verne, France
Tanik Saikh, Indian Institute of Technology Patna, India
Omar Salman, University of Arkansas, USA
Virginie Sans, INRISA/IRISA Université of Rennes 1, France
Lalia Saoudi, Msila University, Algeria
Antonio Sarasa Cabezuelo, Universidad Complutense de Madrid, Spain
Domenico Fabio Savo, Università degli Studi di Bergamo, Italy
Erwin Schaumlechner, DS Development GmbH (part of the HRS group), Astria
Hartmut Schweizer, Institute for Applied Computer Science - TU Dresden, Germany
Filippo Sciarrone, ROMA TRE University, Italy
Marcelo Seido Nagano, University of São Paulo, Brazil
Houcine Senoussi, Quartz laboratory - EISTI, Cergy, France
Luciano Serafini, FBK - Fondazione Bruno Kessler, Italy
Nuno Silva, ISEP - IPP (School of Engineering - Polytechnic of Porto), Portugal
Andrzej M.J. Skulimowski, AGH University of Science and Technology, Krakow, Poland
Koen Smit, Hogeschool Utrecht -Institute for ICT, Netherlands
Christophe Soares, Universidade Fernando Pessoa, Portugal
Darielson Souza, Federal University of Ceará (UFC), Brazil
Gautam Srivastava, Brandon University, Canada
Deborah Stacey, University of Guelph, Canada
Efstathios Stamatatos, University of the Aegean, Greece
Abel Suing, Universidad Técnica Particular de Loja, Ecuador
Marta Silvia Tabares, Universidad EAFIT, Medellín, Colombia
Nelson Tenório, UniCesumar, Brazil
Takao Terano, Chiba University of Commerce / Tokyo Institute of Technology / University of Tsukuba, Japan
Giorgio Terracina, University of Calabria, Italy
Michele Tomaiuolo, Università di Parma, Italy
Christos Troussas, Department of Informatics - University of Piraeus, Greece
Esteban Vázquez Cano, Universidad Nacional de Educación a Distancia (UNED), Spain

Marco Viviani, University of Milano-Bicocca, Italy
Hans Weigand, Tilburg University, Netherlands
Rihito Yaegashi, Kagawa University, Japan
Shuichiro Yamamoto, International Professional University in Nagoya, Japan
Erdem Yörük, Koç University, Turkey / University of Oxford, UK
Zurinahni Zainol, Universiti Sains Malaysia, Malaysia
Brahmi Zaki, Taibah University, KSA
Cecilia Zanni-Merk, INSA Rouen Normandie, France
Elmoukhtar Zemmouri, Moulay Ismail University, Meknes, Morocco
Yu-Dong Zhang (Eugene), University of Leicester, UK
Qiang Zhu, University of Michigan - Dearborn, USA
Beata Zielosko, University of Silesia in Katowice, Poland
Magdalena Zioło, University of Szczecin, Poland
Martijn Zoet, Zuyd University of Applied Science, The Nederland
Mounir Zrigui, Faculté des Sciences de Monastir, Tunisia

Copyright Information

For your reference, this is the text governing the copyright release for material published by IARIA.

The copyright release is a transfer of publication rights, which allows IARIA and its partners to drive the dissemination of the published material. This allows IARIA to give articles increased visibility via distribution, inclusion in libraries, and arrangements for submission to indexes.

I, the undersigned, declare that the article is original, and that I represent the authors of this article in the copyright release matters. If this work has been done as work-for-hire, I have obtained all necessary clearances to execute a copyright release. I hereby irrevocably transfer exclusive copyright for this material to IARIA. I give IARIA permission or reproduce the work in any media format such as, but not limited to, print, digital, or electronic. I give IARIA permission to distribute the materials without restriction to any institutions or individuals. I give IARIA permission to submit the work for inclusion in article repositories as IARIA sees fit.

I, the undersigned, declare that to the best of my knowledge, the article is does not contain libelous or otherwise unlawful contents or invading the right of privacy or infringing on a proprietary right.

Following the copyright release, any circulated version of the article must bear the copyright notice and any header and footer information that IARIA applies to the published article.

IARIA grants royalty-free permission to the authors to disseminate the work, under the above provisions, for any academic, commercial, or industrial use. IARIA grants royalty-free permission to any individuals or institutions to make the article available electronically, online, or in print.

IARIA acknowledges that rights to any algorithm, process, procedure, apparatus, or articles of manufacture remain with the authors and their employers.

I, the undersigned, understand that IARIA will not be liable, in contract, tort (including, without limitation, negligence), pre-contract or other representations (other than fraudulent misrepresentations) or otherwise in connection with the publication of my work.

Exception to the above is made for work-for-hire performed while employed by the government. In that case, copyright to the material remains with the said government. The rightful owners (authors and government entity) grant unlimited and unrestricted permission to IARIA, IARIA's contractors, and IARIA's partners to further distribute the work.

Variation in Job Titles within the Hospitality Workforce

A computation grounded theory approach

Amy Kitchiner, Mădălina Ursache, Evelien Vlijm
Hotel Management School Maastricht,
Zuyd University of Applied Sciences
Maastricht, The Netherlands
jp.hr.analytics@gmail.com

Martijn Zoet
Future Proof Financial
Zuyd University of Applied Sciences
Maastricht, The Netherlands
martijn.zoet@zuyd.

Abstract— **The wide spectrum of job titles worldwide has become the main cause of confusion amongst the general public, organizations, and practitioners of services. Diversity and inconsistency in job titles have implications for the wider perception of the workforce and their career paths. This study aims to understand the variation in job titles in the hospitality industry for management jobs and propose standardization as a means to combat disparity. A dataset of 1.000 job titles has been collected. This has been analyzed by means of grounded theory and computational grounded theory. The results show a number of 210 standardized job titles. Secondly, computational grounded theory can achieve similar results to grounded theory.**

Keywords-grounded theory; job titles; hospitality.

I. INTRODUCTION

It has become apparent that Human Resource (HR) departments in companies worldwide are dealing with challenges concerning human capital, for example, the war on talent. Therefore, the focus of these departments should be on developing data analytics strategies for training, recruiting, and retaining employees. Moreover, acquiring suitable candidates can be difficult as many success factors, such as skills, international experience, achievements, and education, are considered. Additionally, the challenges concerning the HR department: the lack of digitalization of HR processes, innovation within HR departments, the war on talent, and other challenges, make it all difficult for human resource practitioners to excel in their work.

The term 'HR analytics' has been growing at a fast-paced scale amongst human resource practitioners and consultants in the past years [1]. Furthermore, their research describes the desire of HR professionals to access the "magic numbers" that will support them in combating challenges, such as attrition, talent acquisition, and success predictions. The term "HR analytics" has not been given a precise definition, as there are various opinions on its actual meaning [2]. Van Den Heuvel and Bondarouk (2017) define it as "the systematic identification and quantification of the people drivers of business outcomes, with the purpose to make better decisions" [3]. They focus on analyzing human resource data in a systematic way that could benefit decision-making [4].

To reach the goal of analyzing the career paths of management employees, there is a need for standardization. Standardized job titles, departments, and organizational structures, such as a corporate hierarchy tend to differentiate per business, and therefore it is hard to compare [5], [6]. This complexity shows when viewing the websites of hotel chains, such as Marriot, Hilton, and Accor. These chains provide information about people that fill positions within the board of directors and executive management, how these positions are named and distributed, and differentiate per chain. For example, Marriott has separate presidents for both Canada and the US and a group president for these regions together [7]. Hilton, on the other hand, has one president of the Americas, including North, Central, and South America [8]. Moreover, Accor has a "CEO Lifestyle" function [9], whereas Marriot and Hilton do not have this function. Adding to the complexity is that the websites of these chains do not show a structure concerning the job positions. The same goes for department distribution, as big hotel chains categorize them differently than smaller independent hotels. For example, a smaller hotel may have strictly a finance department, whereas a large chain hotel might have separate departments for accounts payable, accounts receivable, budgeting and forecasting, and so on. Likewise, some companies work with a wide variation of job titles that are created just to make an employee happier with their position and title within the company. This forms a large web of titles that are similar and often mean the same thing; therefore, standardized versions of these company structural components are necessary to facilitate the Human Resource process in recruiting and managing talent. If given the means, an HR recruiter would be more effective in analyzing career paths and recruiting the right candidates.

In order to create the pattern libraries, the following research question has been formulated: "How to build pattern libraries that support the open and axial coding of computational grounded theory?" In our research, several products will be built which are defined by the type of coding involved. More specifically, a pattern library for standardizing job titles will be created using open coding, whilst axial coding will define pattern libraries at a department's and hierarchical level.

Section II of this paper describes the research methodology, followed by Section III which will go more in-depth about the data collection and analysis. In Section IV the results of the open and axial coding are written. To continue, limitations can be found in Section V Ending with Section VI where it mentions further research and lastly the Acknowledgements are mentioned.

II. RESEARCH METHODOLOGY

The goal of this research is twofold. The first goal is to identify similarities and dissimilarities in job titles across different lodging enterprises with the objective to formulate a set of standardized job titles. In addition to the goal of the research, also, the maturity of the research field is a factor in determining the appropriate research method and technique. With regards to job titles, this research field is mature. An appropriate focus of research in mature research fields is formal hypothesis testing or reevaluating existing methods[10]. Summarized, to accomplish our research goal, a research approach is needed in which job titles are identified and compared. To accomplish this goal, grounded theory is applied. In total, three cycles of coding were followed: 1) open coding, 2) axial coding and 3) selective coding [11].

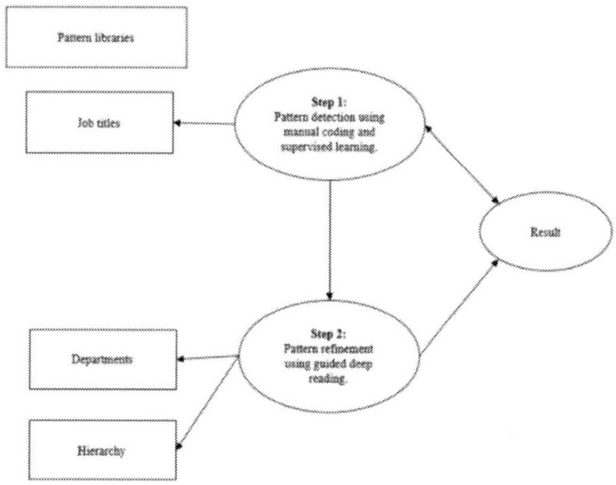

Figure 1. Computational Grounded Theory Model.

The goal of open coding is to create the first level of abstraction from analyzed data. This is realized by analyzing data and merging found instantiations to high-level categories. Identifying more precise categories and relationships among the high-level categories is the goal of axial coding. In our study, axial coding focused on identifying the standardized job titles. Selective coding was conducted to select the core category, relating categories and filling in categories that need further refinement[11]. In our research, this means that standardized job titles are appointed to departments and hierarchy levels. Then, to increase the generalizability 72 round of automated coding through computational grounded theory have been applied [12]. In Figure 1, the process is visualized with the first step resulting in the creation of the pattern library for job titles. This step involves the exploration of text using unsupervised methods and manual coding. Following a chronological order, step 2 will result in the development of the departments and hierarchy which are in essence a cumulus of categories for the job titles. In this phase, guided deep reading facilitates the interpretation of patterns. This is because the researchers can evaluate their analysis of the patterns determined quantitatively in step 1. They can detect whether the patterns are interpreted in a meaningful way and either confirm or reconsider initial patterns [12]. These are also thoroughly analyzed through the means of inter-rater reliability analysis and later translated into text which can be understood by the computer. Inter-rater reliability is a process in which coders/raters consistently distinguish between different items on a measurement scale, with the purpose of analyzing variations between ratings [13]. After both steps have been completed, the testing phase has started which creates rigorous and fully reproducible pattern libraries, measured by an F1 score. The process and results for each stage of coding are discussed in the following section.

III. DATA COLLECTION AND ANALYSIS

Grounded theory states that the first selection of respondents and documentation is based on the phenomenon studied at a group of individuals, organizations, information technology, or *community that best represents this phenomenon* [14]. For the goal of this study, this means the job titles managers use to describe their current job. Therefore, for this study, one real-life data set has been collected from Hospitality.net, between the 1st of June and the 15th of January 2021. The preprocessing of the data involved scraping the raw text descriptions into a .csv file. In this file, the information was sorted by date, job titles and gender, which supported creating the pattern libraries. No further alterations were made, as the goal was to have the data as raw as possible. The method of data collection involves a partially random stratified sampling for the entire population of job postings of management employees, during the period mentioned previously. This population, in the first phase of our data collection, has been divided into different strata depending on job title, level, company, and geographical location. For every strata, several job postings have been scraped and analyzed, totalling 1652 job titles by open coding. Starting from "date emails", the sampling method has been changed. The following phase involved letting the system scrape data and showing the results by means of an automated generated email. The system would scrape newly identified job titles and mention the standardized version. The role of the researchers was to check the accuracy of the system and to standardize new job titles if they were not yet in the system.

First, the patterns with the largest N were added, with N being the number of words in a pattern. For example, the job title pattern "Finance and Accounting Director" has an N of four with the label "Director of Finance". At all times, there is at least one pattern guarantee to match a newly identified job title. If there is no match with a pattern, the job title will be classified as a 999, which is always diverted to the researchers who will either create or assign a label to it.

A. Open Coding

The pattern library for the job titles was created first as it served as a basis for the other two pattern libraries. Hereby the first layer in coding, open coding, was used. In practice, open coding is used to "organize similar words and phrases, concept-indicators, in broad initial thematic domains" [15]. The coding scheme used was designed a priori which was then translated into a code-book/business rules that were then used to hermeneutically categorize the text. Three primary researchers first manually coded the text, whereafter a fourth secondary researcher assessed the coding. The background of the primary researchers encompasses four years of a Bachelor's in Hospitality Industry, with the fourth researcher having more than 10 years of experience in the industry and a PhD in Business Informatics. After, an inter-coder reliability score was measured. An example of one of the standardized job titles is 'CEO', 'New company CEO,' and 'Chief executive Officer' which will be standardized into 'Chief Executive Officer' as a job title. Once this score was satisfactory, the coding of the job titles is translated into patterns that are added into a named entity recognition whereafter the retrieved job titles are automatically coded. If a job title couldn't be coded the system would notify the three coders so that they could add coding to them. In addition, the coders checked the automated codes to see if the system coded the proper elements.

B. Axial coding

Going forward with the axial coding, the pattern library job title is being used as the basis of the other two pattern libraries: 1) Department and 2) Hierarchy. For the axial coding, it has followed the same structure as the open coding by first categorizing the standard job titles by hermeneutic skills and expert opinion, checking this by inter-rater analysis, and by coding it separately. For example, 'Chief Executive Officer' is part of the administrative department; 'Finance Director' is part of the finance department, and 'Director of Human Resource' is part of the human resource department. After completing this process, the axial coding has been automatized by creating the pattern libraries.

IV. RESULTS

The application of the Computational Grounded theory model has resulted in the creation of three pattern libraries. The precision and recall of these products are measured based on a calculated F1 score. Furthermore, the gradual development process is described in the following section.

A. Pattern library for job titles

The results of categorizing the job titles into a pattern library are 210 standardized job titles. Moreover, inter-rater reliability has been applied to ensure rigorous research. This resulted in an inter-rater reliability score of 83,0%. Furthermore, of the percentage of faulty coding, 84.4% were incorrect due to variation in writing; for example, to label the job title 'board of directors, one coder may write 'member of the board of directors', while another writes 'board of directors. On the other hand, 15,6% were more significant faults where titles were labeled entirely differently. An example of this would be labeling the pattern 'pastry chef'. Whereas one would label it as 'chef de cuisine', making it more general, another would keep it specific and label it as 'pastry chef. After this process, more business rules were added, finalizing with 14 rules. Following this, an F1 score was calculated to measure the precision and recall of the pattern library. The pattern library for job titles attained a

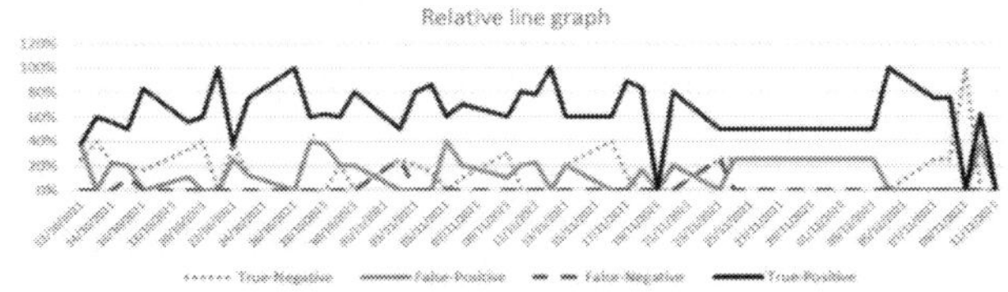

perfect score of 100% after having been observed over 72 times throughout the research.

TABLE I. PRECISION MATRIX

	Positive	Negative
Positive	188 (TP)	47 (FP)
Negative	3 (FN)	48 (TN)

Figure 2. Precision matrix line graph

Whilst the patterns and corresponding labels were in the server, daily e-mails were received, which contained about zero to ten newly identified job titles per day and stated what label had been given to this title. The e-mail shows job titles that have been coded and job titles that have not been coded. For those that had not been coded, new patterns were created. The job titles that were coded were checked against the classification of labeling. In Figure 2, the relative amount of job titles and the outcome of the classification of the labeling is pictured on a timeline, followed by Table 1 which shows the total of newly identified job titles after the pattern library has been created. As seen in the graph, the largest amount was true positives, followed by true negatives, false positives, and finally false negatives.

B. Pattern library for departments

The results of the job title pattern library served as an input for the creation of the department's pattern library and therefore, followed step 2 of Figure 1. During this phase, all the standardized job titles have been categorized per department. This resulted in a count of 17 departments for 210 job titles. To define these departments, inter-rater reliability has been applied by a total of 5 coders starting with conceptualizing a draft version of departments and developing a set of 9 business rules. These business rules have helped the coders define mutually exclusive, qualitative, and complete categories which range from Administrative to Wellness and Recreation. The total number of categorized job titles into departments during inter-rater reliability is 100, representing 10% of the data set at hand. For example, 'Chief Executive Officer' is part of the administrative department.

After the manual process has been finalized, the pattern library has been tested through the means of computation. From the 15th of October until the 15th of January, the pattern library is tested daily to validate the completeness and usefulness against newly identified job titles. If the pattern library cannot recognize what department to classify a standardized job title, the title will be added to the library. This way, the pattern libraries will continuously be developed. For this pattern library, the daily calculated F1 score of the pattern libraries was 100%, meaning that the precision and recall of the pattern library for standardized departments is perfect. Like the job titles, the pattern and label file for the departments was updated when new patterns were discovered. As this pattern library is based on the pattern library for job titles, the outcome of the positives/negatives was the same.

TABLE II. JOB TITLES OVERVIEW BY DEPARTMENTS

Department	Count of Job Title
Administrative	23
Asset Management	3
Business Development Strategy	30
Corporate Affairs	13
Customer Experience	5
Engineering	2
Engineering	2
Events	6
Finance and Accounting	9
Food and Beverage	21
Human Resources	10
Information technology	7
Operations	13
Revenue Management	8
Rooms Division	5
Sales and marketing	29
Wellness and Recreation	3
Other	21
Grand Total	**210**

C. *Pattern Libraries for hierarchy*

The creation of the pattern library hierarchy resulted in three base hierarchy levels. As an organization can be divided into head office (HQ), regional office (RO), and property-based (PB) job levels. Within the HQ level, 26 patterns have been categorized. In RO there are 88 patterns and PB 97 patterns. This resulted in an organizational standardized structure, where "X" refers to the specific job title or department, as for example "Director of Finance". See Figures 3, 4 and 5.

The hierarchy starts with Head Quarters and ends with Property-Based. As every organization is different it was needed to create more detailed levels to place job titles with a similar name in the same hierarchical level. The number shows the level in the hierarchy, where one is the highest, and anything that follows is lower in ranking. The Chief Financial Officer, Chief Human Resource Officer, and Chief Sustainability Officer all come on the same level: HQ1. Followed with HQ2 the President and will go to HQ7. This example explains the details of the standardized hierarchical levels of the Head Quarters, there are also detailed levels for the Regional Office: RO1 being the Group Directors, followed by the Area/Regional Executive Vice Presidents. This goes on till RO8. And Property-Based: PB1: General Manager, followed by the Assistant General Manager on PB2, Going on to the managerial level PB8.

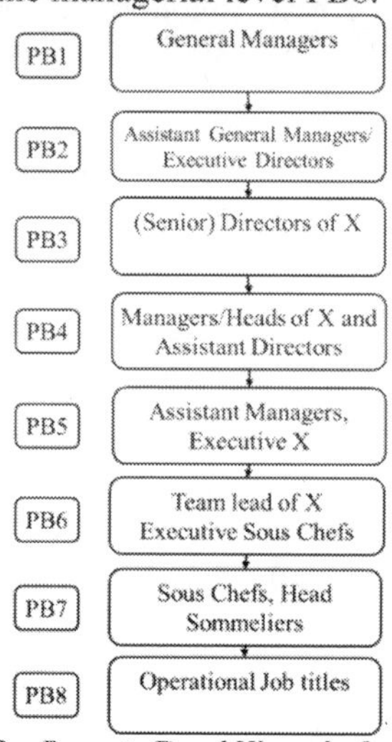

Figure 3. Property-Based Hierarchy Levels

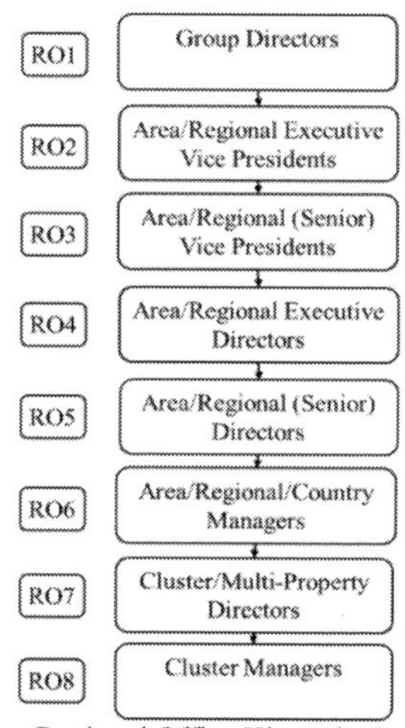

Figure 4. Regional Office Hierarchy Levels

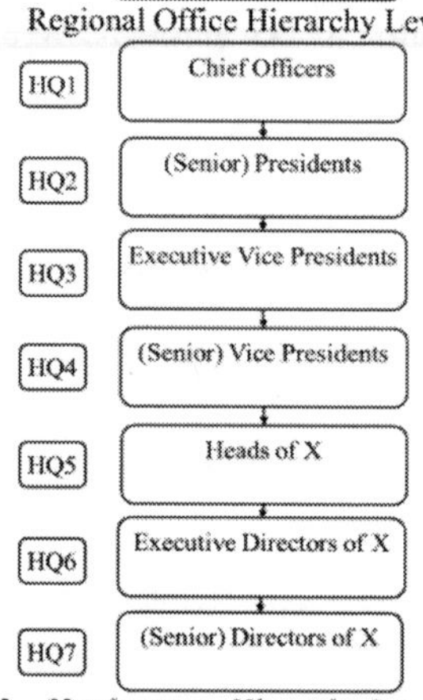

Figure 5. Headquarters Hierarchy Level

For this result, the researchers interviewed four international experienced professors of Hotel Management School Maastricht to validate the hierarchical structure created. The insights given as a response were evaluated based on inter-rater reliability. The result was a score of 82%, meaning that 18% of the answers given amongst the professionals were different. For the 18% of the answers that were different a total of 7 business rules were created. The result of the F1 score of this pattern library also equaled 100%, meaning that this Axial coding recognizes all the existing patterns of the open coding.

V. LIMITATIONS

As this paper has a global scope of analyzing job titles worldwide, it was more difficult to execute during this time period, therefore there were time constraints. Other than that, this research was executed as a cross-sectional study, meaning that longitudinal research is needed to find changes over time to identify trends and adjust this within the patterns. The third limitation is the human bias, due to cultural backgrounds or other interpersonal factors of the researchers that affect the study's validity. This has been reduced because of the inter-rater results. The fourth and last limitation is the sampling technique used in this research. Hospitality.net has been used as sample data that has to be representable for the entire population.

VI. CONCLUSION AND FURTHER WORK

The application of data analytics, measures and, tools has facilitated the process of creating the pattern libraries and, it proves that digitalization in the hospitality industry can be a key tool for solving business problems.

These findings provide a potential mechanism for further development in creating standardization for job titles in the Hospitality industry, in order to combat disparity. Moreover, this paper draws attention to the gaps in the industry, such as the lack of digitalization and innovation in the Human Resources department. The next recommended step would be to compare the findings with similar initiatives in the industry, such as Esco. This enterprise classifies skills, competencies and occupations within the European Union's labour market, which serves a similar scope to the research proposed in his paper [16]. Furthermore, additional resources could be devoted to analyzing the impact certain variables have on job title disparity, such as gender, education, skills and background. On a practical level, the hospitality industry could use all these findings to create a digital platform for businesses worldwide which can compare job titles by department, hierarchy and additional variables as per user preference.

ACKNOWLEDGEMENT

We thank Armand Odekerken and Dennis Trotta for their supervision during this project. We thank Victor Houben and Jannick Hendriks for their assistance during the project. We would also like to thank Eric Mantelaers for sharing his expertise and his guidance.

REFERENCES

[1] J. H. Marler and J. W. Boudreau, "An evidence-based review of HR Analytics," *The International Journal of Human Resource Management*, vol. 28, no. 1, pp. 3–26, 2017, doi: 10.1080/09585192.2016.1244699.

[2] L. Bassi, "Raging Debates in HR Analytics," *Human Resource Management International Digest*, vol. 20, no. 2, pp. 74–80, 2012.

[3] S. van den Heuvel and T. Bondarouk, "'The Rise (and Fall?) of HR Analytics: The Future Application, Value, Structure, and System Support,'" *https://doi.org/10.5465/ambpp.2016.10908abstract*, vol. 2016, no. 1, Nov. 2017, doi: 10.5465/AMBPP.2016.10908ABSTRACT.

[4] D. Ø. Madsen and K. Slåtten, "The Rise of HR Analytics: A Preliminary Exploration by Dag Øivind Madsen, Kåre Slåtten :: SSRN," *Global Conference on Business and Finance Proceedings*, vol. 12, no. 1, pp. 148–159, Jan. 2017, Accessed: Nov. 29, 2021. [Online]. Available: https://papers.ssrn.com/sol3/papers.cfm?abstract_id=2896602

[5] C. v Barrett, S. John, and L. ii, "Job Titles and Education Requirements of Registered Nurses in Primary Care: A Research Practicum," Apr. 2021.

[6] C. Barrett *et al.*, "Job titles and education requirements of registered nurses in primary care: An international document analysis," *International Journal of Nursing Studies Advances*, vol. 3, p. 100044, Nov. 2021, doi: 10.1016/J.IJNSA.2021.100044.

[7] Marriott, "Board of Directors | Marriott International." https://marriott.gcs-web.com/board-of-directors (accessed Oct. 02, 2021).

[8] Hilton, "Hilton – Management." https://ir.hilton.com/corporate-governance/management (accessed Oct. 02, 2021).

[9] Accor, "Accor - Executive Comittee." https://group.accor.com/en/group/our-governance/executive-comittee (accessed Oct. 02, 2021).

[10] A. C. Edmondson and S. E. Mcmanus, "Methodological Fit in Management Field Research Monitor Executive Development," *Academy of Management Review*, vol. 32, no. 4, pp. 1155–1179, 2007.

[11] J. M. Corbin and A. Strauss, "Grounded theory research: Procedures, canons, and evaluative criteria," *Qualitative Sociology 1990 13:1*, vol. 13, no. 1, pp. 3–21, Mar. 1990, doi: 10.1007/BF00988593.

[12] L. K. Nelson, "Computational Grounded Theory: A Methodological Framework:," *https://doi.org/10.1177/0049124117729703*, vol. 49, no. 1, pp. 3–42, Nov. 2017, doi: 10.1177/0049124117729703.

[13] N. Gisev, J. S. Bell, and T. F. Chen, "Interrater agreement and interrater reliability: Key concepts, approaches, and applications," *Research in Social*

and Administrative Pharmacy, vol. 9, no. 3. pp. 330–338, May 2013. doi: 10.1016/j.sapharm.2012.04.004.

[14] B. Glaser, *Theoretical sensitivity: advances in the methodology of grounded theory*. 1978.

[15] M. Williams and T. Moser, "The Art of Coding and Thematic Exploration in Qualitative Research," *International Management Review*, vol. 15, no. 1, 2019.

[16] ESCO, "Homepage." https://esco.ec.europa.eu/en (accessed Jun. 06, 2022).

Towards a Going Concern Assessment Pipeline

Lotte Verhoeven, Eric Mantelaers, Martijn Zoet
Research Group: Future-proof Financial & Auditor
Zuyd University of Applied Sciences
Sittard, the Netherlands
lotte.verhoeven@zuyd.nl
eric.mantelaers@zuyd.nl
martijn.zoet@zuyd.nl

Abstract—**The assessment of the going concern analysis in the audit process is based on the professional judgment of the auditor. To support this individual and personal judgment of the auditor, a more direct source of information in the form of an automated going concern analysis could provide a solution. In this paper a method to automate the going concern analysis was set up, using a combination of 16 forecasting algorithms. To build and validate the forecasting algorithms, 225 administrations have been divided in a train and test set. The results show a confidence percentage of 97.45% for the Gradient Boosting Regressor model, 96.79% for the Decision Tree Regressor model and 77.72% for the AdaBoost Regressor model on the basis of the condition current liabilities for Administration 1.**

Keywords-Forecasting algorithms; Continuity; Going Concern; Forecasting; PyCaret.

I. INTRODUCTION

Research shows that the going concern assessment is one of the most important challenges within the decision-making process of organizations [1]. The law stipulates that management of organizations should value her assets and liabilities based on the principle of the going concern assumption, unless serious doubts concerning the continuity of the organization exists (2:284 paragraph 3 of the Dutch Civil Code). When drawing up financial statements, the going concern assumption is therefore leading, as stated in ISA 2400, ISA 4410 and Title 9, Book 2 of the Dutch Civil Code (Financial Statements and the Management Report) [2][3][4]. The auditor assesses this going concern assumption in both statutory and voluntary audit engagements, but also in review engagements and compilation engagements [5].

Audit quality and the going concern assessment is currently heavily debated worldwide. Past experience shows that, despite the fact that an unqualified audit opinion has been issued, organizations can still go bankrupt in the foreseeable future. An example of this within the Dutch context is the inadequately evaluated going concern assessment of Imtech in 2012. According to the Dutch court [6], some assumptions regarding the going concern assessment did not correspond to the actual figures. Another example are the unseen irregularities within Steinhoff, which eventually led to bankruptcy. In this case, the auditor was accused by the Dutch Authority for Financial Markets (AFM) of not obtaining sufficient and appropriate audit evidence to identify the fraud [7]. In addition, the auditor's unconscious biases, caused by among other things client relations and confidentiality, do not contribute to an independent going concern assessment [8]. With the help of data-driven control, the AFM wants to make the supervision of audit firms more efficient and effective. The Royal Netherlands Institute of Chartered Accountants (NBA) also emphasizes continuity because of the increased social interest. The NBA wants to provide auditors with more tools that the auditor can use in the assessment. In fact, for 2021, the NBA board has set continuity as a mandatory subject for continuing professional education for all auditors (except government auditors). As of the reporting periods starting on or after December 15, 2021 (2020 for public interest entities), the NBA also mandates the inclusion of a separate section "Audit Approach to Going Concern" in the audit report [9]. Regarding the United Kingdom, Brydon's report suggests that the reporting requirements of the current going concern analysis are not sufficiently fit for purpose. Brydon recommended that the current going concern assessment should be expanded in the short term in a transparent manner, which includes material uncertainties without already taking into account mitigating measures [10].

This research focuses on the approach and possible improvements to the going concern assessment. The going concern assessment is still largely dependent on the professional judgment of the auditor, who must assess whether management has made proper considerations. Research shows that technology can contribute to an improvement of audit quality [11]. By automating the going concern assessment, more time and resources can be allocated to the interpretation of the going concern analysis. This maximizes the dual aspects of audit quality: independence and expertise [11][12]. To support the individual and personal professional judgment of the auditor, an additional automated going concern assessment, a more direct source of information with possibly higher reliability, could provide a solution. Automated forecasting of figures and numbers is possible with the use of forecasting algorithms. An algorithm is "a finite, abstract, effective, compound control structure, imperatively given, accomplishing a given purpose under given provisions."[13] An algorithm can be an instruction in the form of code that can be used, among other things, for forecasting time series [14]. This research also focuses on the question of how sufficient and appropriate audit information can be collected using these forecasting algorithms, to analyze the going concern assessment in the (statutory) audit and compilation or review engagements. This can be done with the forecasting algorithms of PyCaret [14]. The use of PyCaret leads to an automated going concern analysis that is less dependent on the individual and personal professional judgment of the auditor, thus a possible improvement of uniformity can be realized. The goal of this research is to achieve an automated going concern analysis and a uniform creation of a more reliable and valid prediction for the going concern analysis. To achieve this, this paper answers the following main question: How can machine learning be used to assess the organizational going concern assessment? Similar to previous research we apply PyCaret to test multiple algorithms in concurrence [15][16].

The remainder of the paper is organized as follows: Section II describes the relevant literature regarding the auditor's evaluation of the going concern analysis and models which give an indication of the going concern. In Section II the method and structure of the algorithms is described, followed by the results in Section IV. The conclusion and future work are presented in Section V.

II. Literature Review

The auditor's evaluation of the going concern analysis consists out of the following four main activities: 1) The auditor concludes whether there is a material uncertainty that could cast doubt on the ability of the company to continue as a going concern. 2) For the purpose of the foregoing analysis, the auditor also performs risk assessment activities and assesses whether the financial, operational, and other events and circumstances cast reasonable doubt on the ability to continue as a going concern. In doing so, the auditor looks at, among other things, the current liabilities position, negative operating cash flows or intentions to liquidate the company. 3) In addition, the auditor assesses other events and circumstances for, for example, changes in relevant laws and regulations and non-compliance with capital or other regulatory requirements. Other examples are included in ISA-570, paragraph A3 [4]. 4) Finally, the auditor should inquire about events after the balance sheet date that may have an effect on the going concern. This is included in ISA-570, paragraph 15 [4].

There are several models available that give an indication about the going concern of a company. A well-known model is the Altman Z-score, which was developed by Altman in 1968 [17]. The model was then designed and tested based on data from manufacturing companies, but further adapted for private Limited Liability Companies (LLCs) and non-manufacturing companies combined with emerging markets. Respectively, the Altman Z'-score Model and the Altman Z"-score Model. The Altman Z-score Model consists of the weighted average of five financial ratios, with each ratio consisting of two conditions. The Altman Z-score provides an indication of the probability of bankruptcy for the company in question. In this, Altman distinguishes three categories: 'Safe Zone', 'Grey Zone' and 'Red Zone'. A score of 3.0 or more leads to the category 'Safe Zone'. A score between 1.8 and 3.0 leads to the 'Grey Zone' and a score below 1.8 to the 'Red Zone'. In which the 'Safe Zone' does not indicate bankruptcy and the 'Red Zone' does indicate bankruptcy [17].

In addition to the Altman Z-score Model, there are several models available for going concern assessment. Using a structured literature review from 238 papers, Mantelaers and Zoet [18] identified 835 conditions that contribute to predicting the going concern. These elements were then analyzed based on the type of element, required information sources and organization type. From this, a top ten of the most commonly used elements for predicting the going concern was formulated. This top ten is shown in Figure 1.

Feature 01: Net income/total assets	85 (papers)
Feature 02: current ratio	74
Feature 03: EBIT/total assets (*)	65
Feature 04: retained earnings/total assets (*)	62
Feature 05: working capital/total assets (*)	60
Feature 06: sales/total assets (*)	46
Feature 07: quick ratio	41
Feature 08: current assets/total assets	39
Feature 09: total debt/total assets	39
Feature 10: cash/total assets	32

Figure 1. Top ten criteria assessing going concern

The ratios indicated with an asterisk are used in the Altman Z-score Model. The fifth element of the Altman Z-score, the market value of equity divided by total liabilities, comes in thirteenth place. This indicates that the elements of the Altman Z- score Model are frequently used. Despite its popularity, the Altman Z-score Model is only suitable for listed companies. Research shows that predicting going concern for mid-sized companies, requires models and procedures that are aimed at the mid-sized segment instead of the general Altman Z-score Model [19]. However, there are only a few going concern models available for predicting the going concern of mid-sized organizations. In this study, the adapted Altman Z-score Model by Altman and Sabato [19] is used.

In this model, the most successful financial ratios to predict the going concern were chosen for each category, namely: liquidity, profitability, leverage, coverage and activity. These financial ratios were incrementally assessed. After which, the financial ratios were logarithmically transformed to reduce the impact of the outliers resulting in an accuracy level of the model of 87% [19].

The Altman and Sabato study also compared the accuracy of the above model with a standard model, in this case a derivative of the Altman Z-score Model, the Z"-score Model was created. Comparing the Z"-score model to the Altman Z-score resulted in a higher prediction accuracy of almost 20% [19]. The conditions derived from the Altman Z-score model [17], the modified Altman Z-score models [19][20], and the top ten criteria from Mantelaers and Zoet's research [18] will be used within this research as input data for the forecasting algorithms. In which the word conditions refer to the various data points that can be used to assess the going concern of an organization. Examples include assets, liabilities, operating income before interest and tax (EBIT) and turnover.

The purpose of this research is to generate an automated going concern analysis. In order to do so the forecasting algorithms of PyCaret are used within this research. PyCaret uses different mathematical models translated into eponymous forecasting algorithms, namely: 1) Extreme Gradient Boosting, 2) CatBoost Classifier, 3) Light Gradient Boosting Machine, 4) K Neighbors Classifier, 5) Random Forest Classifier, 6) Extra Trees Classifier, 7) Gradient Boosting Classifier, 8) Logistic Regression, 9) Linear Discriminant Analysis, 10) AdaBoost Classifier, 11) Ridge Classifier, 12) Decision Tree Classifier, 13) Quadratic Discriminant Analysis, 14) SVM - Linear Kernel, 15) Naive Bayes and 16) Dummy Classifier. Each forecasting algorithm is tailored to specific situations, such as seasonality. In addition, each forecasting algorithm works with its own assumptions and interpretations, resulting in different forecasts [14]. For a detailed explanation we refer to the PyCaret website. By comparing the predictions of each model with each other and the actual realized figures, a ranking can be made with regards to the best performing algorithm. In this way, the most suitable forecasting algorithm can be chosen for each type of input data.

III. METHOD

This paper uses the predictive models of PyCaret, combined with the predefined conditions as input data. In this section, the process from input data to results is explained step by step using the short-term debt condition of Administration 1. The overall process of the system is visually shown in Figure 2. For illustration purposes, the structure of the system is explained for only one administration and condition. However, this process will be repeated for all conditions separately to achieve a complete picture of the organizations' performance regarding the going concern analysis.

To obtain the source data, the existing period balances were exported from Exact Online for eight to thirteen years, depending on the administration and availability. The exported cumulative monthly balance sheets were checked for empty cells. An empty cell can occur if there are, for example, no current liabilities in a period. To avoid errors, the empty cells have been replaced by the amount €0.00. Moreover, the cumulative monthly balance sheets were transposed to obtain the correct input for the algorithm. The beginning and ending balances correspond to months one and twelve of the respective year. To avoid double counting in the dataset, the beginning and ending balances were removed in the transposed file. After cleaning the individual cumulative monthly balance sheets per year, the years were merged into one file. Then, based on the merged cumulative monthly balance sheets per administration, the individual conditions (e.g., current liabilities, equity, sales, etc.) were filtered. This led to a dataset per administration per condition per month.

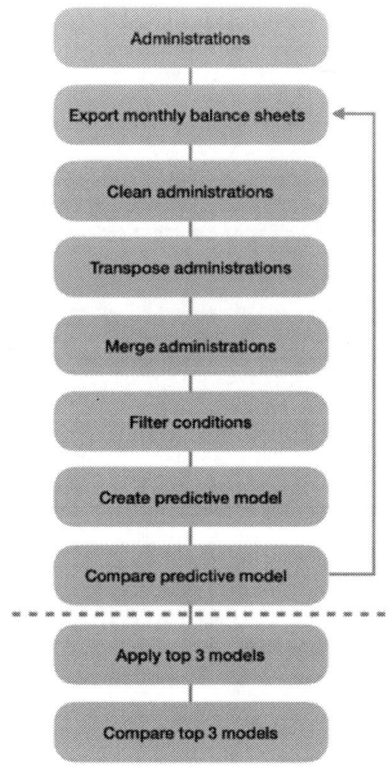

Figure 2. Structure system

The dataset per administration per condition per month for the years present is then presented to PyCaret's regression module (v 2.3.2). The regression module is a supervised machine learning module used for estimating the relationship between a dependent variable and independent variables. PyCaret uses different mathematical models translated into similarly named forecasting algorithms to see which model makes the best predictions.

In doing so, each forecasting algorithm works with its own assumptions and interpretations, resulting in different forecasts. The model that best fits the administration is shown at the top and the model with the least fit is shown at the bottom. The predictions and the true value of each are then stored in one file and compared. To assess the accuracy of the predictions, the (percentage) deviations per month and at the total level were calculated from these real figures.

IV. RESULTS

For the current liabilities condition from Administration 1, the results are explained below. Using PyCaret's regression module, the Gradient Boosting Regressor, Decision Tree Regressor and the AdaBoost Regressor models emerge as the most accurate. The actual current liabilities figures from Administration 1 are visually represented in Figure 3.

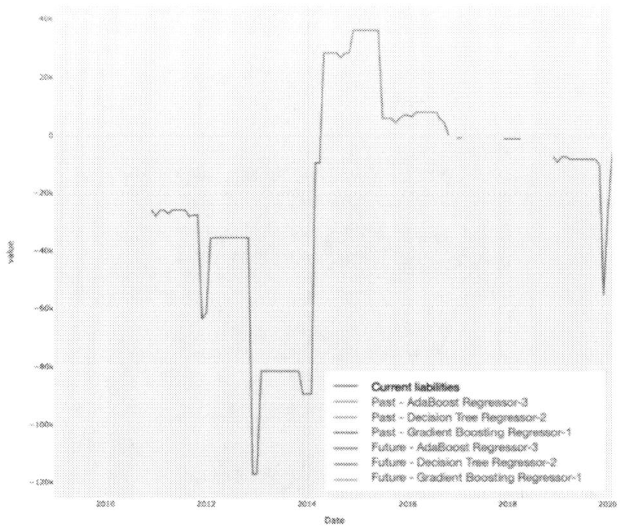

Figure 3. Actual figures current liabilities, Administration 1

The results of the top three models are then added in Figure 4, where the blue line represents the actual short-term debt figures, and the other colored lines represent the predictions. The forecasts within PyCaret consist of two parts per model: Past and Future. Past predicts back into the past based on an adaptive training set consisting out of several years after the predicted year. Future predicts a predetermined time period (in this case six months) based on actual historical figures.

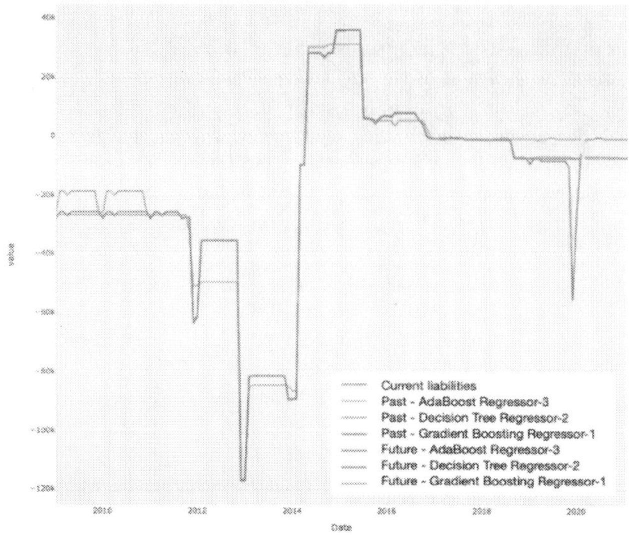

Figure 4. Forecasted figures current liabilities, Administration 1

In addition, the results of the different forecasting algorithms for the current liabilities of Administration 1 were then merged into one CSV file. In addition, the (percentage) deviations were calculated based on the actual figures. In this way, the forecasts are compared with the actual figures. For example, for the period 2010-12-11, the deviation between the AdaBoost Regressor model and the actual value of the current liabilities is €911.00, which represents a deviation of 3.5%. The results for the current liabilities of Administration 1 are visually shown in Table 1.

TABLE I. RESULTS TOP 3 MODELS CURRENT LIABILITIES, ADMINISTRATION 1

Model	Deviation percentage	Confidence percentage
Gradient Boosting Regressor	02.55%	97.45%
Decision Tree Regressor	03.21%	96.79%
AdaBoost Regressor	22.28%	77.72%

On average, a deviation percentage of 2.55% for Gradient Boosting Regressor, 3.21% for Decision Tree Regressor and 22.28% for AdaBoost Regressor was achieved for short-term debt. This leads to a confidence percentage of 97.45%, 96.79% and 77.72%, respectively.

V. CONCLUSION AND FUTURE WORK

Going concern assessment is currently heavily debated all over the world. This within the larger context of the current societal debate on audit quality. With cases such as Imtech and Steinhoff [1][5] proving that going concern assessments needs to be a viable part of the audit. In this article we aim to answer the main question: "*How can machine learning be used to assess the organizational going concern assessment?*" This research presents a first step towards an automated process of going concern assessment. The goal of this research was to predict the different individual variables that affect the going concern assessment of the auditor. A confidence percentage of 97.45% for the Gradient Boosting Regressor model, 96.79% for the Decision Tree Regressor model and 77.72% for the AdaBoost Regressor model was measured on the basis of the current liabilities for Administration 1. This means that the predictions of the algorithms are reliable with 97.45% for the Gradient Boosting Regressor model. The results therefore show that individual variables can be predicted with the various algorithms of the PyCaret Library. This means that the machine learning used in this paper, particularly PyCaret, can be used to assess the organizational going concern assessment.

The insights derived from our study provide a better understanding of the ability to predict numbers based on the general ledger of organizations. This means that the Altman Z-score as a whole can be predicted, resulting in a predictive continuity. Future research should focus on creating an indicator of the going concern assessment. In our study, we draw our conclusions based upon data collected solely from the Dutch context, which limits, in terms of sampling, a broader generalization towards non-Dutch organizations. Future research should focus on further generalization towards other countries. In addition, the sample only consisted of small and medium sized organizations, future research should focus on further generalization towards other industries (non-governmental). Related to the previous limitation is the sample size, which is limited to 221 organizations. Although this is a rather large sample size, the total number of organizations in the Netherlands is much larger. In addition, the predictions are now based on a single variable. For future research, multivariable predictions can be applied to see if this will increase the predictive value. Future research should also focus on comparing the forecast with the going concern paragraphs (used or not) in the financial statements concerned. In this way, it can be determined whether or not there is uncertainty about continuity, or in the accounting policies or events after the balance sheet date, and whether this matches the results of the algorithms.

References

[1] D. E. O'Leary and R. M. O'Keefe, "The Impact of Artificial Intelligence in Accounting Work: Expert Systems Use in Auditing and Tax," *AI Soc.*, vol. 11, no. 1–2, pp. 36–47, 1997, doi: 10.1007/BF02812437.

[2] Dutch government, *Title 9. Financial Statements and the Managing Report; Book 2*. 2022.

[3] IAASB, *Handbook of International Quality Control, Auditing, Review, Other Assurance, and Related Services Pronouncements*. INTL FEDERATION OF ACCOUN, 2021.

[4] International Auditing and Assurance Standards Board, *Handbook of International Quality Control, Auditing, Review, Other Assurance and Related Services Pronouncements*, vol. I. 2020.

[5] E. van der Velden, "Going Concern and Compilation Engagements," *Account.*, no. 7/8, pp. 34–35, 2012.

[6] M. J. G. Princen and M. P. J. Peters, "Ruling of the court dated January 15, 2021 pursuant to Section 38 of the Accountants Disciplinary Act (Wtra) in the complaints received on July 17, 2018 with numbers 18/1193 and 18/1194 Wtra AK," Jan. 15, 2021. https://repository.overheid.nl/frbr/tuchtrecht/2021/ECLI:NL:TACAKN:2021:2/1/pdf/ECLI_NL_TACAKN_2021_2.pdf (accessed Jun. 06, 2022).

[7] Bloomberg, "Ex-deloitte Auditor Faces Disciplinary Action over Steinhoff," 2021. https://www.bloomberg.com/news/articles/2021-04-22/ex-deloitte-auditor-faces-disciplinary-action-over-steinhoff#xj4y7vzkg (accessed Jun. 06, 2022).

[8] D. Bazerman, M.H.; Loewenstein, G.; Moore, "Why Good Accountants Do Bad Audits," *Harvard Business Review*, vol. 97. 2002.

[9] NBA, "Standard 700," in *Regulations Manual Accountancy(HRA)*, 2021.

[10] D. Brydon, "Assess, Assure and Inform: Improving Audit Quality and Efectiveness." APS Group, 2019.

[11] E. Mantelaers, "An Evaluation of Technologies to Improve Auditing," Open Universiteit, 2021.

[12] L. E. DeAngelo, "Auditor Size and Audit Quality," *J. Account. Econ.*, vol. 3, no. 3, pp. 183–199, 1981, doi: https://doi.org/10.1016/0165-4101(81)90002-1.

[13] R. K. Hill, "What an Algorithm is," *Philos. Technol.*, vol. 29, pp. 35–39, 2016, doi: https://doi.org/10.1007/s13347-014-0184-5.

[14] PyCaret, "PyCaret," 2021. https://pycaret.gitbook.io/docs/ (accessed Jun. 06, 2022).

[15] R. Abdullah, Iqbal, F.B.; Biswas, S.; Urba, "Performance Analysis of Intrusion Detection Systems Using the PyCaret Machine Learning Library on the UNSW-NB15 Dataset," Brac University, 2021.

[16] D. T. U. Pol, Dr. U.R.; Sawant, "Automl: Building An Classification Model With PyCaret," *YMER*, vol. 20, no. 11, pp. 547–552, 2021.

[17] E. I. Altman, "The Prediction of Corporate Bankruptcy: a Discriminant Analysis," *J. Finance*, vol. 23, no. 1, pp. 193–194, 1968, doi: 10.1111/j.1540-6261.1968.tb00843.x/pdf.

[18] E. Mantelaers and M. Zoet, "A New Explorative Model to Assess the Financial Credit Risk Assessment," *eKNOW*, vol. The Tenth, pp. 101–106, 2018.

[19] E. I. Altman and G. Sabato, "Modelling credit risk for SMEs: Evidence from the U.S. market," *Abacus*, vol. 43, no. 3, pp. 332–357, Sep. 2007, doi: 10.1111/j.1467-6281.2007.00234.x.

[20] E. I. Altman and E. Hotchkiss, "Defining Corporate Financial Distress and Bankruptcy," in *Corporate Financial Distress; A Study of the Italian Manufacuturing Industry*, 2017, pp. 3–10. doi: 10.1007/978-3-319-67355-4_2.

How to Plot Current Pilots on the Audit Maturity Model?

The Continuum Paradigm

Ed Curfs
Future-Proof Auditor
Zuyd University of Applied Sciences
Sittard, the Netherlands
ed.curfs@zuyd.nl

Eric Mantelaers
Future-Proof Auditor
Zuyd University of Applied Sciences
Sittard, the Netherlands
eric.mantelaers@zuyd.nl

Martijn Zoet
Future-Proof Financial
Zuyd University of Applied Sciences
Sittard, the Netherlands
martijn.zoet@zuyd.nl

***Abstract*—Continuous monitoring, continuous control monitoring, continuous auditing, continuous assurance and continuous reporting and the Continuum Paradigm are topics in which research has been performed for more than 30 years. The possibilities and challenges of these elements have been researched. However, limited studies focused on the holistic view and the status of an pilots, financial as well as non-financial data, in relationship with the Audit Maturity Model have been performed. Based on the existing studies, we defined the following research question: What is the actual status regarding the Continuum Paradigm? Based on a review of pilots and plotting the results of the pilots on the Audit Maturity Model by a focus group, further insight is provided regarding the actual status. The overall conclusion is that the average maturity level for Continuous Monitoring and Continuous Assurance reaches nearly stage 3: Maturing and no research has been performed based on a holistic and fully integrated continuous process.**

Keywords-Audit Maturity Model; Continuous Monitoring; Continuous Auditing; Continuous Assurance; Continuous Control Monitoring; Continuous Reporting; Continuum Paradigm; Financial and Non-financial Data; Sustainability Reporting.

I. INTRODUCTION

Scientific papers in the context of the Continuum Paradigm have often been descriptive in nature in recent years. Common concepts within this research area are Continuous Monitoring (CM), Continuous Control Monitoring (CCM) Continuous Auditing (CA), Continuous Assurance (CAss) and Continuous Reporting (CRe). This whole is now referred to as the Continuum Paradigm [1]. The definition of the Continuum Paradigm is a holistic and pragmatical CA maturity model, which facilitates the assessment of CA capabilities [1].

Only a few studies have been conducted in practice within Continuum Paradigm, combined with results of pilots. What is the actual status regarding the Continuum Paradigm? Based on earlier research the aim is to provide insight in the actual status.

Maturity models [1] [2] can be helpful to provide insight in the actual status. Maturity models enable organizations to assess their current situation and provide handholds for improving and future research. An example of the maturity model is the Audit Maturity Model (AMM) proposed by, Vasarhelyi, Alles, Kuenkaikaew and Littley [2]. For the purpose of our research, we assessed and plotted the outcomes of a number of selected pilots on a maturity model.

The remainder of this paper is structured as follows. Section two summarizes the results of the literature review. The research method is described in section three. Section four, the data collection is described. The results are described in section five. Section six describes areas for future research. Finally, the paper concludes in section seven with the conclusion.

II. LITERATURE REVIEW

The need for ongoing, timely assurance of data and information utilizing CM, CCM, CA, CAss and CRe is becoming more and more apparent.

In the last decades, Vasarhelyi, Kuenkaikaew, Alles and Kattie Willems [3] performed research in the area of CCM, CM, CA, CAss. However, this research was mainly related to financial data. Nowadays management needs more and more data to provide assurance of non-financial data, driven by regulation e.g., regarding climate change and the appetite of stakeholders to be timely informed.

Due to these developments the interests for CM, CA, CAss and CRe grow. When assessing the reliability of data produced by the system, the auditor will review confidentiality, integrity, and availability and how the data is ensured by the system of internal controls. IT technology and the AMM can be used to allocate the current status of CM, CCM, CA, CAss and CRe. The allocation provides insight in the actual level of auditing. This is relevant information to guide research and further developments of these elements.

There are several ideas of what continuous concepts and systems are, and how they work. Each of the concepts has their own definition. CM is "the process and technology used to detect compliance and risk issues associated with an organization's financial and operational environment" [4]. The financial and operational environment consists of people, processes, and systems, working together to support efficient and effective operations. Controls are put in place to address risks within these components. Through CM of the operations and controls, weak or poorly designed or implemented controls can be corrected or replaced – thus enhancing the organization's operational risk profile. Investors, governments, the public and other stakeholders continue to increase their demands for more effective corporate governance and business transparency.

The most widely accepted definition for CA is the one released in 1999 by CICA/AICPA and reads as follows: "a methodology for issuing audit reports simultaneously with, or a short period of time after, the occurrence of the relevant events" [5]. The definition for CAss released by Vasarhelyi is therefore "an aggregate of objectively provided assurance services, derived from continuous online management information structures—the objective of which is to improve the accuracy of corporate information processes. These same services may also provide different forms of attestation including point-in-time, evergreen, and continuous" [6]. CAss and CRe are closely linked. There is no CAss without monitoring and intense measuring of the data and data sources.

The AMM classifies the audit evolution into four stages, which are traditional audit, emerging, maturing, and continuous audit. Per stage seven domains have been considered: objective, approach, IT / data access, audit automation, audit and management sharing, management of audit functions, and analytical methods [7].

The first domain is related to a "level of internal audit organization providing financial reports and monitoring internal controls". The second domain approach is related to a "method of audit review, frequency and technique". The third "domain IT / data access" is related to level and frequency of access to the information system and data. The fourth domain "audit automation" is related to the automated level of auditing, usage of technology to assist the audit review cycle. The fifth domain "audit and management" sharing is related to an internal audit department shares systems and resources with management. They have access and utilize the system together. The sixth domain "management and audit function" is related to the degree of cooperation between financial audit and IT audit, collaboration with other compliance departments. The seventh domain "analytic methods" is related to the level of analytical procedure that an internal auditor performs, techniques, and details. The general purpose of maturity model is to provide guidance for a sustainable implementation and growth for organizations [8]. See Table IV: Audit Maturity Model.

To improve the readiness of the article, all relevant abbreviations are presented in Table I below.

TABLE I. OVERVIEW RELEVANT ABBREVIATIONS OF THE ARTICLE

Abbreviation	*Description*
AMM	Audit Maturity Model
CA	Continuous Auditing
CAss	Continuous Assurance
CM	Continuous Monitoring
CMM	Continuous Control Monitoring
CRe	Continuous Reporting

III. RESREARCH METHOD

The goal of this study is to create an overview of the actual status of the separate elements of the Continuum Paradigm. Maturity models are a well-known instrument to support the improvement of functional domains.

A focus group is a group interview involving a small number of participants who have other common experiences. The focus group should be based on the group of individuals that best represents the phenomenon studied. A focus group existing of 1) a junior researcher, with broad experience in internal and external auditing, 2) a senior researcher (PhD) with broad experience as external auditor and 3) a senior researcher with broad experience on business rules management has been established. Before a focus group is conducted, a number of topics need to be addressed: 1) the purpose of the exercise, 2) the selection of the participants, 3) the number of participants, 4) the protocol of the focus group, 5) the AMM model, 6) the protocol for plotting the pilots on the AMM model and 7) useful pilots for research.

Based on the research performed in the past there are different AMM models available. First, we needed to select which AMM model could be used as reference model for this study. The AMM as described by Mantelaers & Zoet [1] and the AMM as described by Vasarhelyi [2] have been selected as starting point. Both AMM's have been compared. The AMM of Vasarhelyi has been used intensively in research articles since 1990. This AMM has also been used as reference for one other similar study (Metcash's). For that reason, it has been decided to use the AMM of Vasarhelyi.

The next step was to define what pilots could be used to perform this study. Research articles during the period 1990 until 2011 have been selected using the following separate and combinations of the key words: audit, auditing, assurance, combined, control, continuous, data, external, financial, integrated, internal, maturity, model, monitoring, non-financial, pilot(s) and studies. The results have been reviewed by the focus group resulting in seven useful articles. Based on the review of the articles there are limited articles published containing sufficient detailed data and information to make it possible to rank and plot the results in the AMM of Vasarhelyi. The content of the selected articles, the level of detail of the data, level of detail of description of the data collection have been investigated. Based on the defined seven sections of the AMM and the data in the articles we searched for relationships and references. In case identifying that there were sufficient relationships and reference these articles were selected to rank and plot the results in the AMM.

In the article of Hardy and Laslett, the results of the study have been plotted in the AMM [8]. The aim of this paper is to report on the implementation of CA and CM at Metcash Limited, an Australian wholesale distribution and marketing company (hereafter, Metcash). The results for this organization are so far notable: over 100 fully automated tests performed daily, a fully integrated exception management system, advancement from data to predictive analytics, and the use of visualization technologies for enhanced reporting. The results of this study have been used as reference to compare the results.

Every participant followed the same protocol, each starting with an introduction and explanation of the purpose and procedure of the meeting. After the introduction, ideas were generated, shared, discussed, and refined by the participants. Furthermore, the participants were invited to submit secondary data regarding CM, CA, CAss and CRe in the AMM.

Based on the pre-work, two pilots have been identified by the participants useful for plotting the results on the AMM. Each participant plotted the pilots individually. The results have been collected and the average results have been calculated for all three pilots. The average results of the two pilots have been compared with the reference pilot of Metcash's. The results have been shared and discussed with the Focus Group. During this meeting conclusions have been defined and agreed.

IV. Data Collecton

Per pilot further information will be provided as well as the reason why the data has not been used for further research.

A. *Reference Pilot: Metcash's*

The goal of the Metcash pilot (the subject) was to provide key lessons relating to the adoption and implementation of CA and CM because of its advanced maturity. A maturity assessment of Metcash's CA/CM activities was conducted [2]. The results are mapped onto the four stages and seven dimensions.

This research has been performed during 2015 and the articles provided detailed information how to plot the results of a pilot or study [8]. For that reason, the outcome of this study has been used as reference to provide insight in the gap and deviations with other pilots or studies.

Reference research three Pilots: SAPSECURE, CAMAP and BAGHEERA-S™

The goal of this study of the three studies (1) SAPSECURE. (2) CAMAP and (2) Bagheera-S™ is to collect evidence from actual implementations for the need of CA and CM [9]. SAPSECURE was developed to permit auditors to review SAP security settings on a regular basis. It may also be used to provide answers to questions such as, "Who can create a vendor, enter an invoice, and pay it?" SAPSECURE was implemented and tested in a large public-sector organization. The design of CAMAP is based on surveillance of financial transaction data with the intention of profiling and identifying users that violate Segregation of Duties. This CA/CM solution provides an automated, independent mechanism for monitoring key business processes within an organization. Bagheera-S™ has the capability to report on three key business processes: (1) Payroll / Human Resources, (2) Procurement and (3) Finance. The results of the three studies SAPSECURE, CAMAP and BAHEERA-S™ could not be used to plot the results on the AMM as data was missing with regard to approach, IT/Data Access, audit and management sharing and management of the audit function.

B. *Pilot: VODAFONE*

The AICAP published a booklet Audit Analytics and Continuous Audit. In this booklet reference is made to the Vodafone Iceland pilot: Implementing Continuous Monitoring [5]. The scope of the project was to implement exMon for revenue assurance as revenue leakage is a known issue in the telecom industry, to decrease the time required to process the financial closing month-end, fraud detection and to enhance the quality of the Customer Relationship Management. The data of the Vodafone Iceland project was limited and for that reason this could not be used to prepare a AMM rating.

C. *Pilot: Siemens*

Working with Siemens presented an excellent opportunity to test how CA would move from concept to implementation. Vasarhelyi predicted both that ERP-enabled firms are the environments most suited to first deploy CA, and that the course of the implementation would begin with automation of existing audit procedures and then, once the feasibility and value added has been demonstrated, move on to re-engineering the audit to make it more CA ready [3].

At Siemens several hundred procedures regarding Audit Action Sheets are be made up of which describe in considerable detail what the internal auditor is supposed to test for in each SAP system environment. After examination of 25-30 Audit Action Sheets, twelve were chosen as representative of the challenges on automating and reengineering. The Audit Action Sheets are related to inadequate protection for SAP access. Testing one of the major general IT controls, logical access, which is non-financial data. In Visual Basic a prototype has been developed. The Siemens experience indicates that in environments characterized by highly automated business processes, CA can be defined as a process that continually tests controls based upon criteria prescribed by the internal auditor and identifies exceptions for the internal auditor to perform additional procedures. During this project the CM of internal control settings into the CA concepted model have been achieved. This included the treatment of transactional level data (non-financial).

D. *Pilot: HSP*

The HSP project is based on modeling processes required data at a highly disaggregate level, far below the level of account balances that are used in the standard audit analytical procedures. Due to fact that there was access to the full richness of the dataset, it was feasible to create the process-based audit models using as benchmarks. Continuity

Equations (CE), which has been defined by Rogers as stable probabilistic models of highly disaggregated business processes [10]. The CE defined is related to the following strictly enforced business rule of the procurement process: no deliveries are to be accepted without a cross reference to a purchase order. The existence of a deterministic relationship between the counts of purchase orders sent and of the shipments received can be tested. The HSP experience indicates that for CE systems of this level of complexity requires powerful statistical techniques which allow for dynamic set of CEs with multiple time lags and feedback loops. The experience also made clear that CEs to become an essential component in the future CA systems, they will have to be sufficiently easy to implement. This which means that generic CE models developed in the laboratory must be generally applicable to different firms and processes.

E. Plotting Pilots Results on AMM

The focus group used the data of the Siemens Project and HSP project to complete the AMM as the provided data was sufficient to make plotting possible. The outcome is presented in the Table II, which contains an overview of the results per pilot, the reference pilot and average for the seven sections of the AMM.

TABLE II. RESULTS PILOTS AND AVERAGE AMM

	Pilot 1: Siemens	Pilot 2: HSP	Pilot 3: Metcash	Average results
Objectives	2.3	2.5	3.0	2.6
Approach	2.7	1.3	3.0	2.3
IT/Data access	3.0	2.7	3.0	2.9
Audit automation	2.5	2.7	3.0	2.7
Audit and management sharing	2.3	2.3	3.0	2.6
Management of the audit function	2.0	2.0	2.5	2.2
Analytical methods	2.3	2.7	3.0	2.7
Total	19.3	16.0	20.5	18.6
Number of sections	7.0	7.0	7.0	7.0
Average	2.8	2.3	2.9	2.7

Table III provides insight in the elements that have been in scope of the pilot. The first column of Table III refers to the main scope of the pilot, Assurance, Audit or Monitoring. The second column of Table III relates to the part of the Continuum Paradigm in scope of the pilot e.g. CRe, CAss, CA, CM and in addition related elements such as process data, general IT controls, Internal Control System and Enterprise Risk Management system. The elements process data, general IT controls, Internal Control System and Enterprise Risk Management system are added as these are relevant for the external audit to decide the final level of assurance of the audit. The elements process data and general IT controls are defined further in detail. In case 'In scope' is mentioned the related element was part of the pilot. All the other elements were not part of the pilot and for that reason no research has been performed to the Continuum Paradigm based on a holistic view.

TABLE III. SCOPING PILOTS ELEMENTS CONTINUOUS

Scope	Part	IT or Data	Results of the Pilots	
			Pilot 1 Siemens	*Pilot 2 HSP*
Assurance	Continuous Reporting			
	Continuous Assurance			
Audit	Continuous Audit		In scope	In scope
Monitoring	Continuous Monitoring		In scope	In scope
	Process Data	Financial Data		
		Non-Financial Data	In scope	In scope
	General IT Controls	Logical Access	In scope	
		Physical Access		
		Back-up and Recovery		
		Change Management		
	Internal Control System		In scope	In scope
	Enterprise Risk Management System			

V. RESULTS

The overall outcome of plotting both pilots including the reference pilot is that the overall average maturity level is nearly stage 3: Monitoring. Stage 4: Continuous Audit has still not been achieved yet.

There are limited pilots and studies with sufficient detailed data and information available to plot the results and outcome on the AMM. The analysis of the two projects makes clear that the research on CM and CA is still scarce and in maturation and mainly related to non-financial data. Both pilots used for this experiment are related to CM of non-financial data. CAss and CRe are not part of the selected pilots. No pilots or studies based on actual implementations have been set up to perform research in the fields of CM, CA, CAss and CRe as one holistic and fully integrated process. To achieve a successful implementation of the continuous concept it requires an integrations and alignment of all elements of the chain from the start of selection of the data until providing CAss and deliver CRe.

VI. FUTURE RESEARCH

There is an increased need and growing pressure from stakeholders for receiving a continuous flow of assured data and information, specific non-financial data will become more relevant. Compliance, new laws and regulations will become applicable requesting assurance services of financial and non-financial data. As example the development of Corporate Sustainability Reporting, the EU regulation applicable as of 2025 regarding Environmental Social and Governance (ESG), the monitoring of General Data Protection Regulation and current developments regarding Process Robotic Automation. All these new developments included reporting reliability of financial data as well as non-financial data.

CCM can be applied to achieve insight in the existing level of assurance, to make the internal audit function more efficient and possibly, more effective. Auditors are skeptical about reliability of automated controls. There is a need for general audit and assurance models which fit system-based auditing approaches and a Continuous Integrated Assurance

Concept for financial as well as non-financial data. Further research is needed, e.g., blockchain solution, to increase the reliability of the data, financial as well as non-financial data, and the overall level of trust. The outcome could be used to fine-tune the AMM.

New guidance and standards should be defined and implemented in close cooperation and partnership with the developers, producers, users and end users of CM, CA, CAss and CRe to control and manage the levels of expectation.

Further research is needed to get insight in the bottlenecks of why CA has yet not as a fully holistic process been implemented.

VII. Conclusion

The overall outcome was that the average maturity level for CM and CA reaches nearly stage 3: Maturing.

No research was performed based on a holistic and fully integrated process including the status and maturity level of the Line of Assurance at the client.

Limited research has been performed on CMM, CM, CA, CAss and CRe of financial data.

A certain minimum level of the LoA at the client will be required to implement CMM, CM, CA, CAss and CRe.

The holistic and fully integrated process could be very helpful for organizations accountable for reporting of sustainability, non-financial data across the organizations, e.g. usage of CO^2 in the supply chain process or energy process, waste water management, employees (own) and contractors Lost Time Injury Frequency Rate (LTIFR). Research could be performed in combination with automated audit standards is an option to achieve continuous assurance across the organizations and their business processes.

To meet the upcoming requirements of CM, CA, CAss and CRe a comprehensive holistic and fully integrated approach would need to address Line of Assurance testing, CCM testing, continuous internal control testing, continuous data testing, continuous transaction testing and continuous assurance testing.

The AMM could support academics by research and the business by further development of new IT concepts and IT solutions.

References

[1] E. Mantelaers and M. Zoet, "Association for Information Systems AIS Electronic Library (AISeL) Continuous Auditing: A Practical Maturity Model," 2018. [Online]. Available: https://aisel.aisnet.org/mcis2018/40

[2] M. A. Vasarhelyi, M. Alles, S. Kuenkaikaew, and J. Littley, "The acceptance and adoption of continuous auditing by internal auditors: A micro analysis," International Journal of Accounting Information Systems, vol. 13, no. 3, pp. 267–281, Sep. 2012, doi: 10.1016/j.accinf.2012.06.011.

[3] M. A. Vasarhelyi, S. Kuenkaikaew, J. Littley, and K. Katie Williams, "Continuous Auditing technology adoption in leading internal audit organizations," 2008. [Online]. Available: https://www.researchgate.net/publication/229004600

[4] G. Locke and P. D. Gallagher, "Guide for Applying the Risk Management Framework to Federal Information Systems," 2010. [Online]. Available: http://csrc.nist.gov/publications.

[5] AICPA, Audit Analytics and Continuous Audit: Looking Toward the Future. 2015.

[6] M. A. Vasarhelyi, "Chapter 12 CONCEPTS IN CONTINUOUS ASSURANCE."

[7] M. G. Alles, A. Kogan, and M. A. Vasarhelyi, "Putting Continuous Auditing Theory into Practice: Lessons from Two Pilot Implementations," 2008. [Online]. Available: www.businessfinancemag.com

[8] C. A. Hardy and G. Laslett, "Continuous auditing and monitoring in practice: Lessons from Metcash's business assurance group," Journal of Information Systems, vol. 29, no. 2, pp. 183–194, Jun. 2015, doi: 10.2308/isys-50969.

[9] K. Singh, P. J. Best, M. Bojilov, and C. Blunt, "Continuous auditing and continuous monitoring in ERP environments: Case studies of application implementations," Journal of Information Systems, vol. 28, no. 1, pp. 287–310, 2014, doi: 10.2308/isys-50679.

[10] C. Rogers, "Continuous monitoring of business controls: A pilot implementation of a continuous auditing system at Siemens Discussant's comments," International Journal of Accounting Information Systems, vol. 7, no. 2. Elsevier Inc., pp. 167–169, 2006. doi: 10.1016/j.accinf.2006.03.006.

TABLE IV. AUDIT MATURITY MODEL

Stage	*Stage 1*	*Stage 2*	*Stage 3*	*Stage 4*
Domain	*Traditional audit*	*Emerging*	*Maturing*	*Continuous audit*
Objectives	- Assurance on the financial reports presented by management	- Effective control monitoring	- Verification of the quality of controls and operational results	- Improvements in the quality of data - Creation of a critical meta-control structure
Approach	- Traditional interim, and year-end audits	- Traditional approach with some key monitoring processes	- Usage of alarms as evidence - Continuous control monitoring	- Audit by exception
IT/Data access	- Case by case basis - Data is captures during the audit process	- Repeating key extractions on cycles	- Systematic monitoring of processes with data capture	- Complete data access - Audit data warehouse. Production, finance, benchmarking and error history
Audit automation	- Manual processes & separate IT audit	- Audit management software - Work paper preparation software	- Automated monitoring module - Alarm and follow up process	- Continuous monitoring and immediate response - Most of audit automated
Audit and management sharing	- Independent and adversarial	- Independent with some core monitoring shared	- Shared systems and resources with natural process synergies	- Purposeful parallel systems and common infrastructures
Management of the audit function	- Financial organization supervises audit and Matrix to Board of Directors	- Some degree of coordination between the areas of risk, auditing and compliance - IT audit works independently	- Internal Audit and IT audit coordinate risk management and share automatic audit processes - Auditing links financial data to operational processes	- Centralized and integrated with risk management, compliance and SOX / layer with external audit
Analytical methods	- Financial ratios	-Financial ratios at sector level / account level	- KPI level monitoring - Structural continuity equations -Monitoring at transaction level	- Corporate models of the main sectors of the business - Early warning system

Toward a Continuous Measurement Model

Qing Huang, Miklos A. Vasarhelyi
Accounting & Information System Department
Rutgers University
Newark, USA
qing.huang@rutgers.edu
miklosv@business.rutgers.edu

Eric J.H.J. Mantelaers
Research Group: Future-proof Auditor
Zuyd University of Applied Sciences
Sittard, Netherlands
Eric.Mantelaers@zuyd.nl

Abstract— **The business and Enterprise Resource Planning (ERP) system data for accounting and auditing is close to continuous, but the accounting and auditing work is interval-based and loses the close to continuous characteristic of the business measurement process. A series of proxies for more frequent measures have emerged in the increasingly desperate attempt to have very short time market trading superiority. Our objective in this paper is to propose a continuous measurement framework in critical areas of business.**

Keywords- continuous measurement; continuum paradigm; business reporting; cybersecurity; sustainability; ESG.

I. INTRODUCTION

The current accounting and reporting model derives from first mainly legal oriented records of the 12th and 13th centuries from traders from Florence and then more analytic double entry records formalized by Pacioli in late 1400s [4]. At that time, trading was manual, and the determinants for the success of a business were reporting assets and capital structure. Consequently, the traditional accounting and reporting mechanisms worked well for the purposes of record keeping, asset management, supply chain management, loan recording, and profit distribution. However, trading nowadays is real-time, volumes are enormous, and the business environment changes fast. Only relying on annual or quarterly financial reporting is not enough for the algorithms / decision-makers to make good decision [22]. As [11] states:

> *"Over the last few decades, the relationship between market values and traditional financial information has become substantially weaker. [32] had found that income reflected 50% of information in the market while current market studies show relationships in the 5-7% range... [6] has shown that over the years this relationship is less and less relevant and that the inclusion of more firm-specific measures outside of the core four accounting statements, such as intangibles [7] and R&D [8] may provide better matching between market and accounting metrics."*

The progressive adoption of automatic trading by investors, which could entail even close to 70% of daily trading in the markets, as well as index fund trading by algorithms aiming at maintaining these funds representative of their indexes [1] adding probably another 15% of the volume. Financial information is provided today by anachronistic reports published at best once every quarter, trading algorithms [17]. Consequently, trading algorithms must resort to other forms of information as triggers of market actions. Although the rules of trading actions are held very private, it appears that trades tend to focus on very short time frame price changes, volume levels, peer stock behavior, and a series of other factors. These other factors may include market changes relative to the particular equities, and more recently exogenous variables such as social media, weather, internet of things, etc. (see Figure 1). A series of proxies for more frequent measures such as parking lot usage [14], electricity consumption [36] have emerged in the increasingly desperate attempt to have very short time market trading superiority. Many other unorthodox proxy measurements will emerge over time.

These factors largely account for 80 or 90 percent of stock trading leaving traditional stock trading a minor effect and consequently, much of prior research on stock trading and financial reporting by and large obsolete. Furthermore, the very important function of business measurement and reporting principles, which trace back to the Securities Acts of 1933 and 1934 as agent accountability, is being measured by increasingly obsolete and anachronistic rules and measurements.

The Enterprise Resource Planning (ERP) system data for accounting and auditing is close to continuous, but the accounting and auditing work is interval-based and loses the close to continuous characteristic of the business measurement process. If the measurement interval is changed, close to continuous reporting is also possible.

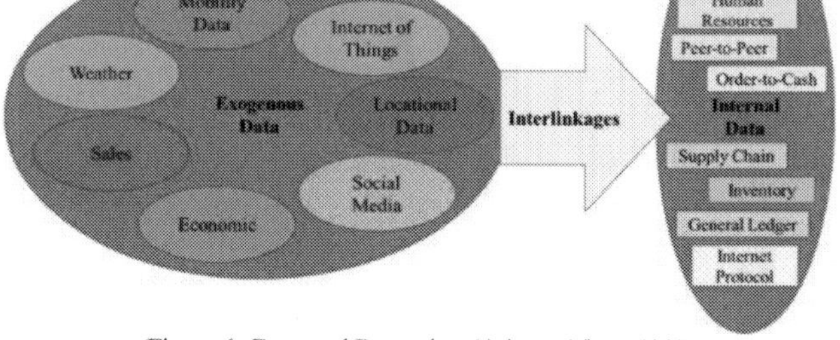

Figure 1. Data and Reporting (Adopted from [11])

However, companies, for obvious reasons, are very hesitant if not mandated, to disclose day-to-day or second-to-second details of their operation even if automatic traders and the modern real-time-economy needs so [26]. Automatic trading algorithms and other modern business issues need real time information, the accounting world is not providing so, consequently new mechanisms are needed [7].

It is not only trading that can benefit of a more continuous schema of measurement, just-in-time production has long been the objective of supply chains where inventory carrying costs tradeoff with periodical ordering and delivering costs.

Although automatic trading is a natural driver for frequent measurement and query-based reporting many processes in the business ecosystem can benefit or demand different methods of measurement, alternative forms of reporting, improved approaches for verification (audit), and automatic actioning algorithms. However, the acceleration and "ad-hoctization" of these processes is not always necessarily desirable. [5] has shown that daily data measurements create instability in models and therefore for certain types of prediction and modeling they are not the most desirable. The objective in this study is to propose a continuous measurement framework that can provide appropriate timely information for both internal and external stakeholders in some business areas that we think are critical.

This paper is structured as follows. Section II summarizes some related literature. Section III elaborate the idea of continuous measurement metrics for critical business areas, and Section IV, classifies and discusses the advantage and disadvantages of both the traditional and proposed measurements.

II. LITERATURE REVIEW

The double entry method for business recording or measurement originated from 12th and 13th centuries [1]. On of the first attempts for a continuous paradigm in accounting and auditing was proposed by Vasarhelyi and Halper at Bell Labs [25]. Later, the Canadian Institute of Chartered Accountants defined continuous auditing as "*a methodology for issuing audit reports simultaneously with, or a short period of time after, the occurrence of the relevant events [9]*". The continuum paradigm covers a wide range of interrelated activities, such as continuous reporting, continuous monitoring, continuous auditing, continuous assurance and so on.

The traditional approach to information technology applications in auditing are characterized by a predominant focus on a singular tool for a singular problem. While a small number of papers focus on a more holistic approach. However, auditing is an evolving process. [13] argue that Continuous Auditing can be represented as a maturity model that consists of five maturity levels and four factors. The progressive maturity levels that can be used in auditing are: 1) initial approach, 2) ad hoc approach, 3) defined approach, 4) managed approach, and 5) optimized approach. The four capabilities are: A) systems, B) data, C) organization, and D) people [13]. That study fills a gap in the literature concerning a more holistic approach on auditing, and it answers the call for more practical oriented research on Continuous Auditing (CA).

Substantial changes in technology, regulation, and business environment led to increased demand for continuous auditing and facilitated the development of a continuous auditing framework [27]. For example, [34] argues for the necessity to provide a reliable real-time monitoring of financial activities resulting in the need for continuous auditing. Emerging technological capabilities also facilitates the usage of other proxy measurements. For example, search volume can be used in firm valuation [31][37], the number of cars in the retailer's parking lots can be a proxy for a timely measure of store performance [19],electricity consumption could detect firm financial misreporting [20], etc.

III. POTENTIAL APPLICATIONS OF CONTINUOUS MEASUREMENT

In the following sections, we discuss how continuous measurement can be used in three critical areas of the enterprise: business reporting, financial and non-financial information related to ESG, and cybersecurity.

A. Continuous Measurement for Business Reporting

Traditional annual business reporting can only provide limited information and is outdated in the real-time economy [24]. Continuous measurements of real-time processes are needed. The emergence of various forms of exogenous data as proxies for business process measurement provides potential sources for state-to-art business reporting. Existing successful applications indicate that business processes and Key Performance Indicators (KPIs) can be used not only to measure but also to improve business performance [35]. Instead of measuring the periodic financial data, we propose a process-based continuous performance measurement framework (PCPM) to measure the business performance. This framework consists of three stages. First, the company needs to construct a business process model; then KPIs will be designed for each process; finally, a continuous monitoring dashboard will be built to monitor all KPIs in real-time.

1) Construct a process model

Each company is a collection of activities that are applied to produce, design, market, deliver, and support its production [30]. But the activities and process models vary from company to company, thus the construction of the process model should follow the company's operational characteristics. [30] provides a value chain model that classifies the company's activities into primary activities and supporting activities. Consequently, the measurements

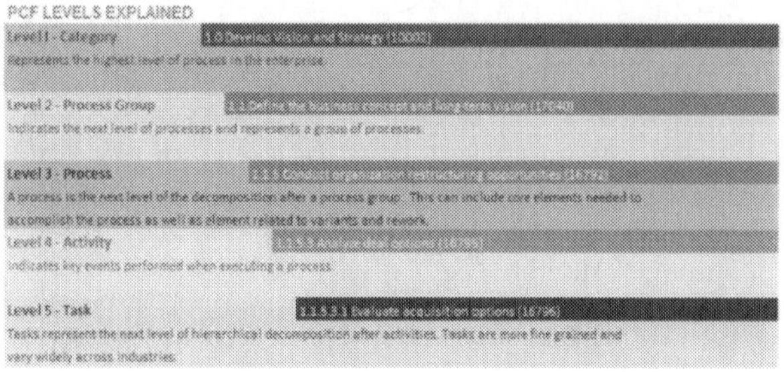

Figure 2: PCF levels explained (adopted from [2])

based on these value activities can provide valuable information to stakeholders. However, these valued activities might be too general for company valuation, thus, a more detailed process model might be needed. The American Productivity & Quality Center (APQC) regularly issues the Process Classification Framework (PCF) [2] for different industries. These frameworks usually have five levels (Figure 2), and for each level, it has detailed activities and evaluation metrics. Companies can construct their specific process model based on this framework.

2) Construc KPI for each process

After all level processes are defined, key performance indicators for each process can be constructed. The KPIs can include not only financial measurements but also customer, internal process, as well as learning & growth perspectives [21].

3) Integration

The last step for the business reporting is to build a continuous monitoring dashboard to monitor all processes and KPIs. The KPIs need to be aggregated at a task, activity, process (group), and category levels to obtain a larger picture of performance at each level (Figure 3). These can also be aggregated in monetary or percentage score formats. The KPI monitoring system can also be combined with process mining, which analyses the compliance and variance of processes[28].

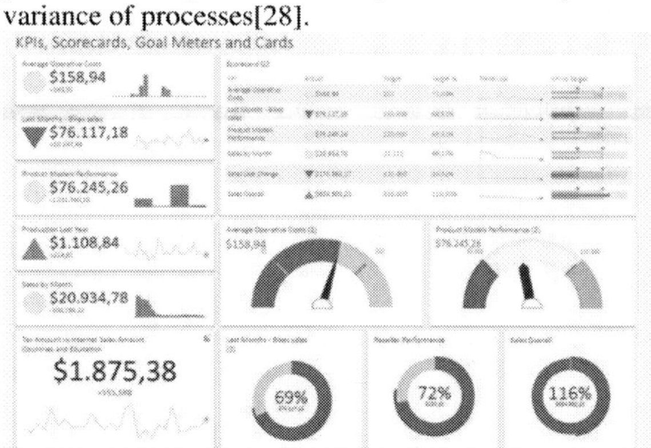

Figure 3: KPI Monitoring Example (Adopted from [23])

B. Continuous Measurement for sustainability reporting

Besides business reporting, sustainability reporting is nowadays also a major concern of information users. Some changes in environmental circumstances can be catastrophic to companies, consequently, the timely monitoring and measurement of the sustainability-related information is very important. There are multiple sources for sustainability or Environment, Social, and Governance (ESG) information, including company annual reports, company websites, regulatory filling, news, etc (Briscoe [15]). These different and highly unstructured data satisfy many requirements but are of very difficult obtention. Thus, a comprehensive measurement system can be very useful for both the usage by the company and its external stakeholders.

The European Union has been working on corporate sustainability for many years. In recent years, the European Financial Reporting Advisory Group (EFRAG) is moving full speed ahead in the development of sustainability reporting disclosure standards and has published many sustainability-related working papers. Companies can follow the proposed topic and subtopics proposed by EFRAG [12] (see Figure 4) to construct their own reporting range and measure related metrics dynamically.

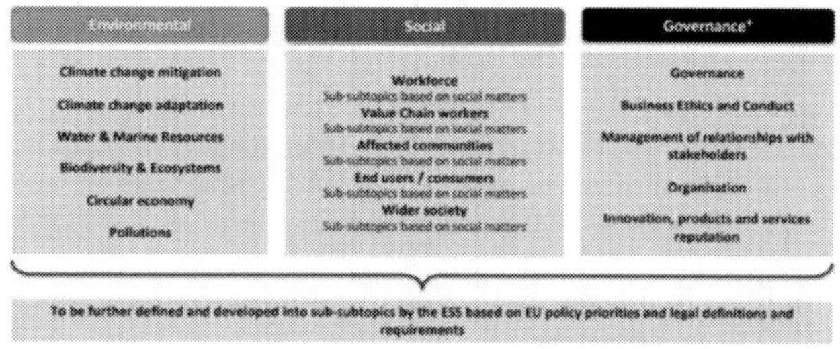

Figure 4: Proposal for a detailed structure for sustainability reporting topics and sub-topics (Adopted from [12])

C. Continuous Measurement for Cybersecurity

Cybersecurity needs had taken very central roles in modern business concerns. Firms that experience cyberattacks or incidents may suffer substantial costs and other negative impacts, such as remediation costs, increased defensive costs, lost business, litigation risks, increased insurance premiums, reputation damage, and so on [33]. According to the 2019 data breach report (IBM [16]), the average cost of a data breach is globally 3.92 million dollars and 8.19 million of dollars for the United States. A cyberattack on May 7, 2021, over a fuel pipeline company caused an emergency declaration in Washington D.C. and 17 states [29].

To respond to the increasing cyberattacks and potential side effects, the AICPA [3] issued cybersecurity risk management description criteria which can provide some guidance on how to measure the cybersecurity-related risks. This guidance consists of nine topic areas, including business operation, cybersecurity objective, governance structure, control process, and so on (see Table I). Companies can continuously measure the listing cybersecurity-related information, and thoroughly understand the organization's cybersecurity status.

TABLE I. CRITERIA FOR CYBERSECUTIRY RISK MANAGEMEN

Nature of Business and Operation • The principal products or services and the methods by which they are distributed
Nature of Information at Risk • The principal types of sensitive information created, collected, transmitted, used, or stored
Cybersecurity Objective • Objectives related to availability, confidentiality, integrity of data, and integrity of processing
Inherent Cybersecurity Risks • characteristics of technologies, connection types, use of service providers, and delivery channels used by the entity • organizational and user characteristics • environmental, technological, organizational and other changes during the period covered by the description at the entity and in its environment.
Cybersecurity risk governance structure • The process for establishing, maintaining, and communicating integrity and ethical values to support the functioning of the cybersecurity risk management program
Cybersecurity Risk Assessment Process • Process for identify and access related risk
Cybersecurity Communications and Quality of Cybersecurity Information • The process for internally and externally communicating cybersecurity information
Monitoring of the Cybersecurity Risk Management Program • Conduct evaluation of the operating effectiveness of key control activities • Evaluate and communicate, in a timely manner, identified security threats, vulnerabilities, and control deficiencies to parties responsible for taking corrective actions, including management and the board of directors, as appropriate
Cybersecurity Control Processes • The process for developing a response to assessed risks, including the design and implementation of control processes

Source: Adopted from [3]

IV. CONCLUSION

The traditional periodic interval measurement is usually yearly or quarterly, and it is standardized, stable, and well regulated, since it has been used for several centuries. However, this measurement is not adequate for the real time economy[10]. Companies may lose great opportunities due to outdated information, and investors may incur in many extra costs to obtain more timely information. Thus, more frequent measurements can benefit both parties. Moreover, the continuous business activities and ERP data, the just-in-time production, and the available exogenous data provide the foundations for short interval or continuous measurement. TABLE II summarizes the advantages and disadvantages of long and short interval measurements. Initial measurement costs might be high but they will decrease over time while the company is getting more familiar with the measurement process. The same will occur for measurement accuracy, which can be low at the beginning, and then improve over time.

TABLE II. LONG INTERVAL AND SHORT INTERVAL MEASUREMENT COMPARSION

	Advantages	Disadvantages
Long interval Measure ment	• Standardized • Well regulated • More stable • More familiar to users	• Outdated • Relies on a series of assumptions and rules (e.g., depreciation)
Short interval measure ment	• Timely • High Transparency • Comprehensive	• Less regulated • Measurement cost might be high at the beginning

To summarize, continuous measurement can benefit both the company and investors in the long run, but there's still a long way to achieve its desired utility. These will have a profound effect on standards. Consequently, future research is needed to further explore questions like what proxies are appropriate for the continuous measurement, what techniques can be used, how the regulations, standards, and assurance professions will be affected, etc.

REFERENCES

[1] A. Frino and D. R. Gallagher, "Tracking S&P 500 index funds", The Journal of Portfolio Management, 28(1), pp. 44-55, 2001.

[2] APQC, American Productivity & Quality Center Process Classification Framework , 2020. Aviable at: https://www.apqc.org/process-frameworks. Accessed on June 3, 2022.

[3] American Institute of Certified Public Accountants (AICPA), Description Criteria for Management's Description of the Entity's Cybersecurity Risk Management Program, 2017, Available at: https://us.aicpa.org/content/dam/aicpa/interestareas/frc/assuranceadvisoryservices/downloadabledocuments/cybersecurity/description-criteria.pdf. Accessed on June 3, 2022.

[4] A. Sangster, "Pacioli's lens: God, humanism, Euclid, and the rhetoric of double entry", The Accounting Review 93, no. 2, pp. 299-314, 2018.

[5] A. Kogan, M. G. Alles, M. A. Vasarhelyi, and J. Wu, "Design and evaluation of a continuous data level auditing system", Auditing: A Journal of Practice & Theory, 33(4), pp. 221-245, 2014.

[6] B. Lev, "On the usefulness of earnings and earnings research: Lessons and directions from two decades of empirical research", Journal of accounting research, 27, pp. 153-192, 1989.

[7] B. Lev and P. Zarowin, "The boundaries of financial reporting and how to extend them", Journal of Accounting research, 37(2), pp. 353-385, 1999.

[8] B. Lev, B and T. Sougiannis, "The capitalization, amortization, and value-relevance of R&D", Journal of accounting and economics, 21(1), pp. 107-138, 1996.

[9] CICA/AICPA. Continuous auditing. Research report, Toronto, Canada. The Canadian Institute of Chartered Accountants, 1999.

[10] D. Y. Chan and M. A. Vasarhelyi, "Innovation and practice of continuous auditing", International Journal of Accounting Information Systems, 12(2), pp. 152-160, 2011. Doi: https://doi.org/10.1016/j.accinf.2011.01.001.

[11] D. Pei and M. A. Vasarhelyi, "Big data and algorithmic trading against periodic and tangible asset reporting: The need for U-XBRL". International Journal of Accounting Information Systems, 37, p.100453, 2020.

[12] European Financial Reporting Advisory Group, EFRAG, "Proposal for a Relevent and Dynamic EU Sustainability Reporting Standard-Setting", February, 2021. Avaliable at: https://www.efrag.org/Assets/Download?assetUrl=%2Fsites%2Fwebpublishing%2FSiteAssets%2FEFRAG%2520PTF-NFRS_MAIN_REPORT.pdf. Accessed on June 3, 2022.

[13] E. Mantelaers and M. Zoet, "Continuous Auditing: A Practical Maturity Model", In MCIS (p. 40), 2018.

[14] H. Bradley, "Startups mine market-moving data from fields, parking lots-even shadows", The Wall Street Journal. https://www.wsj.com/articles/startups-mine-market-moving-data-from-fields-parking-lotseven-shadows-1416502993. Accessed on June 3, 2022.

[15] I. Briscoe, "What Constitutes ESG Data?", Demyst, 2021, https://demyst.com/blog/what-constitutes-esg-data?gclid=EAIaIQobChMIzaaEttLV9QIVrXxvBB0McgCvEAAYAyAAEgLnQvD_BwE. Accessed on June 3, 2022.

[16] IBM, Cost of a Data Breach Report [Press release], 2019. Retrieved from https://www.ibm.com/downloads/cas/ZBZLY7KL. Accessed on June 3, 2022.

[17] J. Brogaard, T. Hendershott, and R. Riordan, "High-frequency trading and price discovery", The Review of Financial Studies, 27(8), pp. 2267-2306, 2014.

[18] J. Dai, A. Medinetz, and M. A Vasarhelyi, " Audit Analytics in the Financial Industry" (Part of the Rutgers Accounting Series). Emerald Publishing, 2019.

[19] J. K. Kang, L. Stice-Lawrence and Y.T.F. Wong, " The firm next door: Using satellite images to study local information advantage", Journal of Accounting Research, 59(2), pp. 713-750, 2021.

[20] K. D. Allee, B. Baik, and Y. Roh, "Detecting Financial Misreporting with Real Production Activity: Evidence from an Electricity Consumption Analysis", Contemporary Accounting Research, 38(3), pp. 1581-1615, 2021.

[21] K. H. Han and J. G. Kang, "A process-based performance measurement framework for continuous process improvement", International Journal of Industrial Engineering, 14(3), pp. 220-228, 2007.

[22] K. Smit, M. Zoet and E. Mantelaers, "An Evaluation of the Added Value of Business Rules Management Principles to Transparency", Journal of Advanced Management Science Vol. 8(1), 2020.

[23] Kyubit Business Intelligence. https://www.kyubit.com/kpi-dashboard. Accessd on June 3, 2022.

[24] L. Zhang, D. Pei, and M. A. Vasarhelyi, "Toward a new business reporting model", Journal of Emerging Technologies in Accounting, 14(2), pp. 1-15, 2017.

[25] M. A. Vasarhelyi and F. B. Halper, " The continuous audit of online systems", Auditing: A Journal of Practice & Theory, 10(1), pp. 110-125, 1991.

[26] M. A. Vasarhelyi and M. Greenstein, "Underlying principles of the electronization of business: A research agenda", International Journal of Accounting Information9Systems, 4(1), pp. 1-25, 2003.

[27] M. Eulerich and A. Kalinichenko, "The Current State and Future Directions of Continuous Auditing Research: An Analysis of the Existing Literature", Journal of Information Systems, Vol. 32, No. 3, pp. 31-51, Fall 2018.

[28] M. Jans, M. A. Vasarhelyi, and M. Alles, "A field study on the use of process mining of event logs as an analytical procedure in auditing", The Accounting Review, 89(5), pp. 1751-1773, 2014.

[29] M. Stuti, "Biden adminstration declares emergency over fuel pipeline hack and warns more attacks will come", Independent. https://www.independent.co.uk/news/world/americas/us-politics/cyber-attack-us-pipeline-biden-b1844775.html. Accessed on June 3, 2022.

[30] M. E. Porter, "The value chain and competitive advantage", Understanding business processes, 2, pp. 50-66, 2001.

[31] P. C. Chiu, S. H. Teoh, Y. Zhang and X. Huang, "Using google searches of firm products to assess revenue quality and detect revenue management", 2020. Available at SSRN 3252314.

[32] R. Ball and P. Brown, "An empirical evaluation of accounting income numbers", Journal of accounting research, pp. 159-178, 1968.

[33] Security Exchange Commision (SEC), Commission Statement and Guidance on Public Company Cybersecurity Disclosures, 2018.

[34] S. Flowerday and R. von Solms, "Real-time information integrity = System integrity + data integrity + continuous assurances", Computers & Security 24 (8), pp. 604–613, 2005, https://doi.org/10.1016/j.cose.2005.08.004

[35] U. S. Bititci, "Modelling of performance measurement systems in manufacturing enterprises", International journal of production economics, 42(2), pp. 137-147, 1995.

[36] Z. Da, D. Huang, and H. Yun, "Industrial electricity usage and stock returns", Journal of Financial and Quantitative Analysis52 (1), pp. 37–69, 2017.

[37] Z. Da, J. Engelberg and P. Gao, "In search of attention", The journal of finance, 66(5), pp. 1461-1499, 2011.

Continuous Monitoring of Counter-Accounts in Hospitality

Assistance with implementation of SDG 5: Gender equality

Anaïs M. Y. Heeren
Hotel Management
Zuyd University of Applied Science
Maastricht, The Nederlands
lectoraat.okb@zuyd.nl

Martijn M. Zoet, Eric Mantelaers
Finance and Control & Accountancy
Zuyd University of Applied Science
Sittard, The Netherlands
martijn.zoet@zuyd.nl

Abstract—**Sustainability reporting has become common practice in organizations. A factor that is associated with the rise of sustainability reporting is greenwashing. In order to counter greenwashing practices, counter-accounting, referring to the use of information produced by actors outside a given organization or industry, aims to help verify statements made by organizations. Although counter-accounting already exists in the toolbox of the auditor, it is mainly applied in an ad-hoc manner and rarely continuous. In this study, a continuous monitoring system for counter-accounts is proposed to measure gender inequality. The application of the system is demonstrated using data from the hospitality sector regarding the fulfillment of different job titles by male and female executives. The presented results shed light on occupational gender segregation and provide a basis from which more continuous counter-accounting systems can be developed.**

Keywords-continuous monitoring; hospitality sector; sustainability reporting; counter-accounting; auditing, job titles; gender segregation

I. INTRODUCTION

Over the last few decades, social and environmental challenges have led to a push in organizations' sustainability-related activities. The consensus regarding organizations' shared responsibility to act in accordance with sustainable purposes for all stakeholders resulted in increased regulations and policies [29] and consequently, also growth in organizations' sustainability reporting. For instance, in 2020, 92% of the S&P 500 companies published sustainability reports or disclosures as opposed to only 20% in 2011 [12]. Such reports are an important part of the conversation between organizations and their stakeholders.

Simultaneously, parallel to the increased sustainability communication, skepticism has grown towards the authenticity of such reporting [20]. A large body of research addresses how some organizations use such sustainability disclosures as "greenwashing" in order to develop a more sustainable image and "window dress" corporate behavior [6] [22]. Hence, greater emphasis has been placed on ensuring the reliability of corporate sustainability reporting. The growing awareness on the reliability of such reports has, for instance, translated into the implementation of a standardized reporting framework with principles to define the content and the quality of reports, as proposed by the Global Reporting Initiative (GRI) [5].

Despite this development, there still remains tension between corporate sustainability discourse and practice [6]. To address the critique regarding the credibility and reliability of sustainability reporting and restore confidence in such disclosures, auditors and assurance providers are introduced to verify the statements made by the reporting organizations [5]. However, given the questioned honesty of corporate disclosures, it becomes increasingly more worthwhile to explore other accounts of organizational activities such as "counter-accounts", that are, contrary to voluntary published corporate reports, outside the control of the organization subject to the account [30]. Counter-accounting through media such as the internet and social media contributes to verifying the organization's legitimacy as it provides an alternative representation of an organization with the aim to rectify otherwise harmful or undesired practices [22] [30]. As previous research suggests, the use of counter-accounts should be further explored [22]. Specifically, to systematically include such counter-accounts when challenging organizations' operations, auditors are in need of an appropriate toolbox existing of a continuous monitoring system [19].

Whereas a continuous monitoring system would be useful to review organizations' disclosures with regard to each and every one of the United Nations' 17 Sustainable Development Goals (SDGs), this paper proposes a continuous monitoring system that addresses the fifth goal, gender equality. Specifically, an application of the system is provided for the hospitality industry, providing insights on occupational gender segregation by mapping the differences in the job titles fulfilled by male and female executives. The research question addressed in this study is the following: "How can a counter-account monitoring system for gender equality in the hospitality industry be designed?".

The remaining part of the paper is structured as follows. Section 2 provides a literature review on counter-accounts, occupational gender segregation, and available monitoring systems. In section 3, a description of the research method is presented. Section 4 gives insight into the data collection and analysis procedure for this application. Section 5 addresses the system architecture and its application. Finally, section 6 concludes the paper.

II. Literature

In 2015, all United Nations Member States endorsed the 2030 Agenda for Sustainable Development, a roadmap for peace and prosperity for both people and the planet, with 17 SDGs at its core [27]. After having defined these integrated, universal goals for sustainable development, the next step toward achieving them was to set specific targets for each goal, which were then in turn further broken down to measurable indicators. However, the incompleteness of the indicators, even after more than three years into the program, make the tracking of the progress towards meeting the SDGs challenging [23].

To assess whether the actions taken by countries and organizations to reach the SDGs are effective and in correspondence with their own reporting, scholars have argued the need to explore new Information, Communication, and Technology (ICT) in combination with multiple data sources to provide a common, continuous, and transparent representation of their efforts [23].

A. *Counter-accounts*

As sustainability becomes an indispensable topic on corporate agendas, growing skepticism toward the authenticity of organizations' sustainability reporting arises. This calls for effective monitoring and auditing in this environment in order to ensure trust and credibility of the information contained in such reports.

With the acceleration of available, real-time information flows, the "archival audit", where the auditor evaluates organizations' yearly reports, is complemented if not replaced by a more real-time evaluation called "continuous auditing" [1]. Together with continuous monitoring, which is described as an ongoing management process to monitor internal controls, continuous auditing aims to provide the organization with a reasonable level of objective assurance [26].

Aside from introducing a continuous monitoring mechanism to provide assurance on these reports and the organizations behind them, scholars have argued the need to explore other accounts, or "counter-accounts", that are outside the control of the respective organization [30]. Counter-accounts are defined as accountings that challenge the representation established by the subject organization and contribute to critically assessing the organization's corporate accountability or lack thereof [22].

B. *Occupational gender segregation*

Over the past decades, one of the most pressing social issues is inequality [2] . Even though inequality is shown in a broad range of forms, this paper focuses on gender equality, the fifth United Nations SDG. A recent study commissioned by the European Parliament's Policy Department for Citizens' Rights and Constitutional Affairs [9], shows not only a difference in the share of employment between working-age men (79%) and working-age women (67%) but also that those women who are employed, are on average paid 14.1% less per hour compared to their male counterparts.

The gender gap, with its key dimension being the gender pay gap, has a considerable impact on individuals' socioeconomic status since gender equality contributes to both economic growth and sustainable development [9]. Evidently, aside from being listed as one of the United Nations SDGs, gender equality is also addressed by the European Commission in the 2020-2025 Gender Equality Strategy which strives for equal access to the economy across genders. In addition, the European Parliament in 2021 called for a new gender pay gap action plan, addressing women's accessibility to study and work in male-dominated sectors, more flexible work arrangements, and improved wages in female-dominated sectors.

The presence of occupational gender segregation and its role in gender inequality has been widely addressed [14] [28], yet there remains little work on the monitoring and auditing process of occupational gender segregation. Therefore, this paper proposes a continuous monitoring system for counter-accounts that allows internal and external auditors to map both the current state of gender division across different jobs and their evolution over time.

C. *Continuous monitoring systems*

Monitoring statements and claims organization communicate on the one hand and monitoring counter-accounts related to the statements on the other hand can provide valuable insights and prevent greenwashing and/or brownwashing [30]. Multiple studies have focused on analyzing such statements and their counter-accounts. For example, reference [22] analyses counter-accounts and responses by various groups to challenge Nestlé on its sustainability actions. Although data analysis is conducted during these studies, commonly the research is performed once, and is singular problem-oriented, meaning that a specific study focusses on one organization and/or one problem, and executes the analyses once for the purpose of the study [13]. At the end of the studies, there is no information system in place that continuously monitors organizations' claims and related external data to compare both. Systems that continuously monitor data and derive results are developed in other studies related to stock prices [24] and political analyses [4]. Also, studies are conducted that focus on extracting the right information from texts to be able to conduct the analyses [24]. Information systems that *"enable independent parties to provide assurance on a subject matter, using a series of reports, issued simultaneously with or a short period of time after, the occurrence of events underlying the subject matter"* are called Continuous Monitoring Systems. In general such systems are used automatically to monitor internal controls within business processes [24].

However, two changes in the current business environment force organizations to start continuous monitoring of external sources. The first change is that organizations are exposed to increased requirements in terms of regulations and business objectives that require managing and monitoring the entire value chain [10]. Second, organizations more and more have to deal with actors that provide counter-accounts through the monitoring of external sources that provide statements about the organization. The focus of this study is automated continuous monitoring of gender equality across job titles and the challenges that occur. To overcome these challenges a system architecture is proposed and its application is presented. Similar to previous research, we consider Named Entity Recognition (NER) as the basis of our system [11] [24].

III. METHODOLOGY

According to the structures of Design Science, designed artifacts must be measured by predefined variables. With regards to the developed counter-accounting system for gender equality, multiple variables can be measured. Examples of such measurements are usefulness, use, mutual exclusivity, completeness, quality, and impact [15]. As design research is a continuous cycle of building and evaluation, it is practically impossible to measure all elements in one study [16]. In this study, the focus is on use, feasibility, and quality. The reason use, feasibility, and quality are chosen, is to determine if a counter-accounting system for gender equality is feasible. The goal of this research is therefore to identify gender equality across job titles. In addition to the goal of the research, also the maturity of the research field is a factor in determining the appropriate research method and technique. With regards to job titles, this research field is mature. An appropriate focus of research in mature research fields is formal hypothesis testing or reevaluating existing methods [8]. Summarized, to accomplish our research goal, a research approach is needed in which first, job titles are identified and compared, and second, a system in which constant comparison (monitoring) of male and female appointments can be achieved.

To accomplish the first goal, grounded theory is applied. In total, three cycles of coding were completed: 1) open coding, 2) axial coding and 3) selective coding [7]. The goal of open coding is to create the first level of abstraction from analyzed data. This is realized by analyzing website data about announcements of employees' appointments to new jobs. In each appointment announcement the job title (e.g. ceo, cfo), job description, and words indicating gender (e.g. he/she/him/her) are collected. For those job appointments in which no gender could be recognized, additional sources such as LinkedIn and company websites have been investigated to identify the gender. Identifying more precise categories and relationships among the high-level categories is the goal of axial coding. In our study, axial coding focused on identifying standardized job titles. For example, the role of 'Chief executive officer' can be described as 'CEO', 'New company CEO', or 'Chief executive officer' in different job appointments. Selective coding was conducted to select the core category, relate categories, and fill in categories that need further refinement [7]. In our research, this means that standardized job titles are appointed to departments and hierarchy levels, see Section 5 for an example. Then, to increase the generalizability, 81 rounds of automated coding through computational grounded theory have been applied [21]. In Figure 1, the process is visualized with the first step resulting in the creation of the pattern library for job titles. This step involves the exploration of text using unsupervised methods and manual coding. Following a chronological order, step 2 will result in the development of the departments and hierarchy which are in essence a cumulus of categories for the job titles. These are also thoroughly analyzed through the means of inter-rater reliability analysis and later translated into text which can be understood by the computer. To achieve the second goal the design for the Continuous Monitoring of Counter-Accounts system has been developed and tested.

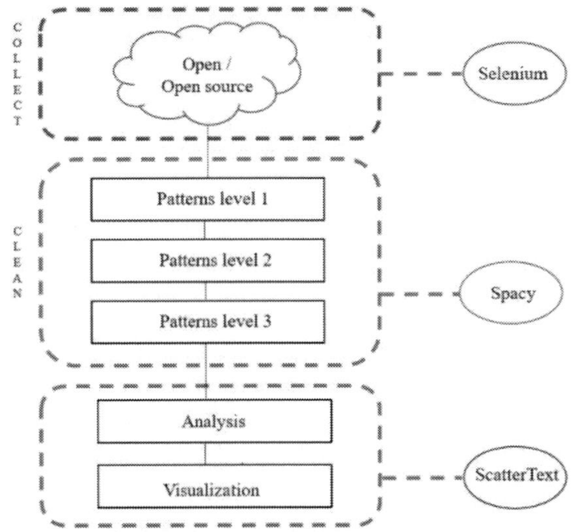

Figure 1. System Architecture: Continuous Monitoring System for Counter-Accounts

IV. DATA COLLECTION AND ANALYSIS

Grounded theory states that the first selection of respondents and documentation is based on the phenomenon studied at a group of individuals, organizations, information technology, or community that best represents this phenomenon. With the goal of this study being the establishment of a counter-accounting system for gender equality, data regarding the job titles of male and female managers had to be collected. Both the data collection and analysis have been performed and supervised by the three authors involved. At the time of writing, the first researcher completes a Master-level degree, whereas the second researcher obtained a Doctoral degree, both having +5 years of experience in Hospitality. The third researcher similarly obtained a Doctoral degree and has 20+ years of experience in Accountancy.

For the model testing, one real-life data set has been collected from Hospitality.net, between the 1st of June 2021 and the 15th of December 2021. The method of data collection involves the entire population of job postings of management employees, during the period mentioned previously. This population, in the first phase of our data collection, has been divided into different strata depending on job title, level, company, and geographical location. For every stratum, several job postings have been scraped and analyzed, totaling 1.000 job titles by open coding. Starting from the 7th of June, the sampling method has been changed. The following phase involved letting the system scrape data and showing the results by means of an automated generated email. The system would scrape newly identified job titles and mention the standardized version. The role of the researchers was to check the accuracy of the system and to standardize new job titles if they were not yet in the system.

V. System Architecture and Application

The architecture to ground the counter-accounting system for gender equality as proposed in this study is visualized in Figure 1. The architecture includes three different sections (Collection, Cleaning, and Analysis and Visualization), that are each supported by a different tool (Selenium, Spacy, and ScatterText). The application of each section is discussed.

A. *Collection of counter-account data*

First, counter-account data, that can counter the statements made by the organization concerning gender equality, need to be identified and collected. For this application, to collect this data, external sources are needed that give insight into the number of males and females appointed to specific job titles. Within the hospitality industry, multiple sources can be used for this, for example, Hospitality.net and LinkedIn. Even though a variety of tools can be used to collect this data, for this application, Selenium, a tool for automated web scraping is employed to extract useful information from the identified sources.

B. *Cleaning of counter-account data*

The second section of the model includes the cleaning of the collected counter-account data. For the job title data, a wide variety of linguistic variations need to be reduced to a manageable amount of job titles. Therefore, by making use of pattern lists, also called 'business rules' that exist of a set of reoccurring words with a predefined annotation, job titles are standardized, appointed to departments, and appointed to levels. To automate this process, a tool called Spacy is used [11].

1) Standardize the job titles: When information on job title data is collected at a large scale, it becomes apparent that organizations give different titles to the same job. For example, when a person is a 'Chief executive officer' this can be described as 'CEO', 'New company CEO', or 'Chief executive officer'. To allow for comparison, these small linguistic variations need to be standardized. Specifically, as for the previous examples, these job titles would be standardized to 'Chief Executive Officer'. In total, the NER system now incorporated 210 standardized job titles [18]. This NER needs to be updated regularly to adjust for both new job titles such as 'vice president sustainability', and for new title variations of existing jobs such as the examples mentioned above. A process to realize these updates has been put into place [18].

2) Appointment to departments: In addition to the job titles, also the department to which the job is appointed needs to be taken into account. Similarly, a standardized appointment of job titles per department needs to be developed. For example, 'Chief Executive Officer' is part of the administrative department, 'Finance Director' is part of the finance department, and 'Director of Human Resource' is part of the human resource department. Having determined the allocation of job titles per department, the axial coding has been automatized through the creation of pattern libraries. Finally, the system now includes a total of 17 departments [18].

3) Appointment to levels: Lastly, aside from department allocation, the job titles can also be categorized based on the hierarchical level to allow for multi-level analysis. The creation of the pattern library hierarchy resulted in three base hierarchy levels. As an organization can be divided into head office (HQ), regional office (RO), and property based (PB) job levels. Within the HQ level, 22 patterns have been developed. In RO there are 24 patterns and for PB there are 32 patterns.

The hierarchy starts with HQ and ends with PB. As every organization is different, it was necessary to create more detailed levels to place job titles with a similar name in the same hierarchical level. The 'Chief Financial Officer', 'Chief Human Resource Officer', and 'Chief Sustainability Officer' all come on the same level: HQ1. Followed with HQ2 the 'President' and will go to HQ7. This example explains the details of the standardized hierarchical levels of the HQ, there are also detailed levels for the RO: RO1 being the 'Group Directors', followed by the 'Area/Regional Executive Vice Presidents'. This goes on till RO8. And PB: PB1: 'General Manager', followed by the 'Assistant General Manager' on PB2, going on to the managerial level PB8 [18].

C. *Analysis and Visualization*

Finally, after having the data collected, standardized job titles, and appointed to departments and levels, the final step involves the comparative analysis of job titles fulfilled by males and females. To visually present the counter-account data, the system makes use of ScatterText [17]. This interactive scatter plot allows distinguishing between job titles fulfilled by male and female executives. Figure 2 presents a visualization of the model outcome based on job titles; however, this can also be performed based on departmental or hierarchical levels. The outcome of the counter-account analysis can be of value to auditors and assurance providers in their assessment of the reporting organizations' credibility and reliability. For this application, this refers to the verification of statements made about gender equality efforts in the hospitality industry.

Results from the counter-account monitoring of gender equality in the hospitality workforce confirm some of the stereotyped occupational gender segregation. For example, in line with arguments in reference [14] regarding women's presence in occupations characterized by high warmth and low competence and evidence showing women tend to be excluded from fields like science, technology, engineering, and mathematics [9], results in Figure 2 show job titles like 'Head of Human Resources', 'Spa Director', and 'Sales and Marketing Manager' to be more frequently fulfilled by females, whereas job titles like 'Chef de Cuisine', 'Senior Vice President of Operations', 'Director of Food and Beverage', 'Executive Vice President', and 'Chief Development Officer' are substantially more often fulfilled by males.

Even though there are clear signs of a gender division in the hospitality workforce, there are also some remarkable evolutions regarding female presence in higher executive level jobs. Women are traditionally strongly present in the hospitality industry, a service industry, yet struggled to fulfill higher-level positions. Figure 2, presenting the current gender division of the hospitality workforce, shows how positions like 'General Manager', 'Director', and 'President' are roughly equally fulfilled by males and females.

Lastly, relatively new positions such as 'Vice President of Sustainability' and 'Chief Sustainability Officer' do not appear to be appointed to any gender specifically. Mapping the gender division on a continued basis allows for tracking changes in occupational gender segregation within organizations or industries.

VI. CONCLUSION

This research aims to find an answer to the following research question: "How can a counter-account monitoring system for gender equality in the hospitality industry be designed?". To answer this question, a system has been designed and tested. The research has several limitations. Limitations on the subject matter of hospitality and limitations on the actual counter-account system. First, the results are based on 1.000 new functions that became available to the public during a relatively short time frame (June-December, 2021). Although 1.000 new functions can be enough, it is possible that specific functions have not become available during this period. Future research should focus on collecting more and different function names to improve the current system, which is an integrated part of the application. Besides this, the sample contained only functions that have been posted on Hospitality.net. Therefore, results might not be fully representative of the sector and future research should attempt to extend sources

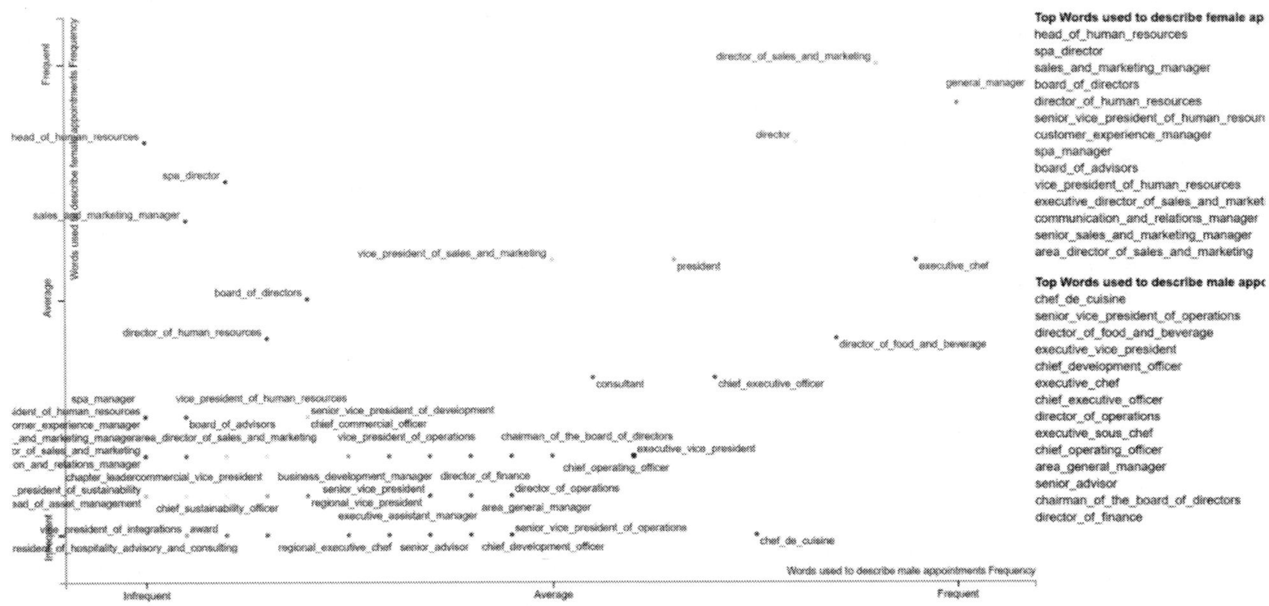

Figure 2. ScatterText Visualization of Gender Segregation on Job Title Level for Hospitality Industry

and generalize the results. Additionally, future research could focus on additional sectors to see expand the results.

References

[1] M. G. Alles, A. Kogan, and M. A. Vasarhelyi, "Feasibility and Economics of Continuous Assurance," Auditing, vol. 21, no. 1, pp. 125-138, March 2002, doi: 10.2308/aud.2002.21.1.125.

[2] A. B. Atkinson, Inequality: What can be done?, Cambridge (Mass.) Harvard University Press, 2015, pp. 384.

[3] A. B. Atkinson, T. Piketty, and E. Saez, "Top Incomes in the Long Run of History," Journal of Economic Literature, vol. 49, pp. 3–71, March 2011, doi: 10.1257/jel.49.1.3.

[4] A. Bermingham and A. Smeaton, "On Using Twitter to Monitor Political Sentiment and Predict Election Results," Proc. Workshop on Sentiment Analysis where AI meets Psychology (SAAIP 11), AFNLP press, November 2011, pp. 2-10.

[5] O. Boiral, I. Heras-Saizarbitoria, and M. C. Brotherton, "Assessing and Improving the Quality of Sustainability Reports: The Auditors' Perspective", Journal of Business Ethics, vol. 155, no. 3, pp. 703-721, March 2019, doi: 10.1007/s10551-017-3516-4.

[6] C. H. Cho, M. Laine, R. W. Roberts, and M. Rodrigue, "Organized Hypocrisy, Organizational Facades, and Sustainability Reporting," Accounting, Organizations and Society, vol. 40, no. 40, pp. 78–94, January 2015, doi: 10.1016/j.aos.2014.12.003.

[7] J. M. Corbin and A. Strauss, "Grounded Theory Research: Procedures, Canons, and Evaluative Criteria," Qualitative Sociology, vol. 13, no. 1, pp. 3-21, March 1990, doi: 10.1007/BF00988593

[8] A. C. Edmondson and S. E. McManus, "Methodological Fit in Management Field Research," Academy of Management Review, vol. 32, no. 4, pp. 1246-1264, October 2007, doi: 10.5465/amr.2007.26586086.

[9] European Parliament, "Reporting obligations regarding gender equality and equal pay," 2021, Retrieved: May, 2022 from https://www.europarl.europa.eu/RegData/etudes/STUD/2021/698641/IPOL_STU(2021)698641_EN.pdf.

[10] European Commission, "Proposal for a Directive of the European Parliament and of the Council amending Directive 2013/34/EU, Directive 2004/109/EC, Directive 2006/43/EC and Regulation (EU) No 537/2014, as regards corporate sustainability reporting, COM (2021) 189 final," 2021b, Retrieved: May, 2022 from: https://eur-lex.europa.eu/legal-content/EN/TXT/?uri=CELEX:52021PC0189. Accessed on June 26, 2021.

[11] A. Fantechi, S. Gnesi, S. Livi, and L. Semini, "A SpaCy-based Tool for Extracting Variability from NL Requirements," Proc. ACM International Systems and Software Product Line (SPLC 21), ACM Press, September 2021, pp. 32-35, doi: 10.1145/3461002.3473074.

[12] Governance & Accountability Institute, "Sustainability reporting in focus 2021," 2021, Retrieved: April, 2022 from: https://www.gainstitute.com/fileadmin/ga_institute/images/FlashReports/2021/Russell-1000/G_A-Russell-Report-2021-Final.pdf?vgo_ee=1GwDh4sTgtYj0oCrAM%2BSEBwUnRnlmwiuCIJkd9A7F3A%3D.

[13] G. Goncharenko, "In the spotlight: Rethinking NGO accountability in the #MeToo era," Critical Perspectives on Accounting, March 2021, in press.

[14] J. C. He, S. K. Kang, K. Tse, and S. M. Toh, "Stereotypes at Work: Occupational Stereotypes Predict Race and Gender Segregation in the Workforce," Journal of Vocational Behavior, vol. 115, pp. 103318, December 2019, doi: 10.1016/j.jvb.2019.103318.

[15] A. Hevner and S. Chatterjee, Design research in information systems, 1ste ed. Springer New York, 2010.

[16] A. Hevner, S. March, J. Park, and S. Ram, "Design Science in Information," MIS Quarterly, vol. 28, no. 1, pp. 75-105, March 2004, doi: 10.2307/25148625.

[17] J. S. Kessler, "Scattertext: a browser-based tool for visualizing how corpora differ," ArXiv, April 2017, unpublished.

[18] A. Kirchner, M. Ursache, E. Vlijm, and M. Zoet, "Variation in Job Titles within the Hospitality Workforce," The Fourteenth International Conference on Information, Process, and Knowledge Management (eKNOW 22) IARIA, June 2022.

[19] J. Kuhn, J. Courtney, and B. Morris, "A Theory of Complex Adaptive Inquiring Organizations: Application to Continuous Assurance of Corporate Financial Information," The Knowledge Engineering Review, vol. 30, no. 3, pp. 265–296, May 2015, doi: 10.1017/S0269888913000428.

[20] T. P. Lyon and A. W. Montgomery, "The Means and End of Greenwash. Organization & Environment, vol. 28, no. 2, pp. 223-249, March 2015, doi: 10.1177/1086026615575332.

[21] L. K. Nelson, "Computational Grounded Theory: A Methodological Framework. Sociological Methods & Research, vol. 49, no. 1, pp. 3-42, Novermber 2017, doi: 10.1177/0049124117729703.

[22] S. Perkiss, C. Bernardi, J. Dumay, and J. Haslam, "A Sticky Chocolate Problem: Impression Management and Counter Accounts in the Shaping of Corporate Image," Critical Perspectives on Accounting, vol. 81, pp. 102229, December 2021, doi: 10.1016/j.cpa.2020.102229.

[23] R. Saner, L. Yiu, and M. Nguyen, "Monitoring the SDGs: Digital and Social Technologies to ensure Citizen Participation, Inclusiveness, and Transparency. Development Policy Review, vol. 38, no. 4, pp. 483-500, February 2019, doi: 10.1111/dpr.12433.

[24] X. Sibande, R. Gupta, R. Demirer, and E. Bouri, "Investor Sentiment and (Anti) Herding in the Currency Market: Evidence from Twitter Feed Data," Journal of Behavioral Finance, pp. 1-17, May 2021, doi: 10.1080/15427560.2021.1917579.

[25] C. Sumana, S. M. Reddy, S. Sahaa, and P. Bhattacharyyaa, "Why pay more? A simple and efficient Named Entity Recognition System for Tweets," vol. 167, pp. 114101, April 2021, doi: 10.1016/j.eswa.2020.114101.

[26] The Institute of Internal Auditors, "Global technology audit guide continuous auditing: Implications for assurance, monitoring, and risk assessment", 2005.

[27] United Nations, "The 2030 Agenda and the Sustainable Development Goals: An opportunity for Latin America and the Caribbean," January 2018, Retrieved: May, 2022, from https://repositorio.cepal.org/handle/11362/40156.

[28] P. Valet, "Social Structure and the Paradox of the Contented Female Worker: How Occupational Gender Segregation Biases Justice Perceptions of Wages. Work and Occupations, vol. 45, no. 2, pp. 168-193, January 2018, doi: 10.1177/0730888417753048.

[29] C. van Aartsen, R. Bauer, T. Bauer, and M. Olaerts, "Sustainability Embedding in Dutch Listed Companies. Vba Journaal, vol. 37, no. 149, pp. 32-38, October 2021, doi: 10.2139/ssrn.3957250.

[30] E. Vinnari and M. Laine, "The Moral Mechanism of Counter Accounts: The Case of Industrial Animal Production," Accounting, Organizations and Society, vol. 57, pp. 1-17, February 2017, doi: 10.1016/j.aos.2017.01.002.

Blockchain in e-Health: Review

Rees Mangena, Nidhal Taferguennit, Samia Aitouche, Seyf El Islam Bousiouda, Fadhila Djouggane, Morri Farida
Laboratory of Automation and Manufacturing, Industrial Engineering Department, University Batna 2, Batna, Algeria
e-mail: mangenarees@gmail.com, nidhaltaferguennit@gmail.com, s.aitouche@univ-batna2.dz,
bousioudaseyfelislam@gmail.com, djouggane fadhila@gmail.com, mourrisihame@gmail.com

Abstract— **Certain researchers consider the blockchain technology as an Industry 4.1 revolution, because it benefits from the Industry 4.0 revolution and its technologies, in a decentralized manner. It is a revolution in digital world. In this paper, authors addressed a review of the use of blockchain technology in electronic health (eHealth) because of its importance for the comfort of citizens and the promotion of a healthy society, especially after the pandemic experience of COVID-19, where the necessity and the importance of telework and, Information and Communications Technology (ICT) became more essential than ever before. The review begins by the essence of eHealth and the problems encountered in it. It responds to how blockchain can promote eHealth in terms of management of patient data, its privacy, gains in time and because of how it is a facility without a central authority. The decentralized management of the blockchain does not mean a mess or a loss of data; on the contrary, it means the accountability of all members and partners of the blockchain (patient, doctor, medical institution, etc.). This is guaranteed by the good choice of the consensus algorithms to minimize time, energy consumption and consequently minimize costs. Several algorithms and other issues are discussed in this review paper to help researchers and software developers to discover and use the opportunity of blockchain in eHealth. All the used rules consented by the partners of blockchain system for eHealth are automatically applied in the form of smart contracts. These latter allow the treatment of citizens by the same way, without subjectivity and favoritism.**

Keywords-blockchain; eHealth; e-Health; telemedecine; EHR; electronic health record.

I. Introduction

In 2008, the cryptocurrency Bitcoin [1] launched the blockchain technology, which has inherited properties such as decentralization, transparency, and anonymity. Bitcoin represents a good use-case for blockchain technology, with close to 400 million completed transactions as of March 19, 2019 [2]. As a result, there have been talks and suggestions that blockchain technology could be useful in a variety of other data-driven sectors, others as big as healthcare [3].

Healthcare has had a reputation for being a traditional business that is difficult to evaluate due to the realities of change and it's resistance to new ideas. Healthcare issues (such as privacy, quality of care, and information security) have gotten a lot of attention in recent years all around the world. Blockchain technology is becoming more widely recognized as a means for addressing current information mismanagement difficulties. It has the potential to improve immediate healthcare practices, such as health service delivery and care support quality. The blockchain's immutability is a critical feature for healthcare data. It can protect health records, clinical trial outcomes, and regulatory compliance. Smart contracts are being utilized to show how blockchain can help with real- time patient monitoring and medical interventions [12]. Health Insurance Portability and Accountability Act (HIPAA) compliant solutions provide record protection while enabling access to patients and medical professionals.

Further blockchain applications include the pharmaceutical supply chain and the development of anti-counterfeiting mechanisms. While the development of new pharmaceuticals incurs significant expenditures connected to trials to evaluate the drug's safety and efficacy, the usage of smart contracts allows for a more efficient informed consent approach, as well as improved data management and quality [13]. Providing patients with access to manage their own identities allows the informed consent method to be integrated while preserving the privacy of individual health data. In the pharmaceutical industry, blockchain has the potential to assist the pharmaceutical business deal with the rising risks of counterfeit and unapproved pharmaceuticals. With integrated Global Positioning System (GPS) and chain-of-custody logging, smart contracts for pharmaceuticals can be formed and then identified, similar to device tracking.

Within clinical trials, blockchain can be used to address issues, such as falsified results and data removal that contradict the researcher's bias or the funding source's objective. Clinical studies will be more reliable as a result of this. It also enables for the creation of an irreversible log of trial subject consent. It is estimated that identifying a chain-of-custody in the supply chain may save the pharmaceutical sector $200 billion [7]. Many sectors of health insurance could benefit from a reliable record of events surrounding the patient pathway, such as improved incident reporting and automated underwriting operations. Contracts, such as automated payments for segments of the patient journey, could also be precisely stated and then implemented.

This paper is organized as follows; Section 2 gives a view on the meaning of eHealth and some problems encountered in it. Section 3 clarifies the need of blockchain in eHealth to solve some of these problems. Some types of used blockchains in eHealth are given in Section 4. Section 5 points the more adapted and benefic consensus or algorithms to eHealth. Section 6 highlights the use of smart contracts in eHealth. The methods of accessing and storing data are presented in Section 7. Section 8 inspects the benefits of IOT in eHealth and blockchain. Section 9 is devoted to Electronic Health Records. Section 10 analyses blockchain eHealth's respect of General Data Protection Regulation (GDPR) rules. Then we finished by general remarks in a conclusion Section.

II. Problems In e-Health

The use of the Internet and other technologies in the health-care industry is referred to as eHealth [8]. eHealth is an evolving field at the intersection of medical informatics, public health, and business. It refers to health services and information distributed or enhanced through the Internet and associated technologies. According to the World Health Organization (WHO), eHealth is "the cost-effective and secure use of information and communication technologies in support of health and health-related fields, such as health-care services, health surveillance, health literature, and health education, knowledge, and research."

Many government health institutions have developed frameworks to ensure a high level of security and privacy. For example, the United States (US) Congress proposed the Health Insurance Portability and Accountability Act (HIPAA) in 1996 as a federal law that applies to the US healthcare industry. For effective use of eHealth, a set of valuable security and privacy requirements must be put in place in accordance with HIPAA guidelines [32].

- **Accessing and Sharing Health Data:** Data must be transferred between healthcare providers, third parties, insurers, and patients while adhering to data protection regulations in the healthcare sector.
- **Nationwide Interoperability:** Having a single standard for patient data exchange facilitates data exchange between healthcare providers, which legacy systems frequently do not provide.
- **Medical Device Tracking:** Medical device tracking from the supply chain to decommissioning enables quick retrieval of devices, avoidance of unnecessary repurchasing, and fraud analytics.
- **Drug Tracking:** Blockchain like medical devices, allows for the tracking of the chain of custody from the supply chain to the patient, allowing for frictionless recalls and the prevention of counterfeit drugs.

Furthermore, blockchain based health care systems face additional challenges, such as system evolution, privacy leakage, energy consumption, and communication scalability, due to the complexities associated with healthcare engagement and laws [28].

III. The Use of Blockchain Technology in e-Health

There are many problems in today's healthcare that may be solved using blockchain. Two of the major focuses that must be addressed are: Data security and Data ownership. Others include health data interchange, nationwide operability, Medical Device tracking, Drug Tracking, Clinical trials and Health Insurance. Currently, sensitive medical records lack a secure structure, resulting in data breaches with serious consequences. For example, in 2018, the Office for Civil Rights (OCR) at the Department of Health and Human Services (DHHS) received notification of numerous data breaches that exposed 13 million total healthcare records.

The second source of concern is that patients are currently unable to fully own their own medical data, a concept that is becoming more relevant with the rise of personalized medicine and wearables. Both of these issues have significant moral ramifications that must be addressed. Blockchain technology could be the answer to both these problems.

Another key challenge as tagging medical equipment with a usable ID and integrating trust in device identification and tracking. When a device, such as an infusion pump, is shown to have malfunctioned, tracking the device can reveal the source of the problem and prevent unnecessary repurchasing in the case of lost devices. These threats are likely to be reduced by a strong trust infrastructure based on medical device identification. According to the report, only 20% to 30% of medical devices are connected within hospitals due to security and privacy concerns.

Blockchain can also assist the pharmaceutical industry in overcoming the growing risks associated with counterfeit and unapproved drugs. As with device tracking, smart contracts for drugs can be defined and then pill containers identified using integrated (GPS) and chain-of-custody logging.

Another use of blockchain in healthcare could be in clinical trials to overcome problems such as fraudulent results and the removal of data that does not support the researcher's bias or the funding source's intention. This will enforce clinical trial integrity. Furthermore, it allows for the keeping of an immutable log of trial subject consent. The pharmaceutical industry is expected to save $200 billion by defining a chain-of-custody in the supply chain. Health insurance could also benefit from a trusted record of events surrounding the patient pathway, such as improved incident reporting and automating underwriting activities. Contracts, such as automated payments for parts of the patient pathway, could also be clearly defined and then implemented [11].

Table 1 [25] shows the benefits of blockchain to the eHealth systems, relative to the traditional system. Privacy, security, transparency and reliability are guaranteed in the blockchain system.

All pharmacists will potentially be impacted by this technology and therefore should have a strong interest in it. Pharmacists could have prescriptions that cannot be forged. Pharmacists in research laboratories could use this technology to prove the progress of their research without disclosing it. Finally, industrial pharmacists will be able to ensure the authenticity of medicines throughout their journey [26].

TABLE I. Comparison Of Traditional, Centralized, And Blockchain Supported eHealth

criterion	Traditional Healthcare System	Centralized Telemedicine System	Blockchain Supported Telemedicine
Cost	High	Low	Low
Patient Waiting Time	Very High	Low	Low
Fault Tolerence	No	No	Yes
Requirement for In-	Yes	No	No

Person Visiting			
Data Provenance	No	No	Yes
Health Record Manipulation	Yes	Yes	No
Documentation	Yes	Yes	No
System Administration	Centralize d	Centralized	Decentralized
Audit Trials	No	No	Yes
Data Privacy & Security	Hard	Hard	Easy
Transparency	No	No	Yes
Reliability & Integrity	Low	Low	High

Blockchain Supported telemedecine is better for the comfort of patients and healthcare personel.

IV. eHealth Types of Blockchains

Blockchains are classified into three types: public (permissionless), consortium (public permissioned), and private. They differ in terms of who has access to, writes to, and reads data on the blockchain [30]. Everyone can see the data in a public chain, and anyone can join and contribute to both consensus (in theory) and changes to the core software. The public blockchain is widely used in cryptocurrencies, and the two most popular cryptocurrencies, Bitcoin and Ethereum (the main chain), are public permissionless chains. A consortium blockchain is partially centralized in the sense that only a select group of entities has access to view and participate in the consensus protocol. The network in a private blockchain is distributed but frequently centralized [31]. Only selected nodes can participate in the network, which is frequently managed by a single central authority. The debate over the definition and categorization of the various types of blockchains presented here is still ongoing. There is currently no broad agreement on which distributing characteristics and consensus mechanisms are required to label a technology as "blockchain".

V. Algorithms (Consensus) Used In eHealth Systems

The way data entries are accepted onto the distributed ledger by a distributed consensus protocol validating the data entries is a critical component of blockchains. There are several proposed and used consensus protocols, the three most commonly used being Proof-of-Work (PoW), Proof of Stake (PoS) and Practical Byzantine Fault Tolerance (PBFT) [34].

Because of its integration in Bitcoin, Proof-of-Work (PoW) is the consensus protocol most strongly associated with blockchain. When the PoW protocol is used, so-called miners compete to solve a computationally difficult puzzle. Miners use brute force to try to find a hash of the proposed block that is less than a predetermined value. The miner who computes this hash value first validates the transactions (or other entries) in the block and receives a reward. When used on a large blockchain, the PoW protocol consumes a significant amount of energy. This is demonstrated by the fact that the current electricity used for Bitcoin mining is comparable to the needs of a smaller country [33].

The selection of an approving node in Proof of Stake (PoS) is determined by the stake each node has in the blockchain. The stake in crypto-currencies is represented by the balance of a given currency. This, however, may give the "richest" node an unfair advantage. To account for this, several hybrid PoS versions have been proposed, in which the stake is combined with some randomization to choose the approving node. Ethereum, the second largest cryptocurrency, intends to switch from PoW to PoS [35]. A Byzantine agreement protocol underpins Practical Byzantine Fault Tolerance (PBFT). Because all nodes in PBFT must be known to the network, this consensus protocol can only be used in a public blockchain. The PBFT consensus process can be divided into three stages: pre-prepared, prepared, and commit. To progress through the three phases, each node must receive two-thirds of the votes cast by all nodes. Hyperledger Fabric currently employs PBFT [36].

Due to the high cost of PoW algorithm in terms of hardware and energy, there was a need for an efficient but low-cost protocol. A promising candidate is the proof of elapsed time protocol made by INTEL which is secure and fast in processing and approving transactions, and low in energy consumption considering the huge number of blocks needed to be created and data to be stored in the health industry. However, this algorithm lacks decentralization, which is the main philosophy of the blockchain technology because this protocol depends only on INTEL hardware. A hybrid protocol with the same properties but independent of INTEL will have promising results [37].

There is one other candidate that can be used which is the proof of weight protocol that has the speed and security needed to store and approve medical data and is low in terms of energy consumption. But the only down side for this algorithm is that it doesn't reward miners. However, finding an alternative way of paying them will make this protocol an optimal choice for the health industry [19].

VI. Smart Contracts

Smart contracts are supported by some blockchain infrastructures, such as Ethereum. These are self-executing contractual agreements that formalize previously agreed-upon provisions in source code. Because smart contracts are automatically enforced based on these pre-agreed provisions, they operate without the involvement of a third party or intermediary. This function within a smart contract can be activated in a blockchain transaction, and its use appears to be appealing to the health domain [10]. In [4], authors design secure payment protocols by performing blockchain-based smart contract enabling the patients and hospital to reliably pay the diagnostic and storage service efficiently. In general, the smart contracts in eHealth can be involved in [27]:

- Health Record Creation Contact to generate digital health records.
- Health Record Storage Contract for secure storage and rapid access
- Update permission Contract that can provide access at emergency situations.
- Data sharing Permission Contract for exchange of health records between different stakeholders and

VII. Methods of Accessing and Storing Data

A. *Using a blockchain tree*

This is done by using a principal block on the main chain containing basic information of the patient and a sub block on the sub chain containing the medical record accessed only by using Proof Of Authority (POA) protocol to ensure the registration of any successful or unsuccessful attempts of access to the records, as illustrated in Figure 1 [20].

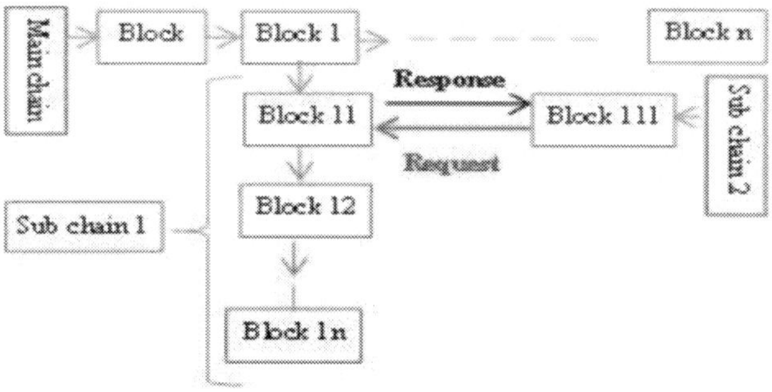

Figure 1. Blockchain tree structure

B. *Practical Byzantine fault tolerance*

Here, all nodes participate to the voting (2/3 must accept the transaction) which may cause a delay in the transaction processing and slow the whole operation.

Delegated byzantine fault tolerance

Not all nodes most vote which leads to a fast transaction acceptance but with a risk of centralization [21].

C. *Adoptive leader election algorithm : (ALEA)*

This algorithm is based on electing a leader via Leader Election Algorithm (LEA) to grant him permission to create, access, copy, move, edit and delete data. This type of algorithm is using bully leader election method to minimize energy consumption.

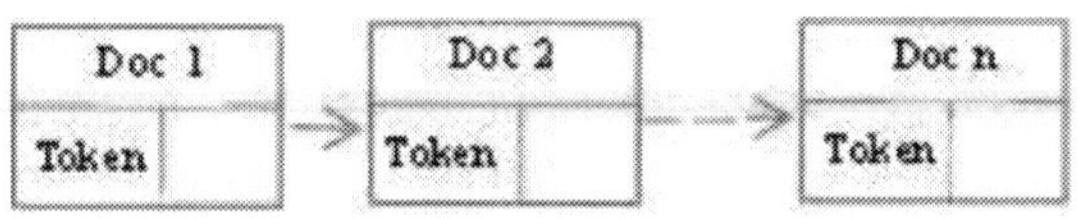

Figure 2. Leader election queue

These algorithms are characterized by:

- 0% failure: due to blockchain technology if a node fails others can do the work
- Ownership can't change if the owner dies or loses consciousness
- High and slow response using ALEA [22]

D. *Using two types of chains*

A private one that contains the real ID of the patient and a public one which has health data of the patient under a temporary ID, under the control of a hyper ledger fabric framework, noting that only the trusted nodes can access the private chain, as shown in Figure 3.

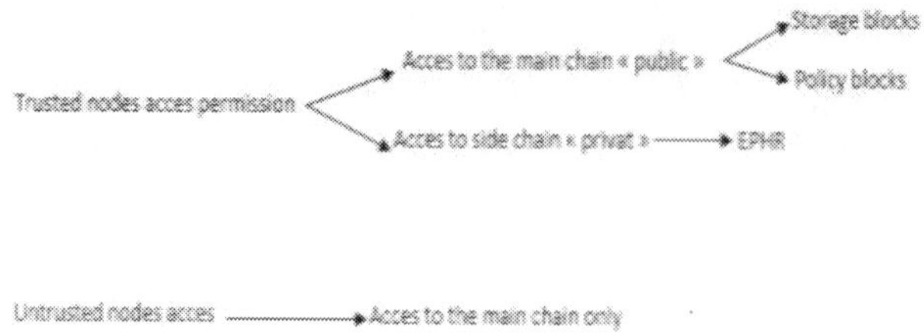

Figure 3. Types of permission for trusted and untrusted nodes

Storage block: The main chain is used to secure the data from modification as it creates storage blocks containing the temporary ID, patient digital signature approving the transaction, medical institution signature and information about the current block and the previous one.

Policy block: It contains a form of contract about the storing policies of the institution who store the data, signed by both it and the patient then approved by the trusted nodes and broadcasted on the main chain [23].

VIII. Using Internet Of Things (IOT) in eHealth

In this section, we will try to see how can we introduce IOT and blockchain to the health care system, first we must refer to some existing platforms such as OmniPHR [38] which is a platform that allows the sharing of EPHR on a universal scale or GemOS which is used as an access platform to a medical chain owned by the patient and contains his EPHR. many researchers have developed BC-enabled IoT eHealth systems and explored the application of BC technology in diverse fields of eHealthcare. The general idea is to equip patients, post-hospitalization, with equipment easy to use that collect data for example "heart rate, blood pressure, etc. and puts them on the blockchain while having a well put web platform that offers the link for authorized persons (medical staff) to access the patients' data and monitoring his medical status leading to the lowering of the cost of post-hospitalization by roughly 113B$ just in the US (Fig. 4). Cybersecurity is a critical consideration for all users of EHRs, particularly for patients. With the advent of Healthcare 4.0, which is based on IOT and sensors, cyber resilience has become a key requirement in ensuring the protection of patient data across devices [6].

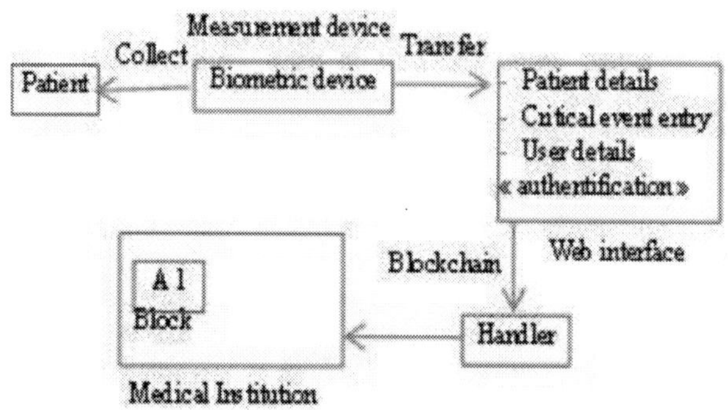

Figure 4. IOT and blockchain health platform

One of many developed methods of collecting patient data and storing them or delivering them in real time to medical institution to ensure the best performance of health care towards the patient is Wireless Body Area Network (WBAN) [18]. It is mainly a collection of wireless sensors placed on or in a human body and is used to exchange data from patient to remote stations (Fig. 5).

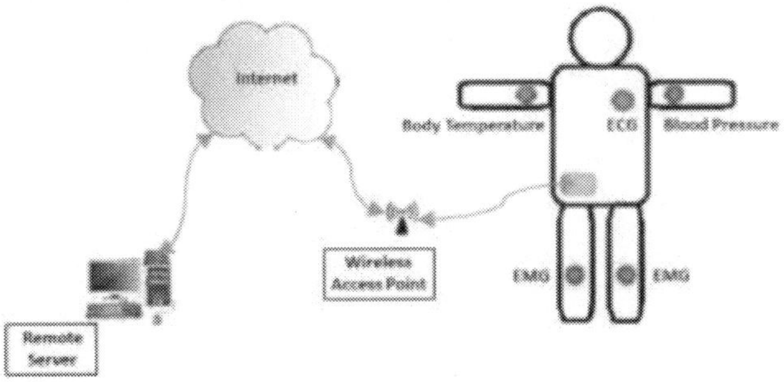

Figure 5. Wireless body area network scheme [29]

Afterwards, all these data are then transferred using blockchain technology to ensure proper security and confidentiality.

IX. Health Records And The Integration Of Blockchain Technology

In a general point of view, e-health is an integration of computing methods and systems to provide solutions to the industry of health care, such as managing patient files but due to the huge amount and diversity of files provided by medical institutions, it has become a challenge to share and store data without failing or breaking the rules of privacy [15]. These files are called EHRs, i.e., a digital format of a patient information such as medical history, current and past medication, etc., that are sourced to cloud but cloud based EHRs aren't secure enough and their current cryptographic methods aren't sufficient enough [18]. Thus, blockchain technology has emerged as a promising solution in terms of privacy and data security since it is independent of third parties such as governments or banks. However, this doesn't mean that it is an optimal solution since it is in its early years and needs more development in terms of performance, energy consumption and offering guaranteed confidentiality since in medical health care no one is allowed to read or see patient files without the proper permission [16].

X. Blockchain Technology And The GDPR Rules

After the rise of blockchain technology, all over the world, a tension was created between this technology and the GDPR. This tension was mainly because of two overarching factors. First, the GDPR is based on assuming that there is always someone who controls data thus adding more protection as commanded by data subjects; however, blockchain has a philosophy of decentralization, which means there is no more governance but many players who control these data, which can make accountability difficult.

Secondly, the GDPR requires the possibility to erase or modify data in certain circumstances but blockchains are designed for the exact opposite purpose where they make the modification or deletion data difficult or even impossible, which makes it hard to reconcile with GDPR requirements [17]. The crucial challenges that companies face to achieve compliance with GDPR, and specifically to i) let data owners full visibility and control on the consents related to their own personal data, and ii) design services that can cope with consents that may change or be revoked dynamically. In [39], authors proposed a solution that relies on the blockchain technology to let data owners grant, access and rectify their consents in a decentralized peer-to-peer fashion, while guaranteeing consensual agreement of data owners and companies on the status of the relevant consents at any time. Although blockchains let all users access all contents freely.

XI. Conclusion

Blockchain is a new technology has the potential to disrupt a variety of data-driven industries, including the healthcare sector. The efficient management of EHRs is critical for patient telecare, which includes medicine for chronic patients, long-term telecare for special patients, and study of patients infected with a specific disease, among other things. The sharing of EHRs with medical practitioners can improve diagnosis accuracy; however, the system's privacy and security preservation of patients' records are drawbacks. Blockchain technology, due to its immutability, has recently been offered as a promising method for accomplishing EHR sharing while maintaining privacy and security [5]. Cyber resilience has become a major requirement in assuring the protection of patient data across devices, thanks to the introduction of healthcare 4.0, which is based on IOT and sensors. To all users in the network, blockchain provides crypto-enforced security, data immutability, and smart contracts-based business logic characteristics [6]. There are several other areas of healthcare and well-being that could be enhanced using blockchain technologies. Accessing and sharing health data, device tracking, clinical trials, pharmaceutical tracing, and health insurance are just a few examples. For accessing and sharing health data, patients can have their EHRs in a decentralized blockchain which any hospital can access instead of having their records scattered in different centralized hospital systems where they are difficult to access all at once and where they are susceptible to privacy breaches and alterations.

In this paper, authors tried to give a review about the usage of blockchain in eHealth to resolve problems of central bureaucratic authority, replaced by a peer-to-peer network allowing decentralized responsibility, even including the end user in certain blockchain solutions, while maintaining patient privacy and protecting the confidentiality of their health folder. Blockchain is still promising in the future of the healthcare domain as well as in other domains.

References

[1] S. Nakamoto, "Bitcoin: A peer-to-peer electronic cash system. Decentralized Business Review", 2008, 21260.

[2] Blockchain.com [retrieved: May, 2022]. Available on: https://www.blockchain.com/, charts/n-transactions-total.

[3] M. Mettler, "Technology in healthcare: The revolution starts here. In: 2016 IEEE 18th international conference on e-health networking", applications and services (Healthcom). IEEE, 2016. p. 1-3..

[4] G. Zhang, Z. Yang, and W. Liu, "Blockchain-based privacy preserving e-health system for healthcare data in cloud", Computer Networks, 2022, 203: 108586.

[5] S. Shamshad, Minahil, K. Mahmood, S. Kumari, and C. M. Chen, "A secure blockchain-based e-health records storage and sharing scheme", Journal of Information Security and Applications", 2020, 55: 102590.

[6] N. Venkatachalam, P. O'connor, and S. Palekar, "Cyber Security and Cyber Resilience for the Australian E-Health Records: A Blockchain Solution. In: Handbook of Research on Advancing Cybersecurity for Digital Transformation", IGI Global, 2021. pp. 61-78.

[7] Frost and Sullivan, "Why Healthcare Industry Should Care About Blockchain?" 2017. [Online]. Available on: https://ww2.frost.com/files/8615/0227/3370/Why_Healthcare Industry_Should_Care_About_Blockchain_Edited_Version. [retrieved : June 2022]

[8] eHealth: Definition, History, Characteristics, Scope, Benefits and Challenges, September 5, 2019.

[9] S. Subashini and V. Kavitha, "Review: a survey on security issues in service delivery models of cloud computing", J Netw Comput Appl, 2011; vol. 34(1), pp. 1-11.

[10] A. Hasselgren, et al., "Blockchain in healthcare and health sciences—A scoping review". International Journal of Medical Informatics, 2020, vol. 134: 104040.

[11] L. Bell, W. J. Buchanan, J. Cameron, and O. Lo, "Applications of blockchain within healthcare. Blockchain in healthcare today", 2018.

[12] K. N. Griggs, et al., "Healthcare blockchain system using smart contracts for secure automated remote patient monitoring". Journal of medical systems, 2018, vol. 42. Issue 7, pp. 1-7.

[13] N. B. A. Razak, G. Jones, M. Bhandari, M. C. Berndt, and P. Metharom, Cancer-associated thrombosis: an overview of mechanisms, risk factors, and treatment. Cancers, 2018, 10.10: 380..

[14] E. F. Coutinho, et al. "Modeling blockchain e-health systems", Proceedings of the 10th Euro-American Conference on Telematics and Information Systems. 2020.

[15] F. Yahmed and M. Abid, "Trust Execution Environment and Multi-party Computation for Blockchain e-Health Systems", International Conference on Smart Homes and Health Telematics. Springer, Cham, 2020.

[16] F. Michèle, "Blockchain and the General Data Protection Regulation, Can distributed ledgers be squared with European data protection law?", Panel for the Future of Science and Technology EPRS | European Parliamentary Research Service Scientific Foresight Unit (STOA) PE 634.445 – July 2019 ENEPRS

[17] B. Arunkumar and G. Kousalya, "Blockchain-Based Decentralized and Secure Lightweight E-Health System for Electronic Health Records", Intelligent Systems, Technologies and Applications. Springer, Singapore, 2020. pp. 273-289.

[18] M. R. Yuce and J. Khan, eds. , "Wireless body area networks: technology, implementation, and applications", CRC Press, 2011.

[19] S. M. H. Bamakan, A. Motavali, and A. B. Bondarti, "A survey of blockchain consensus algorithms performance evaluation criteria", Expert Systems with Applications, 2020, vol. 154: 113385.

[20] L. Hirtan, P. Krawiec, C. Dobre, and J. M. Batalla, "Blockchain-based approach for e-health data access management with privacy protection", In: 2019 IEEE 24th International Workshop on Computer Aided Modeling and Design of Communication Links and Networks (CAMAD). IEEE, 2019, pp. 1-7.

[21] T. Hyla and J. Pejas, "eHealth integrity model based on permissioned blockchain", Future Internet, 2019, vol. 11.3: 76.

[22] L. Xu, A. Bagula, O. Isafiade, K. Ma, and T. Chiwewe, "Design of a Credible Blockchain-Based E-Health Records (CB-EHRS) Platform", In: 2019 ITU Kaleidoscope: ICT for Health: Networks, Standards and Innovation (ITU K). IEEE, 2019, pp. 1-8.

[23] B. Assiri, "Using Leader Election and Blockchain in E-Health, Advances in Science", Technology and Engineering Systems Journal, vol. 5, no. 3, pp. 46-54 (2020).

[24] M. M. Neto, E. F. Coutinho, L. O. Moreira, and J. N. de Souza, "Toward blockchain technology in iot applications: An analysis for e-health applications", In: IFIP International Internet of Things Conference. Springer, Cham, 2019, pp. 36-50.

[25] R. W. Ahmad, et al. "The role of blockchain technology in telehealth and telemedicine", International journal of medical informatics, vol. 148, 2021, 104399.

[26] S. Tessier, Operation of the blockchain and its interest for the pharmaceutical world, PhD thesis in pharmacy, UFR pharmaceutical sciences, university Bordeau, France, Sciences du Vivant, 2019, dumas-02296520

[27] U. Chelledurai, S. Pandian, and K. Ramasamy, "A blockchain based patient centric electronic health record storage and integrity management for e-Health systems", Health Policyand Technology, 2021, vol. 10, n° 4: 100513.

[28] M.S. Rahman, M. A. Islam, M. A. Uddin, and G. Stea, "A survey of blockchain-based IoT eHealthcare: Applications, research issues, and challenges", Internet of Things, 2022, 100551.

[29] M. Javed, G. Ahmed, D. Mahmood, M. Raza, K. Ali., and M. Ur-Rehman, "TAEO-A thermal aware & energy optimized routing protocol for wireless body area networks", Sensors, vol. 19, n° 15, 2019, 3275.

[30] https://www.techtarget.com/searchcio/feature/What-are-the-4-different-types-of-blockchain-technology

[31] https://www.investopedia.com/news/public-private-permissioned-blockchains-compared/

[32] https://www.cdc.gov/phlp/publications/topic/hipaa.html

[33] https://www.investopedia.com/terms/b/blockchain.asp

[34] https://www.investopedia.com/terms/p/proof-work.asp

[35] A. Hasselgren, K. Kralevska, D. Gligoroski, S. A. Pedersen, and A. Faxvaag, Blockchain in healthcare and health sciences—A scoping review. International Journal of Medical Informatics, 2020, vol. 134, 104040.

[36] https://www.geeksforgeeks.org/practical-byzantine-fault-tolerancepbft/

[37] D. P. Oyinloye, J. S. Teh, N. Jamil and M. Alawida, Blockchain consensus: An overview of alternative protocols. Symmetry, vol. 13 n° 8, 2021, 1363.

[38] A., Roehrs, C. A. Da Costa, and R. da Rosa Righi, "OmniPHR: A distributed architecture model to integrate personal health records", Journal of biomedical informatics, vol. 71, 2017, pp. 70-81.

[39] M. Calani, G. Denaro and A. Leporati, "Exploiting the Blockchain to Guarantee GDPR Compliance while Consents Evolve under Data Owners' Control", In ITASEC, 2021, pp. 331-343.

Analysis of Blockchain in Solar Energy Systems

Nidhal Taferguennit, Seyf El Islam Boussiouda, Samia Aitouche, Rees Mangena, Fadhila Djouggane, Nesrine Sersa
Laboratory of Automation and Manufacturing, Industrial Engineering Department, University Batna 2, Batna, Algeria
e-mail: nidhaltaferguennit@gmail.com, bousioudaseyfelislam@gmail.com, s.aitouche@univ-batna2.dz, mangenarees@gmail.com, djougganefadhila@gmail.com, nesrinesersa05@gmail.com

Abstract— **This paper is a descriptive review of utilisation of blockchain technology in solar energy (photovoltaic) systems. The 42 studied papers where extracted from the database SCOPUS using the research expression "Blockchain AND (PV OR photovoltaic OR "solar energy")", in titles of the papers, at April 22nd, 2022. A quantitative analysis is elaborated about authors, affiliation, journals, countries and authors keywords. A qualitative analysis of papers is more elaborated manually extracting the main problems encountered in solar energy systems and how blockchain technology brings some solutions. This study may help researchers and practitioners to direct their studies and solutions in a way to take advantage to the emergent blockchain technology.**

Keywords- ***blockchain; renewable energy; solar energy system; photovoltaic; PV, solar energy trading.***

I. Introduction

By this review, we are trying to shed light on the usage of the blockchain technology in the solar energy systems represented by the photovoltaic systems. The information is extracted from 42 papers from SCOPUS database. We used abstracts and full papers to study quantitative and qualitative aspects. The general principle is self-consuming [1] the solar energy and trading the surplus, this system is called prosumer. Other papers combine PV (Photovoltaic) operators and consumers of energy (Fig.1).

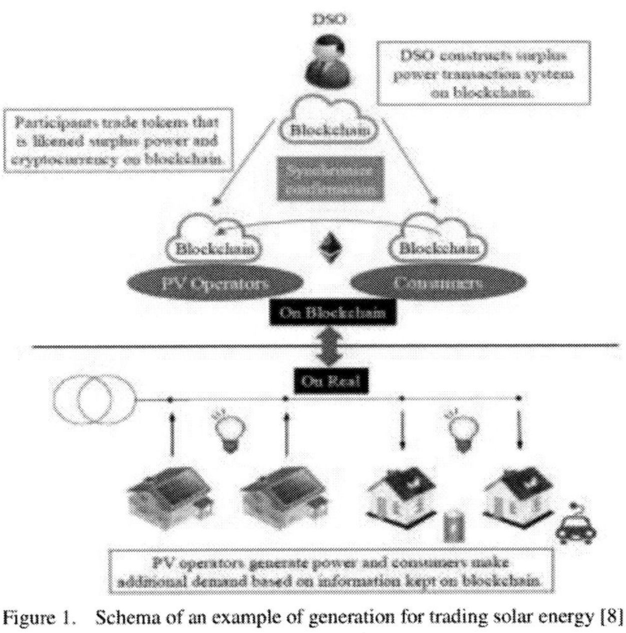

Figure 1. Schema of an example of generation for trading solar energy [8]

The paper treats two aspects. Section 2 offers a quantitative study of the papers (scientific production by year, author, affiliation, country, document type, subject area and citations). Section 3 is a citation analysis of papers, Section 4 is an authors' keywords analysis, then a qualitative analysis containing problematics and their solutions is presented in Section 5. The final section is a conclusion about the limits and trends on applying blockchain on solar systems.

II. Scientific Production Analysis

In this section we'll show which year was the most productive in term of literature, which authors contributed more, which country is more interested in this topic and many other quantitative properties.

A. *Scientific production by year*

In the collection of papers, 2019 was the most productive year (13 papers). The decrease of production in 2020 is explained by the crucial pandemic situation. The increase in 2021 comes from the transformation of scientists and industrials to teleworkers. An increasing is expected in 2022, in a post-pandemic situation due to the awareness of industrials and governments about the importance of digitalization and comfort of the citizen's sides of life.

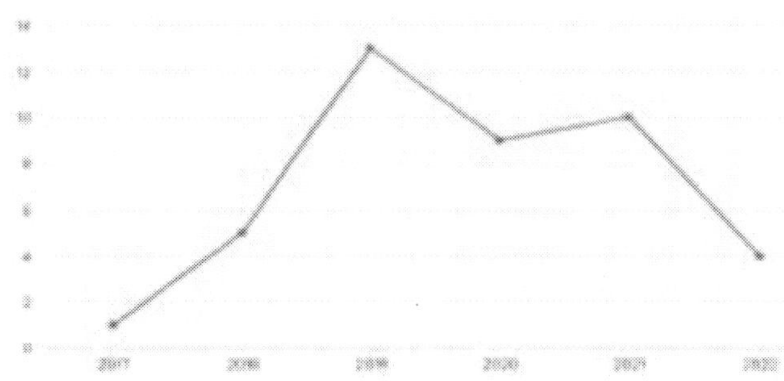

Figure 2. Production by year

B. *Number by source*

The shape of the graph is monotone; all sources are ex aequo in number of papers (1 paper per source), only one source (the journal of energy reports) has 2 papers related to the blockchain used in PV system. This fairness is explained by the consciousness of all the scientific communities about the advantages of blockchain in the management of PV energy.

Figure 3. Papers by year by source

C. *Number by author*

The analysis of authors (Fig. 4) shows that the first author in blockchain in PV energy (5 papers) is "Kim Taesic" affiliated to "Texas A and M University-Kingsville, Kingsville, United States" since 2017. His research interests are principally: engineering, energy, computer science and Mathematics.

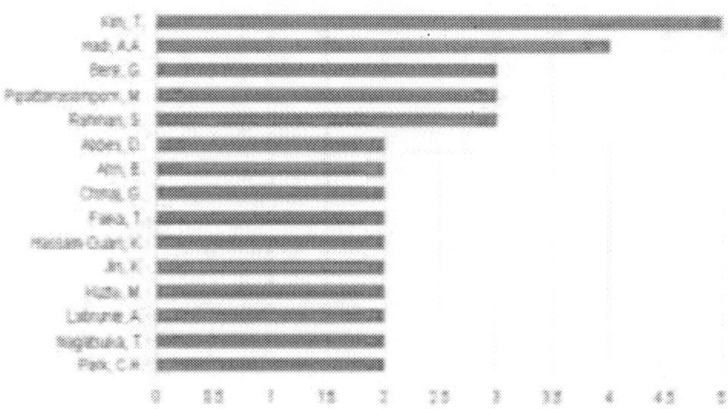

Figure 4. Papers per author

He has an h-index of 16 and 1033 citations on 71 published papers (Fig. 5), on energy and other domains.

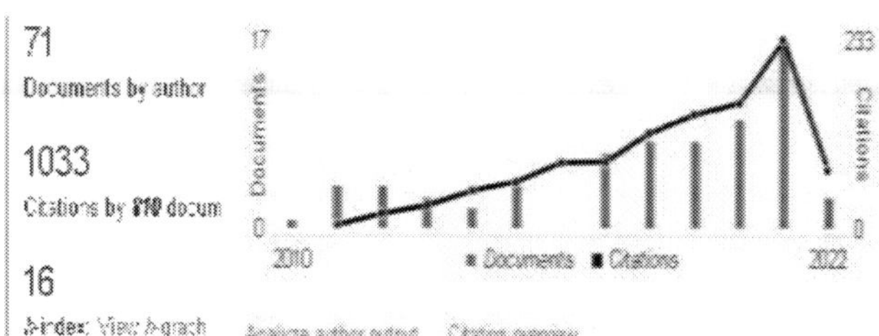

Figure 5. Sc

The second most productive in this collection of papers is "Hadi, Abdullah Al" by 4 papers, also affiliated to "Texas A and M University-Kingsville, Kingsville, United States". Even his novelty (since 2019) in research, He has 8 papers cited 52 times and an h-index of 4 (Fig. 6). His interests of research are: Engineering, Energy, Computer Science and Chemical Engineering.

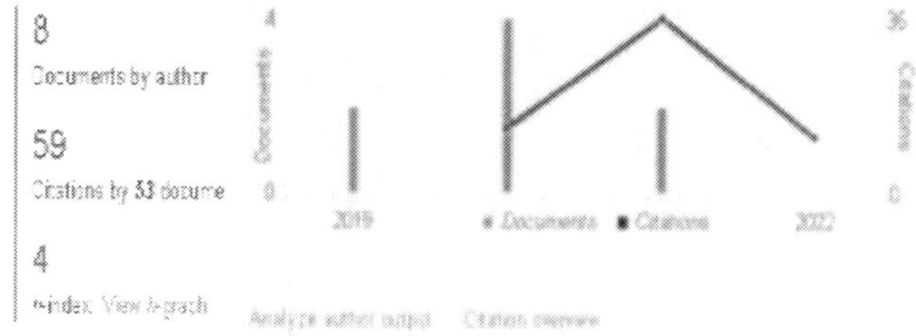

Figure 6. Scientific metrics of the author Hadi, Abdullah Al in SCOPUS

In the Third position (with 3 papers in the studied collection), comes the authors shown in Table 1.

TABLE I. AUTHORS IN THIRD POSITION

Author	Affiliation	Papers	h-index	Citations
Bere, Gomanth	Texas A and M University-Kingsville, Kingsville, United States	11	3	24
Pipattana sompon, Manisa	Chulalongkorn University, Bangkok, Thailand	105	35	5362
Rahman, Saifur	Virginia Polytechnic Institute and State University, Blacksburg, United States	365	48	11155

We notice that the fifth and the last author in table 1, has the highest number of citations. Even He is the low productive in Top 5 authors, He has the highest impact on scientific community.

D. *Number by affiliation*

The universities and laboratories look for the primary ranking positions, to be more visible and attractive to the international scientific competencies of lecturers and researchers.

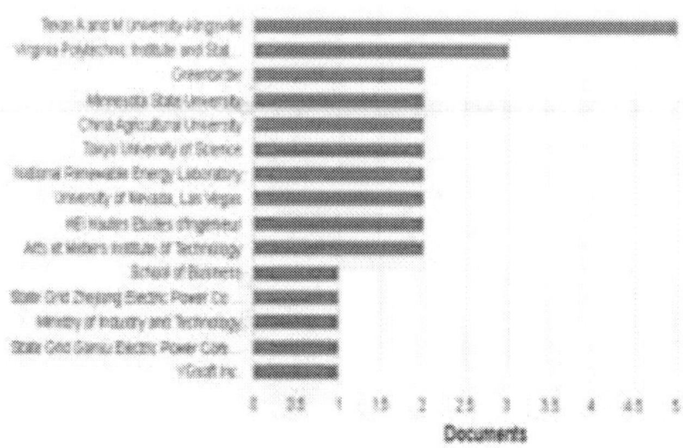

Figure 7. Papers by affiliaion

The first productive university with 5 papers is "Texas A and M University-Kingsville". The university has a hole institute "institute for sustainable energy and the environment" interested in the issues of renewable energy and blockchain. It is followed by "Virginia Polytechnic Institute and State University" with 3 papers, and, the third position with 2 papers by 8 universities (Fig. 7), and then come the remaining affiliations by 1 paper.

E. *Number by country*

United States is the most productive country (Fig. 8) with 12 papers among 42, followed by China (10 papers) and India (5 papers).

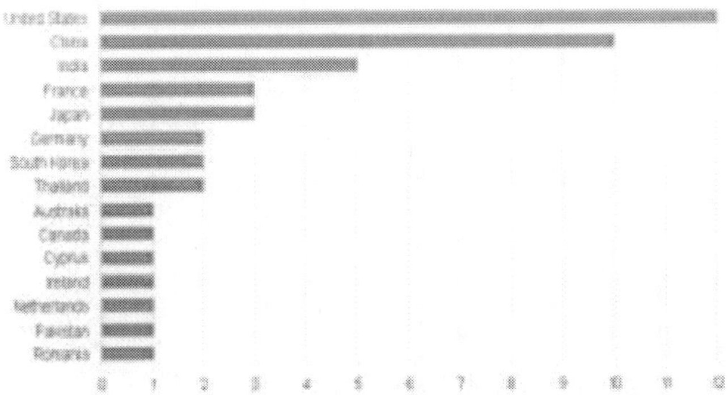

Figure 8. Papers by country

F. *Number by document type*

The conference papers are majority (64,3%), ie 27, followed by journal articles (31%), ie 13 papers. It is remaining 1 paper as a review and 1 paper as a note (Fig. 9).

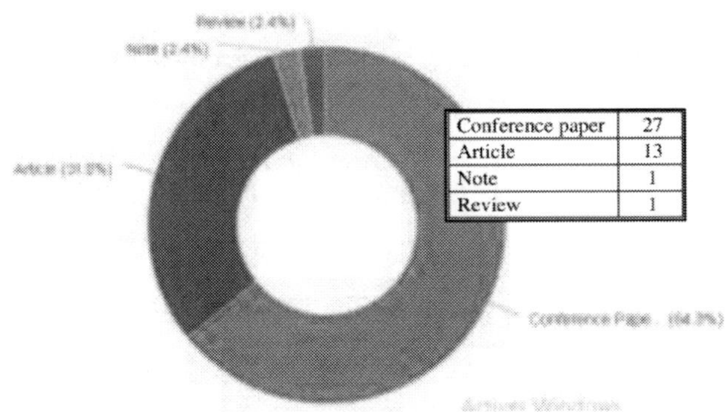

Figure 9. Papers by document type

G. *Papers by subject area*

The papers are divided fairly on the subject areas of energy (27 papers) and Engineering (26 papers), in third position comes the computer science (20 papers). The remaining papers (Fig. 10) are shared on mathematics (8 papers), social science (5 papers), environmental science (4 papers)…etc.

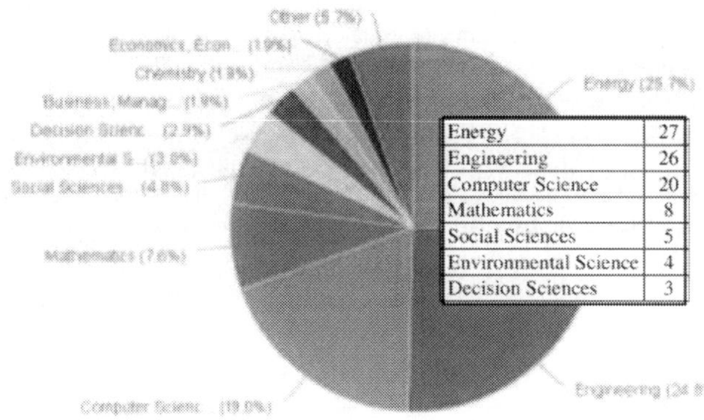

Figure 10. Papers by subject area

III. CITATION ANALYSIS

The citation analysis is the examination of the frequency and impacts of a scientific document over time. In this section we'll show different citation criteria to determine which paper contributed the most and in which year it appeared the most in others scientific documents.

A. *Citations by year*

Figure 11 shows that the citations are increasing over the years, showing a growing interest in strong and valid papers about energy, energy trading and blockchain technology. This was especially true in 2021 where all eyes were headed towards cryptocurrency and blockchain.

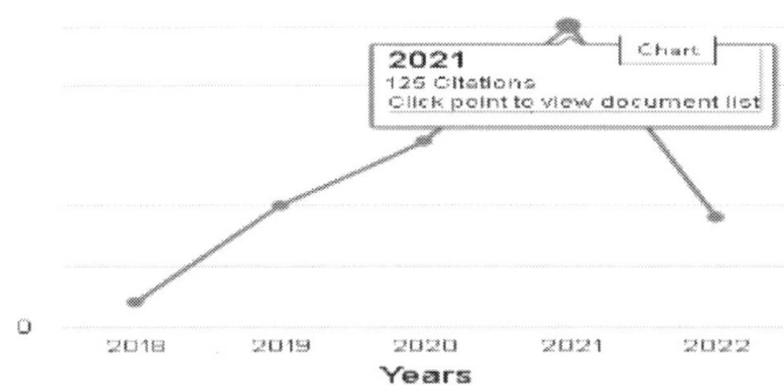

Figure 11. Citations per year

B. *Citations by papers*

The most cited paper (86 citations) is entitled "Energy trading for fun and profit buy your neighbor's rooftop solar power or sell your own-it'll all be on a blockchain". The reasons are: (1) the notoriety of the paper (2012), (2) the usage of blockchain in managing the photovoltaic system was relatively new, (3) the paper responded to the questions: Would you pay slightly more for your electricity if you knew it was sourced from photovoltaic panels on your neighbor's roof? Or, if you are that neighbor, would you use your solar power to charge a battery and dump that energy back onto the grid at peak hours, when the price was highest? [24]. The second most cited paper [11] is entitled "Applying the blockchain technology to promote the development of distributed photovoltaic in China" (31 citations). Even though it is relatively recent (2018), but it was cited thanks to: (1) it is a review paper, it is more read than other papers, (2) it gives strengthens and weakenesses of the distributed PV system, by region and several environments like economic, social and technical one, (3) It explains what are the threats and how blockchain comes to improve the existing PV system. The third position of citations are two papers concerning the trading of PV energy in a hybrid system (self consumption and injection in a public grid) [23] [25], with 28 and 27 citations respectively (Fig. 12).

	Documents	Total
		[illegible]
1	Energy trading for fun and profit buy your neighbor's rooftop ...	86
2	Applying the blockchain technology to promote the developmen	31
3	[Photovoltaic Trading Mechanism Design Based on Blockchain-b	28
4	Distributed Solar Self-Consumption and Blockchain Solar Ener...	27
5	Trading solar energy within the neighborhood: field implemen...	21
6	Implementing blockchain technology in irrigation systems tha...	13
7	Internet of Things (IoT) Enabled Solar Micro Inverter Using ...	11
8	A Blockchain-based Platform for Exchange of Solar Energy: La...	10
9	Blockchain-Based Communication and Data Security Framework f...	9
10	Comparative Analysis of Blockchain-based Smart Contracts for...	8
11	Application of Blockchain Technology in Peer-to-Peer Transac...	8
12	Blockchain in solar energy	7
13	A Novel Framework for Monitoring Solar PV based Electric Veh...	6
14	Blockchain-based Solar Electricity Exchange: Conceptual Arch...	6

Figure 12. Most cited papers

IV. KEYWORDS ANALYSIS

The keyword analysis is a quantitative and qualitative analysis of a paper. The most used words in the titles are "blockchain" and "solar energy"; of course, they are contained in the request introduced in the research zone in SCOPUS database. "block-chain" is appeared 10 times. The remaining keywords are "Smart contracts" to explaiin the automated rules concerning the generation and trading of the solar energy (Solar power generation, Electric power transmission networks, power markets,...etc.). The keywords also concern "Internet Of Things", consensus and the most used cryptocurrency in them "ethereum".

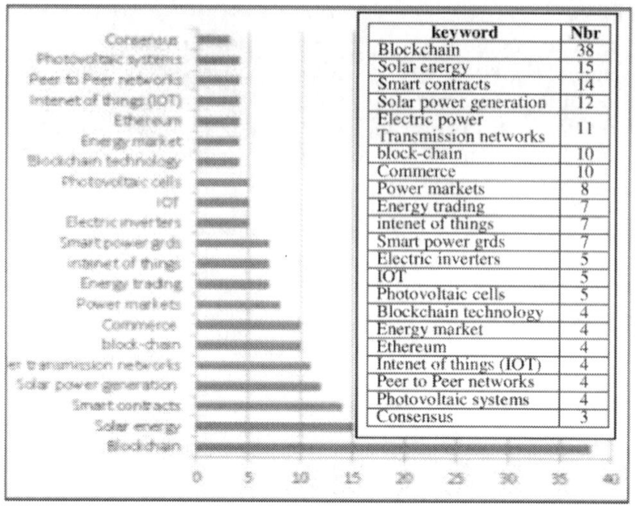

keyword	Nbr
Blockchain	38
Solar energy	15
Smart contracts	14
Solar power generation	12
Electric power Transmission networks	11
block-chain	10
Commerce	10
Power markets	8
Energy trading	7
intenet of things	7
Smart power grds	7
Electric inverters	5
IOT	5
Photovoltaic cells	5
Blockchain technology	4
Energy market	4
Ethereum	4
Intenet of things (IOT)	4
Peer to Peer networks	4
Photovoltaic systems	4
Consensus	3

Figure 13. Authors' keyword frequencies

We can notice that blockchain is appeared like "blockchain" (38) and like "block-chain" (10) and like "blockchain technology" (4), in total 52 times. We find also that "peer to peer network" (4) is appeared because it supports the blockchain solution.

V. QUALITAIVE ASPECTS OF THE ANAYSIS

The remaining of the paper concerns a qualitative study, concerning aspects extracted after a full exploration of the papers.

A. *Energy generation or energy trading*

Twenty papers treat the problem of trading solar energy jointed to self-consumption. Two among them are surveys and eighteen papers treat the self-consumption of solar energy and other aspects.

Figure 14 shows the sequence diagram for the energy trading.

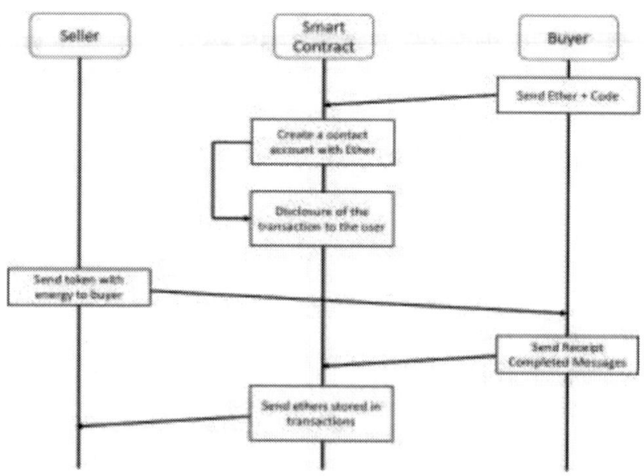

Figure 14. Sequence diagram for the energy trading [2].

In the energy trading platform, some participants have superfluous energy that they wish to sell to the platform as sellers, whereas others do not have sufficient energy to meet their demands and must buy the shortfall from the platform as buyers. Specifically, first, the buyer defines and sends Etherium and code so that smart contracts can be created.

B. Solar Energy System 4.0 (IOT and Blockchain)

Establishing a system using IOT (Internet Of Things) devices that produce the excess of energy. It consists of two parts: energy generation which maximizes the produced energy and energy trading using blockchain trading model ethereum based application. Enegy generation gains 35% [2]. There are 6 papers related to the IOT. [20] Provides continuous monitoring, data exchanging, and optimal operation in smart grid environments and in the IOT-enabled PV systems.

C. Other treated Ploblematics And Solutions

This section illustrates the encountered problems in solar energy systems, proposed solutions and the findings after applying these solutions. To avoid similarities, only 13 papers are explicited.

In [1], none of the existing studies provides a complete blockchain-based multi-dimensional P2P transaction mechanism. Fully open P2P trading mode and decentralized electricity price mechanism are adopted in day-ahead market, and P2P pool trading mode and electricity price mechanism based on supply/demand ratio are adopted in real-time market. The transaction mechanism designed can effectively realize P2P power transactions between producers and consumers, and promotes the enthusiasm of producers and consumers to participate in the P2P day-ahead market in order to maximize the benefits for prosumer target to achieve transactions between users according to different transactions. The objective of [2] is balancing power supplement from the solar energy's intermittent and unpredictable generation. A solar energy generation and trading platform EggBlock is proposed. It achieves reliable and transparent energy trading on the blockchain and converges to the optimal direction with short iterations. The average energy generation gain of 35% is obtained. How to optimise energy exchanges on a local energy community in a distributed way? [5]. It is possible to solve the optimization problem also with a distributed method using game theory, where each element of the grid tries to reach its own objectives, using real consumption and production data. It is possible to determine not only anomalies but also to create clean dashboards that can help on reporting how each classroom/auditorium is being used and who are the biggest offenders when it comes to power consumption and warning with alarms. The integration of distributed energy resources (DER) into centralized power markets on the large scale is challenging. The contribution of [6] is meeting future electricity demand. It provides valuable guidelines for the integration of DER into future sustainable energy markets. How to manage surplus PV output? The aim of [8] is to find consumers of surplus PV output and to match electricity supply and demand with market mechanism. Authors propose a new contract processing algorithm to calculate the nodal price in the area with surplus power transaction.

Abandoning solar energy in rural regions and increasing voltage fluctuation have become more prominent [3]. To increase the local electricity consumption of the photovoltaic generation, the incentive mechanism using an optimal internal electricity price is proposed with blockchain technology. The simulation result shows that the comprehensive revenue is increased, and the local electricity consumption rate of distributed photovoltaic generation is significantly raised.

Alao and Cuffe [12] investigate the impact of the delay resulting from a blockchain, and proposes a promising security measure, for a hierarchical control system of inverters connected to the grid. The blockchain communication network is designed at the secondary control layer for resilience against cyberattacks. A temperature-based weather derivative swap DeFi instrument is proposed in [13], it can serve as an effective volumetric risk hedging instrument at a negligible cost. It is only elucidative of the type of flexible hedging arrangements that can be enabled by blockchain, as any other weather index could be employed if required. In the same context [15], simulation method for smart inverters and blockchain network using a proposed framework as cooperative control approach, responded to different operating conditions.

In [16], authors adopt an appropriate mechanism that allows benefiting from the excess energy produced by these base stations and simplifies the process of energy trading while also making it cost-optimal.

A direct communication-based LCOE (BLCOE) is proposed in [17]; it is a model as the least-cost solution that measures the impact of energy reliability on generation cost. It considers daily variations in the cost of solar modules and battery storage across sub-Sahara Africa (SSA). Simulation results show the reduction of energy costs by approximately 95% for battery and 75% for the solar modules.

To avoid repetitions, the remaining papers are not presented because of the similarities with the presented ones.

VI. CONCLUSION

We saw in this paper how fast intrests in energy are growing. Many papers are published about this topic and many other technologies other than blockchain are integrated, which will lead to a mass distribution of the idea of exchanging excess solar energy with neighbours via a blockchain network using a proper coin. The main barrier here is how to transform a simple consumer to a prosumer. A P2P network is the most adequate architecture to support this platform. A cryptocurrency will make the trading more fluent. The prices of energy generally depend to the rules of offer/demand of the local or metropolitan market of solar energy. Knowing that the blockchain technology itself is a big consumer of energy, it is important to be autonome and a consumer of renewable energy like solar energy. This work may be usefull to developper of blockchain platforms and the producer of energy solar to take benefits both from their combination and to find exactly how to do so since the word blockchain can be difficult to combine with energy production In a future work, we will show other studies aspects from this collection of papers like: used protocols and consensuses, smart contracts, statistical methods, used data in blockchains…etc.

REFERENCES

[1] X Xiong, G. Qing,., and H Li,. "Blockchain-based P2P power trading mechanism for PV prosumer. Energy Reports", vol 8, pp. 300-310, 2022.

[2] S Kwak, J. Lee, J. Kim, and H. Oh, "EggBlock: Design and Implementation of Solar Energy Generation and Trading Platform in Edge-Based IoT Systems with Blockchain", Sensors, vol 22(6), 2410, 2022.

[3] T. Zhang, J. Yang, J. Li, Z. Yang, and K. Jin, "Research on local consumption method of distributed photovoltaic generation for benefits of multi parties based on blockchain", Energy Reports, vol 7, pp. 185-190, 2021.

[4] F. M. Enescu, N. Bizon, A. Onu, M. S. Răboacă, P. Thounthong, A. G. Mazare, and G. Șerban, "Implementing blockchain technology in irrigation systems that integrate photovoltaic energy generation systems", Sustainability, vol 12(4), 1540, 2020.

[5] A. Labrunie, and B. Robyns, "Increasing Photovoltaic Self-consumption: An Approach with Game Theory and Blockchain. In Sustainable Energy for Smart Cities: First EAI International Conference, SESC 2019, Braga, Portugal, December 4–6, 2019, Proceedings (Vol. 315, p. 180). Springer Nature., 2020.

[6] A. Wörner, A. Meeuw, L. Ableitner, F. Wortmann, S. Schopfer, and V. Tiefenbeck, "Trading solar energy within the neighborhood: field implementation of a blockchain-based electricity market", Energy Informatics, vol 2(1), pp. 1-12., 2019.

[7] R. Jain, and A. Dogra, "Solar energy distribution using blockchain and IoT integration", In Proceedings of the 2019 International Electronics Communication Conference, pp. 118-123. 2019, July.

[8] T. Nagatsuka, K. Kushino, M. Sano, and N. Yamaguchi, "Congestion Dissolution of Distribution Systems in Local Power Exchange Systems for Surplus Photovoltaic Output Using Blockchain", In 2019 3rd International Conference on Smart Grid and Smart Cities (ICSGSC), pp. 193-199. IEEE, 2019, June.

[9] Y. Huang, P. Yang, Z. Liu, Y. Lyu, and Y. Chen, "A design of photovoltaic plants financing platform based on blockchain technology", In 2018 International Conference on Power System Technology (POWERCON), pp. 4251-4256, IEEE, 2018, November.

[10] C. Gao, Y. Ji, J. Wang, and X. Sai, "Application of blockchain technology in peer-to-peer transaction of photovoltaic power generation", In 2018 2nd IEEE Advanced Information Management, Communicates, Electronic and Automation Control Conference (IMCEC), pp. 2289-2293, IEEE., 2018, May.

[11] J. Hou, H. Wang, and P. Liu, "Applying the blockchain technology to promote the development of distributed photovoltaic in China", International Journal of Energy Research, vol 42(6), pp. 2050-2069, 2018.

[12] N. Gajanur, M. Greidanus, G. S. Seo, S. K. Mazumder, and M. A. Abbaszada, "Impact of blockchain delay on grid-tied solar inverter performance", In 2021 IEEE 12th International Symposium on Power Electronics for Distributed Generation Systems (PEDG), pp. 1-7, IEEE., 2021, June.

[13] O. Alao, and P. Cuffe, "Towards a Blockchain Weather Derivative Financial Instrument for Hedging Volumetric Risks of Solar Power Producers", In 2021 IEEE Madrid PowerTech, pp. 1-6, IEEE., 2021, June.

[14] K. S. Thu, and W. Ongsakul, "Simulation of Blockchain based Power Trading with Solar Power Prediction in Prosumer Consortium Model", In 2020 International Conference and Utility Exhibition on Energy, Environment and Climate Change (ICUE), pp. 1-10, IEEE., 2020, October.

[15] A. A. Hadi, G. Bere, B. Ahn, and T. Kim, "Smart Contract-Defined Secondary Control and Co-Simulation for Smart Solar Inverters using Blockchain Technology", In 2020 IEEE CyberPELS (CyberPELS), pp. 1-6, IEEE, 2020, October.

[16] V. Hassija, V. Gupta, V. Chamola, and S. Kanhare, "A blockchain-based framework for energy trading between solar powered base stations and grid", In Proceedings of the Twenty-First International Symposium on Theory, Algorithmic Foundations, and Protocol Design for Mobile Networks and Mobile Computing, pp. 315-320, 2020, October.

[17] O. Samuel, N. Javaid, R. Khalid, M. Imran, and M. Guizani, "Case Study of Direct Communication based Solar Power Systems in Sub-Saharan Africa for Levelled Energy Cost Using Blockchain.", In ICC 2020-2020 IEEE International Conference on Communications (ICC), pp. 1-6, IEEE, 2020, June.

[18] A. A. Hadi, G. Bere, T. Kim, J. J. Ochoa, J. Zeng, and G. S. Seo, "Secure and cost-effective micro phasor measurement unit (pmu)-like metering for behind-the-meter (btm) solar systems using blockchain-assisted smart inverters", In 2020 IEEE Applied Power Electronics Conference and Exposition (APEC), pp. 2369-2375, IEEE, 2020, March.

[19] A. A. Hadi, U. Sinha, T. Faika, T. Kim, J. Zeng, and M. H. Ryu, "Internet of Things (IoT)-enabled solar micro inverter using blockchain technology", In 2019 IEEE industry applications society annual meeting, pp. 1-5. IEEE, 2019, September.

[20] U. Sinha, A. A. Hadi, T. Faika, and T. Kim, "Blockchain-based communication and data security framework for IoT-enabled micro solar inverters", In 2019 IEEE CyberPELS (CyberPELS), pp. 1-5, IEEE, 2019, April.

[21] M. Pipattanasomporn, M. Kuzlu, and S. Rahman, "A blockchain-based platform for exchange of solar energy: Laboratory-scale implementation", In 2018 international conference and utility exhibition on green energy for sustainable Development (ICUE), pp. 1-9, IEEE., 2018, October.

[22] J. Lin, M. Pipattanasomporn, and S. Rahman, "Comparative analysis of blockchain-based smart contracts for solar electricity exchanges", In 2019 IEEE Power & Energy Society Innovative Smart Grid Technologies Conference (ISGT), pp. 1-5, IEEE., 2019, February.

[23] C. Plaza, J. Gil, de F. Chezelles, and K. A. Strang, "Distributed solar self-consumption and blockchain solar energy exchanges on the public grid within an energy community", In 2018 IEEE International Conference on Environment and Electrical Engineering and 2018 IEEE Industrial and Commercial Power Systems Europe (EEEIC/I&CPS Europe), pp. 1-4, IEEE., 2018, June.

[24] M. E. Peck, and D. Wagman, "Energy trading for fun and profit buy your neighbor's rooftop solar power or sell your own-it'll all be on a blockchain", IEEE Spectrum, vol 54(10), pp. 56-61, 2017.

[25] B. Qi, Y. Xia, B. Li, D. Li, Y. Zhang, and P. Xi, "Photovoltaic trading mechanism design based on blockchain-based incentive mechanism", Autom. Electr. Power Syst, vol 43(9), pp. 132-139, 2019.

[26] SCOPUS database, www.scopus.com for the extraction of papers and some metrics, visited at April 22th, 2022.

Blockchain based Decentralized Home Energy Management System using Double Auction

Sweta Malik, Subhasis Thakur, John Breslin
Insight Centre for Data Analytics
National University of Ireland
Galway, Ireland
e-mail: m.sweta1, subhasis.thakur, john.breslin@nuigalway.ie

Maeve Duffy
Electrical and Electronic Engineering, School of Engineering
National University of Ireland
Galway, Ireland
e-mail: maeve.duffy@nuigalway.ie

***Abstract*—Due to increasing concern about climate change, the local energy market has been revolutionized with the increase in solar photovoltaic, electric vehicles, smart home appliances, and demand response. These technologies used in the residential sector provides new opportunities for Home Energy Management System (HEMS) to manage peak hours and gain incentives. In this paper, we develop a blockchain-based smart meter and HEMS that can collaboratively participate in energy consumption to maximize energy from renewable sources and reduce peak load. A fully decentralized blockchain-based system is used for trading energy using a double auction. Smart meters are enabled with a lightweight blockchain client that provides detailed information about energy consumption and controls the appliances from installed HEMS. Lightweight blockchain clients can be deployed on the smartphones of the owner of these smart meters. Regulations may prevent renewable electricity injection into the electricity grid. Hence, we investigate how to reduce energy consumption from the electricity grid. A test-bed is constructed and the simulations are done for two seasons: winter and summer. Different case studies and scenarios are carried out to show the proposed model's effectiveness. The results show that blockchain-based trading algorithms can impact individual users to manage energy consumption with high incentives.**

Key words - Blockchain, Home Energy Management System, double auction, energy trading, incentives, trading algorithm

I. INTRODUCTION

Due to the increasing usage of renewable energy, the local energy market has been revolutionized with the increase in the use of solar photovoltaic, electric vehicles, smart home appliances, and demand response. These technologies used in the residential sector provide new opportunities for an Energy Management System (EMS) [1] to manage peak hours and gain incentives without causing discomfort. The Energy Management System plays a significant role in maintaining the balance between demand and supply. Energy trading [2], [3] is a suitable method to balance demand and supply in EMS. Suppliers, also known as prosumers, provide surplus energy to the distribution network to satisfy the demand. Consumers and prosumers; both are rational and, therefore, try to maximize their revenues from incentive-based schemes. In a similar incentive-based trading mechanisms, energy price is a crucial component of Energy Management .

There are various incentive based approaches [4], [5] available in the literature, such as, game theory [6], auction [7] and negotiation. To model the trading mechanism, in this work, we are using double auction mechanism, which is able to maximize revenue for individual users in trading. The main contribution of this paper are as follows:

- A novel Home Energy Management System (HEMS) problem for a microgrid is presented, which is able to maximize the energy consumption from DERs and reduce peak load.
- A fully decentralized blockchain-based system is used for trading energy using double auction. Smart meters are enabled with a lightweight blockchain client that provides detailed information about energy consumption and controls the appliances from installed HEMS.
- The objective of the proposed trading algorithm is to optimize the energy demand according to real time prices. The trading algorithm is optimized using double auction mechanism.

The paper was organised as follows: We introduced pricing mechanism for decentralized HEMS using blockchain in section II with related literature. In section III, we discussed the double auction trading algorithm and blockchain architecture in section IV. The implementation, simulations and results were discussed in section V. Finally, in section VI, we presented conclusions and future work.

II. RELATED LITERATURE

A. Pricing mechanism

Pricing is a powerful mechanism to simulate prosumers and consumers to achieve high economic value. At the time of peak hours, electricity prices are high, users reschedule their load and the demand decreases. As the demand of microgrids keeps changing, electricity prices vary with time. In real-time pricing [8], the price keeps on varying with respect to energy demand and is suggested as one of the best approaches to improve the performance in the local energy market. Information regarding the change in price is timely informed to the users in the microgrid. Instead of flat-rate pricing, smart grids are now shifting towards market-driven pricing schemes where the kilowatt-hour cost changes with the day, time, weather conditions and demand. Since dynamic pricing is a concept that can be wisely used with respect to the ToU, it serves as a significant mechanism in demand-side management techniques. Another pricing scheme is the Time of Usage (ToU) tariff [9], which is based on energy demand for an extended time, like an hour, daytime and nighttime. Information regarding ToU is provided in advance to the users in the microgrid and stays constant for a more extended time.

B. Decentralized HEMS

Figure 1 illustrates the applications of customer based HEMS in smart appliances, demand flexibility, energy storage, and electric vehicles. Furthermore, HEMS also helps in managing peak demand, shifting the load to non-peak hours, and save energy. HEMS can be controlled using two main approaches: centralized and decentralized. The decentralized approach [10] objective is to achieve high social welfare while providing the best possible revenue to the users and Distributed Energy Resources (DERs). In the centralized approach, main grid or third party act as a controller to provide the relevant information, such as, energy demand, energy generation, forecasting information to the user in the microgrids in order to decide the price and energy according to the predefined preferences of the user [11]. In a microgrid having HEMS, which is the focus of this work, a high level of trust and transparency is required among the users and DERs, which makes decentralized approach the most suitable approach. Simply by expanding the DERs into centralized approach will not be effective for the distribution network. Some of the challenges of the centralized system are: (a) Lack of information from devices to optimize (b) Limited or delayed real time information (c) High transaction cost for settlement mechanism (d) No flexibility. Therefore, an improved, innovative, and decentralized solution is required. As a distributed ledger technology, blockchain provides such a solution. [12] proposes a decentralized energy management system problem for a distribution system with networked microgrids. The problem is solved using a stochastic decentralised bi-level algorithm that takes into consideration the intermittent outputs of DERs, the uncertain load consumption, and the coordinated operation points of all interdependent systems. [13] have explored a decentralised coordinated energy management approach for networked microgrids and future distribution system that is solved using the alternating direction method of multipliers (ADMM).

C. Blockchain

In recent years, Blockchain, the technology that nurtures the success of Bitcoin and many other cryptocurrencies, has emerged as research topic in the energy sector [14]. Blockchain is a database that stores information in blocks that are linked together. A new block is created for new data, and once the transactions are recorded in the block, it is linked in a chain with the previous block. This current block with transaction details chained into the blockchain is irreversible and is accessible to all the users in the network, making it a decentralized network. Blockchain eliminates the aggregator of the centralized network from the trading platform by keeping track of energy and price. All the transactions recorded are transparent to all the nodes/users (consumers and prosumers) in the network [15]. This transparency allows consumers and prosumers to have a network where users in the network can settle transactions without having trust on each other. With a self-executing and self-enforcing program, also referred to as the 'smart contract', blockchain can facilitate and verify the transactions.

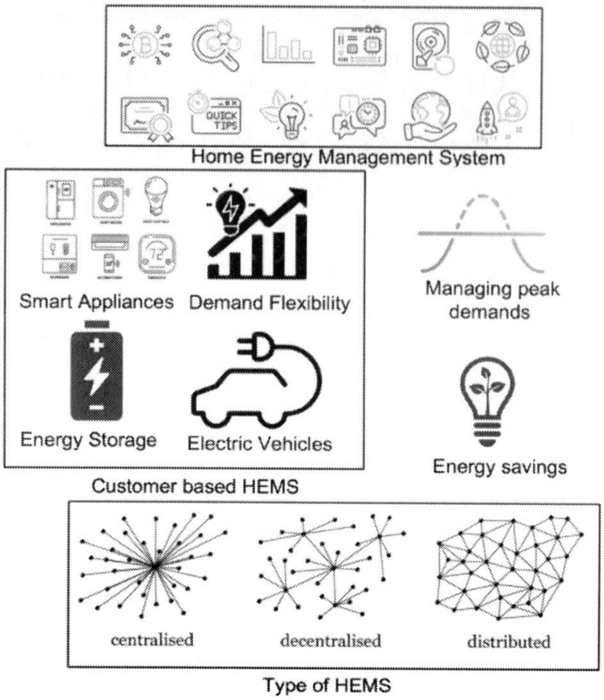

Fig. 1. Home Energy Management System.

The smart contract is a set of self-executing transaction protocols which are intended to run with respect to the terms of nodes present in the network directly written into the codes. Smart contracts exists in a distributed, decentralized blockchain network. First, the validity of each user is checked by the smart contract. When a user sends a request to trade energy, the smart contract checks for the surplus and deficit energy of that user. When a prosumer sends a surplus energy request, the smart contract calls for the seller function. The seller function stores the prosumer data, such as, surplus energy, selling price, geographical location of the prosumer, and the lowest selling price available in the network. Similarly, when a consumer sends an energy demand request, the smart contract calls for the buyer function. The buyer function stores the consumer data, such as, deficit energy, buying price, geographical location of the consumer, and the highest buying price available in the network. When bidding ends the trading price/market clearing price is calculated using a clear market function. To further extend the scope and harness the potentials of microgrid with blockchain innovations in fostering the clean energy transition, challenges, approaches, and future directions are presented in [16] from the technical, social, and economic dimensions. [17] developed a cost analysis method for blockchain-based peer to peer energy trade systems by examining the tradeoffs between the cost of the blockchain network, the appropriate throughput required for the blockchain, and profit from a user low energy price provided to another prosumer.

III. Home Energy Management Model

A. *Control levels of Microgrid*

Microgrids are cluster of loads and DER coordinated and operated by a third party or the main grid. Grid connected and isolated/stand alone are two type of microgrids. Microgrids are controlled by three levels of hierarchical structure: Primary, Secondary and Tertiary are illustrated in Figure 2. Primary level includes output control stage that tracks voltage, current and power imbalances. Smart meters in primary level uses smart bi-directional power flow for providing information. Secondary level is HEMS controls the economical operation and management of DER. Tertiary level is responsible for the coordination between the third party/ community aggregator/ main grid and the user. The community aggregator is responsible for coordination between the residential users in the microgrid and providing data to the blockchain platform.

HEMS is used to control, monitor and schedule smart appliances, extract energy generated information, while meeting the customers requirement. HEMS receives data like energy demand, foretasted weather details, real time prices, ToU prices from the community aggregator. Smart appliances can be divided into critical loads and schedule loads. Loads like air conditioner can be shifted to non peak hours by changing the thermostat level. Other high demand loads like washing machine, dish washer are also considered as time shiftable loads.

B. *Double auction based Trading Algorithm*

In Double Sided Auction (DSA), multiple consumers and prosumers gets an opportunity to trade energy simultaneously at a single time interval. According the bidding price of both the players, DSA mechanism provides efficient market scenario. DSA market asks consumers to submit the bid price i.e., the maximum price they are willing to pay and prosumers to submit sell price i.e., the minimum price they want to receive for selling surplus energy. The auctioneer(aggregator) collects the data from both the players, sorts the price and pairs consumer's bid price to prosumers selling price. It allows single consumer to buy energy from multiple prosumers to complete its demand and similarly, single prosumers can sell the surplus energy to multiple consumers in the network. Here all the users are in equilibrium, which is the state in which all the users find their required optimal energy while meeting all the user preferences. Once all the users are in equilibrium state, no user can further improve its utility by deviating from its current position. Nash Equilibrium is a state where no user can improve the revenue by changing its current positions, with respect to other users. In this section, a trading algorithm is proposed, that allows users to trade energy from

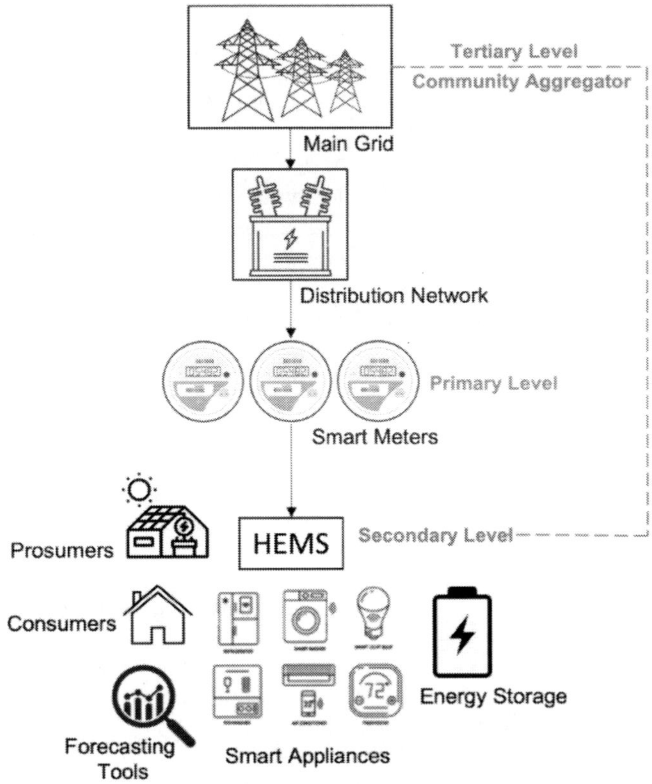

Fig. 2. Control levels of a microgrid.

each other using double auction mechanism. At each time interval (iteration), a user (U) chooses its best strategy to fulfill its energy demand and sell the surplus energy.

This trading algorithm presented in Algorithm 1 will run for two cases: Summer and Winter. Smart meters connected with blockchain network will send information regarding energy demand, surplus energy, and price to the community aggregator. The collaboration algorithm of DSA and blockchain will run as follows:

Step 1: Smart meter connected with the blockchain network will send the information regarding energy generated, surplus energy available to trade, and energy demand.

Step 2: Community aggregator will announce real time energy prices, energy load status on the grid or any other incentive that can help to low or high the load on electricity grid.

Step 3: The aim of the community aggregator is to maximize the use of solar rooftop generation to complete energy demand and minimize the energy imported from the main grid. Community aggregator will commit such incentives (including price of electricity) using the offline channel network.

Step 4: End users may update their energy use preference to the HEMS. The user have an option to take energy from the grid, or to trade from other users, or be a part of demand response.

Step 5: The HEMS will collaborate as optimal electricity

consumption plans will be generated via computation offloading to edge servers. HEMS will match and make pairs to trade energy within users.

Step 6: Data from smart meters will be used to validate end user compliance with planned energy consumption.

Step 7: Finally offline channel network will be used to share the incentives among the end users(such fund or token may be kept on the home energy device or smartphone of the user).

Algorithm 1: HEMS algorithm

```
For T=5 minutes
Initialization: Energy demand and energy generated, Input
buying price and selling price
Check status of consumers and prosumers
function peak hours () {
        Announce real time energy price for peak hours
for grid and Trade }
function non-peak hours () {
        Announce real time energy price for non-peak
hours for Grid and Trade }
function clear market () {
        HEMS does matching and call calculated users to
distribute energy }
function match bid () {
        Exchange energy with paired user }
Function sell energy () {
        Calculate Trading price
        Send price to blockchain }
Calculate incentives
Send incentives to the blockchain network
    End procedure
```

Fig. 3. HEMS using double auction algorithm.

IV. Blockchain Architecture

We will use Blockchains and decentralised data storage to execute the auction-based energy trade. We will use a permissioned blockchain with prosumers, Distribution System Operator (DSO), utility companies, and miners as the participants. We will use Inter-planetary File Systems (IPFS) as a decentralised data store. Figure 4 shows the overview of the proposed decentralised method:

1) The regulator (for example DSO) will store Hashes of a set of keys in the blockchain by creating a transaction with these hashes in the data field of the transaction.
2) The HEMS will ask the DSO for encryption keys (symmetric encryption).
3) DSO will verify the identify of the HEMS (possibly by its public key) and send a set of keys (hashes of these keys are kept a transaction in the blockchain).
4) HEMS will send information regarding bids/ asking price and amount of energy to be traded to the auctioneer. It will also send the Hash of a key which will be used to encrypt energy consumption data by the HEMS.
5) The Auctioneer will announce the outcome of the auction and HEMS.

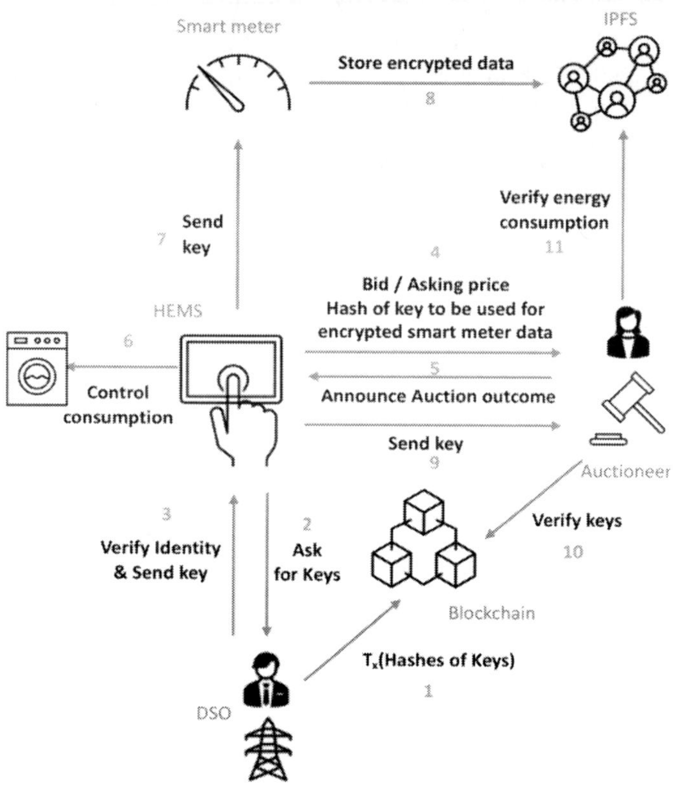

Fig. 4. Blockchain architecture.

6) HEMS will control its energy consumption according to the outcome of the auction.
7) After the energy consumption the HEMS will send the key (which it got from the DSO and reported Hash of it to the auctioneer) to encrypt smart meter data.
8) Smart meter will store will use this key to encrypt electricity meter reading and store it to the IPFS. It will get the ID of this information from IPFS and inform the ID to HEMS.
9) HEMS will send this ID and key used to encrypt the meter reading to the auction.
10) Auctioneer will verify the validity of the key by searching transactions created by the DSO.
11) Auctioneer will verify compliance with outcome of auction by decryption of the smart meter reading in the IPFS.

V. Simulations Results and Discussions

In this section, a microgrid is considered and simulated. To demonstrate this proposed trading algorithm, let us consider a microgrid consisting of N = 100 users, where 25 users have solar rooftop and 75 users are customers over a period of 288 time slots of 5 minute intervals. The trading simulations has been modeled and solved using MATLAB 2022. The energy transactions are blockchain based double auction mechanism proposed in this paper. The designed blockchain based HEMS

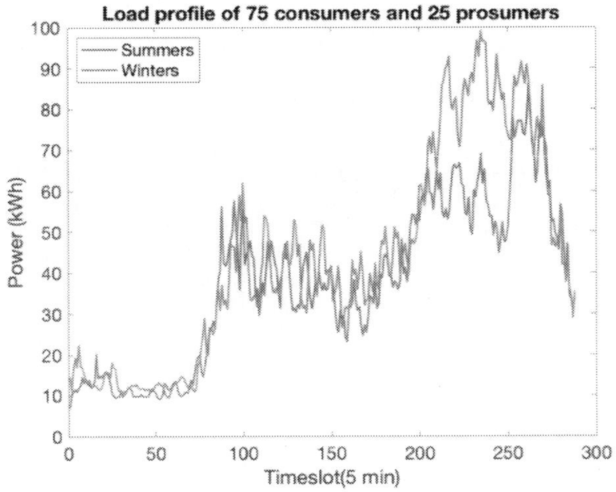

Fig. 5. Load profile for summer and winter for a microgrid with 75 consumers and 25 consumers.

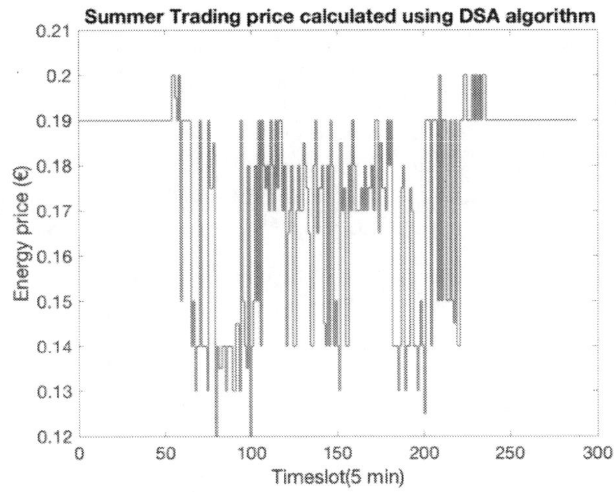

Fig. 6. Trading price in summer.

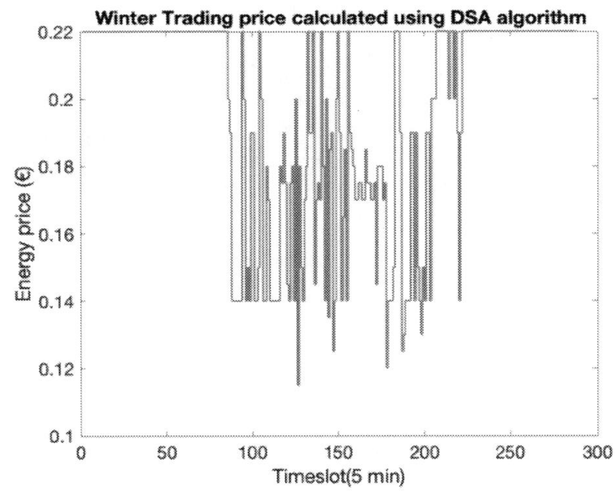

Fig. 7. Trading price in winter.

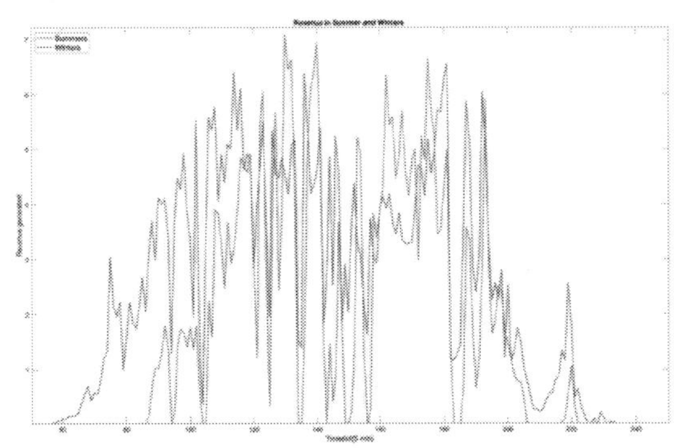

Fig. 8. Incentives distributed by blockchain.

for a microgrid is tested on low voltage network data having summer and winter load analysis and generation. For this simulation, an update time interval is chosen as 5 minutes, which is suitable with the intermittent nature of renewable sources and can collect fluctuations as well. Therefore, every 5 minutes the HEMS action is triggered by blockchain, and trading algorithm is solved according to the real time prices and the preferences of the users. Using 5 minutes time intervals, the entire horizon results in 288 time slots and incentives are distributed for each slots using blockchain. In this paper, data for 24 hours is used for summer and winters for the HEMS problem. Thus, smart meters captures energy generated and demand of the user and provide real time prices for trading.

The load profile of microgrid in summer and winter is shown in Figure 4. We can see that the peak hours are mostly during the night time. The peak load can be shifted to the non-peak hours either by shutting down schedule loads or shifting the loads to non-peak hours according to the real time prices. The Real time prices of Ireland is shown in Table 1 below. The electricity cost for day and night in winter and summer are shown in Table 1.

TABLE I
REAL TIME PRICES FOR SUMMER AND WINTER

	Summer	Winter
Day price	€0.18/unit	€0.2255/unit
Night price	€0.0924/unit	€0.1113/unit

For comparison purposes, the trading energy algorithm is run for two cases: summer and winter. In summer analysis, the solar generation is high and energy demand is fulfilled by energy generated by solar rooftop. However, during winter, energy demand is high, and solar rooftop is not able to fulfill the energy demand of the microgrid. Figure 5 and 6 show the trading price for both the scenarios. The ToU tariff for peak hours as shown in Figure 3 lies between 0.16€ to 0.2€ and for no-peak hours it lies between 0.09€ to 0.15€. The trading price is calculated as the average price of the asking price and selling price of the pair selected for trading. In Figure 7, the comparison of incentive generated in both, summer and winter scenario is presented. In the day time, the sum of incentive generated in summer is higher than in winters. The average revenue generated by the microgrid is 1175 Euros in 24 hours.

The total simulation time of this trading algorithm is 76 sec for 288 iterations of the HEMS, thus yielding an average computational time of 0.26 sec per iteration, making it suitable for real time price and smart appliances.

VI. CONCLUSIONS

This work has shown the modelling of integrated blockchain based on HEMS where users are able to trade energy, save their electricity bill, generate revenue, and shift from peak hours to non-peak hours. Type of pricing mechanism and importance of decentralized HEMS are introduced in this study. Microgrids are controlled by three levels of hierarchical structure: Primary, Secondary and Tertiary. HEMS is used to control, monitor and schedule smart appliances, extract energy generated information, while meeting the customers requirement. A trading algorithm is proposed in this work, that allows users to trade energy from each other using double auction mechanism. We used Blockchain and decentralised data storage to execute the auction-based energy trade. A test-bed is constructed with 100 users, with 25 houses with 3kWp rooftop PV. The simulations are done for two seasons: winter and summer. Different case studies and scenarios are carried out to show the proposed model's effectiveness. The results show that blockchain-based trading algorithms can impact individual users to manage energy consumption with high incentives. In future, we will provide a detailed formal security analysis of the blockchain-architecture of the energy trade. Moreover, the proposed work will be compared with other HEMS available to check its effectiveness.

ACKNOWLEDGMENT

This publication has emanated from research supported in part by a grant from Department of Business, Enterprise and Innovation, under the Government of Ireland's Project 2040, co-funded by the European Regional Development Fund, and also by a grant from Science Foundation Ireland under Grant Number SFI/12/RC/2289_P2. For the purpose of Open Access, the author has applied a CC BY public copyright licence to any Author Accepted Manuscript version arising from this submission.

REFERENCES

[1] S. K. Rathor and D. Saxena, "Energy management system for smart grid: An overview and key issues," *International Journal of Energy Research*, vol. 44, no. 6, pp. 4067–4109, 2020.

[2] M. Elkazaz, M. Sumner, and D. Thomas, "A hierarchical and decentralized energy management system for peer-to-peer energy trading," *Applied Energy*, vol. 291, p. 116766, 2021.

[3] S. Malik, M. Duffy, S. Thakur, B. Hayes, and J. G. Breslin, "Cooperative game theory based peer to peer energy trading algorithm," in *The 12th Mediterranean Conference on Power Generation, Transmission, Distribution and Energy Conversion (MEDPOWER 2020)*, vol. 2020. IET, 2020, pp. 135–142.

[4] M. Eissa, "First time real time incentive demand response program in smart grid with "i-energy" management system with different resources," *Applied energy*, vol. 212, pp. 607–621, 2018.

[5] B. Shakerighadi, A. Anvari-Moghaddam, E. Ebrahimzadeh, F. Blaabjerg, and C. L. Bak, "A hierarchical game theoretical approach for energy management of electric vehicles and charging stations in smart grids," *Ieee Access*, vol. 6, pp. 67 223–67 234, 2018.

[6] S. Malik, M. Duffy, S. Thakur, B. Hayes, and J. Breslin, "A priority-based approach for peer-to-peer energy trading using cooperative game theory in local energy community," *International Journal of Electrical Power & Energy Systems*, vol. 137, p. 107865, 2022.

[7] B. P. Hayes, S. Thakur, and J. G. Breslin, "Co-simulation of electricity distribution networks and peer to peer energy trading platforms," *International Journal of Electrical Power & Energy Systems*, vol. 115, p. 105419, 2020.

[8] B. Xu, J. Wang, M. Guo, J. Lu, G. Li, and L. Han, "A hybrid demand response mechanism based on real-time incentive and real-time pricing," *Energy*, vol. 231, p. 120940, 2021.

[9] L. Chebbo, A. M. Bazzi, A. Yassine, S. H. Karaki, and N. Ghaddar, "Tou tariff system using data from smart meters," in *2021 IEEE Power and Energy Conference at Illinois (PECI)*. IEEE, 2021, pp. 1–5.

[10] F. Z. Harmouch, N. Krami, and N. Hmina, "A multiagent based decentralized energy management system for power exchange minimization in microgrid cluster," *Sustainable cities and society*, vol. 40, pp. 416–427, 2018.

[11] D. Espín-Sarzosa, R. Palma-Behnke, and O. Núñez-Mata, "Energy management systems for microgrids: Main existing trends in centralized control architectures," *Energies*, vol. 13, no. 3, p. 547, 2020.

[12] Z. Wang, B. Chen, J. Wang *et al.*, "Decentralized energy management system for networked microgrids in grid-connected and islanded modes," *IEEE Transactions on Smart Grid*, vol. 7, no. 2, pp. 1097–1105, 2015.

[13] H. Gao, J. Liu, L. Wang, and Z. Wei, "Decentralized energy management for networked microgrids in future distribution systems," *IEEE Transactions on Power Systems*, vol. 33, no. 4, pp. 3599–3610, 2017.

[14] M. Andoni, V. Robu, D. Flynn, S. Abram, D. Geach, D. Jenkins, P. McCallum, and A. Peacock, "Blockchain technology in the energy sector: A systematic review of challenges and opportunities," *Renewable and Sustainable Energy Reviews*, vol. 100, pp. 143–174, 2019.

[15] A. Esmat, M. de Vos, Y. Ghiassi-Farrokhfal, P. Palensky, and D. Epema, "A novel decentralized platform for peer-to-peer energy trading market with blockchain technology," *Applied Energy*, vol. 282, p. 116123, 2021.

[16] Y. Wu, Y. Wu, H. Cimen, J. C. Vasquez, and J. M. Guerrero, "Towards collective energy community: Potential roles of microgrid and blockchain to go beyond p2p energy trading," *Applied Energy*, vol. 314, p. 119003, 2022.

[17] S. Thakur and J. G. Breslin, "Cost analysis of blockchains-based peer to peer energy trade," in *2020 IEEE International Conference on Environment and Electrical Engineering and 2020 IEEE Industrial and Commercial Power Systems Europe (EEEIC/I&CPS Europe)*. IEEE, 2020, pp. 1–6.

A Decentralised Reputation Management System for Internet of Things Data Marketplace

Subhasis Thakur
National University of Ireland, Galway
Galway, Ireland
email: subhasis.thakur@nuigalway.ie

John Breslin
john.breslin@nuigalway.ie
Galway, Ireland
email: john.breslin@nuigalway.ie

Abstract—**A correct reputation management system can differentiate between low-quality and high-quality data providers in an Internet of Things (IoT) data marketplace. There are challenges in designing an unbiased and secure reputation management system that can not be manipulated by wrong feedbacks or wrong aggregation of feedbacks. In this paper, we develop a decentralised reputation management system for the IoT data marketplace that prevents biased selection and aggregation of reputation feedback. The proposed reputation management system uses blockchain offline channels, which makes the solution secure, unbiased, scalable, and least costly. We prove the security and correctness of the proposed reputation management system and present its experimental evaluation using simulation of data marketplace and blockchains.**

***Index Terms*—IoT, Data marketplace; Reputation management; Bitcoin; Lightning Network; Blockchain Offline channels.**

I. Introduction

In an Internet of Things (IoT) data marketplace there are three entities (1) data providers, (2) data consumers, and (3) data brokers. The data brokers act as match-makers between a data provider and a data consumer. The quality of data in a data marketplace is a big concern. A correct reputation management system can identify bad data providers. However, malicious behaviour of data consumers and data brokers may also affect the correctness of a reputation management system. In this paper, we propose a reputation management system that considers all such malicious entities.

Blockchains can be a useful platform to host a decentralised IoT data marketplace. Smart contracts are commonly used to act as a data broker in such a decentralised IoT data marketplace. However, executing data trade operations via smart contracts may be costly. Also, public blockchains such as Ethereum, Bitcoin have a scalability problem. In this paper, we develop a decentralised reputation management system for the IoT data marketplace. We advance the state of the art in reputation management for IoT data marketplace as follows:

- Correlated reputation: We proposed a reputation management system that correlates reputations of data providers, data brokers, and data consumers in such a way that if one entity had given negative feedback about another entity but the reputation of the other entity is eventually increased then the entity who had provided negative feedback loses its reputation.
- Economical feasibility: We used data brokers in this reputation management system. The proposed reputation management system uses a blockchain offline channel network, and these brokers invest to build such a network. In return, they get a financial benefit for executing the reputation management operation.
- Scalability: We execute the proposed reputation management algorithm in blockchain offline channels. It significantly improves the scalability of the solution as the number of transactions needed to be recorded in the blockchain is greatly reduced.
- Low fee: As we execute the reputation management system in blockchain offline channels we reduce the cost of executing the reputation management operations by reducing the number of transactions.
- Competitive reputation score calculation: In the proposed reputation management system, the data brokers act as betting houses where the data buyers place bets on the reputation of the data sellers. The data broker may deploy its own algorithm to find the accurate reputation of the data sellers and announce the betting odds accordingly. The accuracy of the algorithm to predict the reputation of the sellers will determine the revenue for the data brokers. This allows the proposed solution to be extended further by data brokers as they may deploy machine learning-based algorithm to accurately find the reputation of the data sellers.

The paper is organised as follows: in Section 2 we discuss related literature, in Section 3 we describe our solution, in Section 4 we present an analysis of the solution, in Section 5 we present an experimental evaluation of the proposed solution, and we conclude the paper in Section 6.

II. Related Literature

In [1] the authors developed a flexible reputation management model for IoTs, which chooses the best reputation model based on the current environment of the sensor. In [2] the authors developed a reputation model for a peer-to-peer network where one peer provides feedback about service provided by another peer. In [3] the authors developed a decentralised infrastructure for edge computing and IoTs. In [4] the authors proposed group formation among IoTs based on their reputation using blockchains. In [5] the authors developed proposed a centralised trust management system for IoTs using a centralised trust manager. In [6] the authors developed a trust management system for social IoTs. In [7] the authors developed a social IoT model [8] using trust relations among the sensors. In [9] the authors proposed a trust calculation method where a user may have personal and non-personal trust values. In [10] the authors developed a reputation system for IoT data marketplace using Ethereum. In [11] the authors developed a smart contract-based reputation management method for IoTs. In [12] the authors developed a decentralised IoT data marketplace with blockchain. In [13] the authors developed a smart-contract-based data trade model for IoT. In [14] the authors proposed a payment settlement method in IoT data marketplace using blockchains. In this paper, we used proof of work-based blockchains. Proof of work-based blockchains was proposed in [15]. There are several variations of blockchains in terms of consensus protocols. Offline channels for Bitcoin, i.e., Bitcoin Lightning network was proposed in [16], which allows peers to create and transfer funds among them without frequently updating the blockchain. Similar networks were proposed for Ethereum [17] and credit networks [18].

III. Decentralised Reputation Management

A. Blockchain and IoT networks

An IoT data marketplace will consist of a set of data buyers, data sellers, and a set of betting houses that will manage the reputation of the buyers and the sellers. In this paper, we will use Bitcoin or proof of work-based public blockchain as the blockchain. The buyers in this IoT data marketplace, are the devices or applications seeking IoT data and the sellers are IoT devices providing sensing data. We will denote the buyers as the set $B = (B_1, \ldots, B_n)$ and the sellers as the set $S = (S_1, \ldots, S_m)$. The betting houses will allow the buyers to bet on the reputation of the sellers and they will maintain the betting odds of the sellers. The betting odds of the sellers will denote the reputation of the sellers. The reputation of the buyers will be their investments, i.e., the bets they have placed. All actors of this IoT data marketplace will establish uni-directional channels with each other to place bets on the reputation of the sellers.

B. Unidirectional Offline Channel

Blockchain offline channels [16] uses multi-signature addresses to open an offline channel among peers of the blockchain. This offline channel [16] is bidirectional and potentially infinite, i.e., it can execute the infinite number of transfers between two peers provided they do not close the channel and each of them has sufficient funds. We construct an offline channel for proof of work-based public blockchain with the following properties:

- We construct a uni-directional channel between two peers, i.e., only one peer can send funds to another peer of this channel.
- We construct a uni-directional channel that can be used for a finite number of transfers from a designated peer to another peer.

The procedure for creating the uni-directional channel from A to B (A transfers token to B)is as follows: Let A and B are two peers of the channel network H. $M_{A,B}$ is a multi-signature address between A and B. This is a unidirectional channel from A to B.

1) A creates a set of k (k is a positive even integer) random strings $S_A^1, \ldots, S_A^k$. Using these random strings A creates a set of Hashes $h_A^1 = Hash(S_A^1)$, $h_A^2 = Hash(S_A^2), \ldots, h_A^k = Hash(S_A^k)$ where $Hash$ is Hash function (using SHA256). A creates a Merkle tree height $D = Log_2 k$ using these Hashes. In this tree there are k leaf nodes and $k-1$ non-leaf nodes of this Merkle tree. We denote the non-leaf nodes as $H_A^1, \ldots, H^(k-1)_A$.
2) B creates a set of $D-1$ random strings and corresponding Hashes $H_B^1, \ldots, H_B^{D-1}$ such that there is a lexicographic order among these Hashes with $H_B^i \leq H_B^{i+1}$. We will call H_B^x is ranked more than H_B^y if the lexicographic order of H_B^x is more than H_B^y.
3) A will create a Hashed time locked contract as follows:
   a) Let A wants to transfer $1-d/D$ tokens to B where $d \leq D$.
   b) From the multi-signature address $M_{A,B}$ 1 token will be given to A after time T(will be measured as the number of new blocks to be created from the current block in the blockchain) if B does not claim these tokens by producing the key to any non-leaf node H_A^x of the Merkle tree created by A, which is at a distance d from the root of the Merkle tree.
   c) If B produces the key to such a Hash H_A^x at depth d then $(1-d/D)$ tokens will be given to B and remaining d/D tokens will be given to A if it can produce the key to a hash H_B^x in the set $H_B^1, \ldots, H_B^{D-1}$, which is ranked more than d hashes in this set.
4) A will sign this Hashed Time Locked Contract (HTLC) and send it to B.
5) Now A will send a transaction to $M_{A,B}$ of amount $1+\epsilon$ token with the Merkle tree mentioned in the transaction. B will send ϵ tokens to $M_{A,B}$ with $H_B^1, \ldots, H_B^D$ in the transaction data field where ϵ is the transaction processing fee. More than 1 token can be transferred by A. We are using 1 token as an example.
6) Before the next transfer from A to B, A will send the keys to the subset of Hashes $h_A^1, \ldots, h_A^k$, which can generate the Hash H_A^x. Fig. 1b(b) shows the sequence of subsets of non-leaf nodes of the Merkle tree, which A should reveal before each transfer of amount $1/D-1$. It will be possible for A to transfer multiples of $1/D-1$ tokens to B, in such a case multiple subsets of non-leaf Hashes of the Merkle tree will be revealed by A.

Note that,

- B signs and publishes the HTLC to claim the tokens. It gets the most number of tokens by using the last known

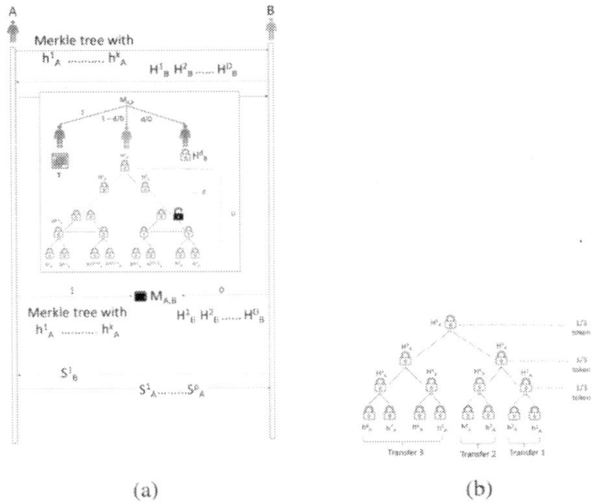

Fig. 1: (a) Procedure of creating unidirectional offline channels, (b) sequence of keys given by A to transfer fund to B .

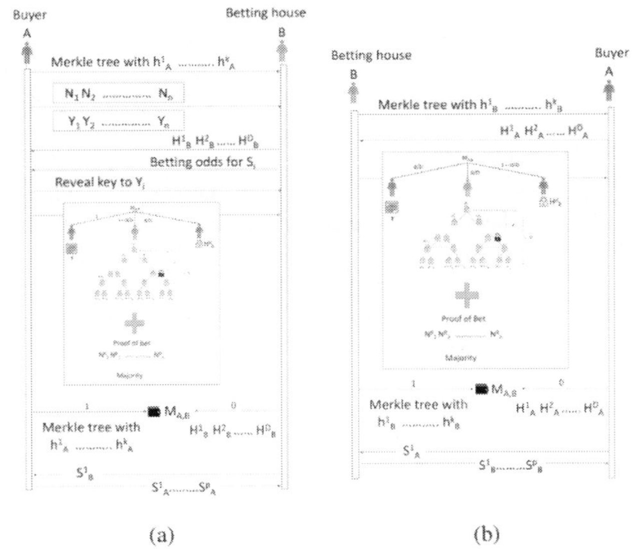

Fig. 3: (a) Channel creation from a buyer to a betting house, (b)Channel creation from a betting house to a buyer.

keys of the Merkle tree leaf nodes. Thus, B will always use the last known keys of this Merkle tree leaf node.

- The channel is secure as A can not transfer to B more than the current balance of the channel as B will know the current balance by finding the non-leaf nodes from the keys supplied by A and depth of such a non-leaf node.
- All peers of the blockchain will know the existence of this channel and Hashes used in creating the channel as transactions to $M_{A,B}$ are visible to all peers.

C. Channel network formation

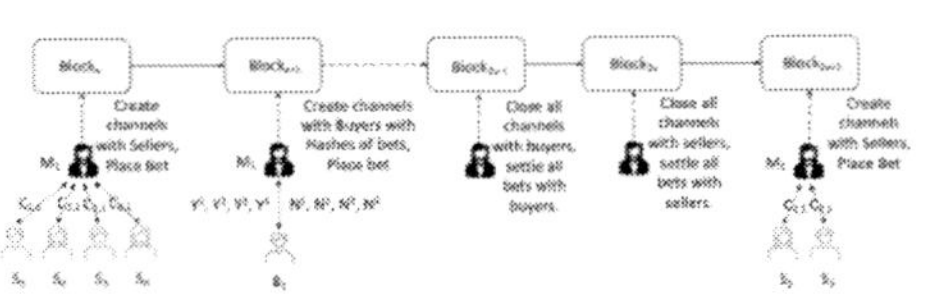

Fig. 2: Sequence of channel network creation in the IoT data marketplace

The channel network among the data buyers, sellers, and brokers (betting houses) will be constructed as follows:

1) The unidirectional channels with the betting houses will have a life span of x new blocks.
2) A betting house at the block $Block_{x-1}$ will settle all bets and close all channels. Channels can be closed by publishing HTLCs to the blockchain.
3) A betting house will create channels with all sellers and these channels will be created in the block $Block_x$. No further channels with the sellers will be created after the creation of the block $Block_x$. A betting house will create two channels 'to' and 'from' each seller.
4) Each betting house can open channels with all sellers.
5) From block $Block_{x+1}$ to $Block_{2x}$ any buyer can establish a channel with a betting house and place a bet on the reputation of a seller.
6) At the block $Block_{2x}$ all channels to and from the betting house will be closed.
7) The betting house can again facilitate betting on the reputation of the sellers by repeating the above steps.

D. Channel between a buyer and a betting house

The procedure to open a channel between a buyer and a betting house is as follows:

1) The procedure is the same as opening a uni-directional channel with these additional steps.
2) The buyer can check the set of sellers who established a channel with the betting house as the sellers should establish channels with the betting house before any buyer can do the same. The buyer can check the previous blockchain head for the existence of such channels.
3) Let there are n sellers who have established channels with the betting house.
4) The buyer will create two sets of n Hashes $(N_1, \ldots, N_n)$ and $(Y_1, \ldots, Y_n)$. If it reveals the key to the Hash N_i then it will mean it is betting against the reputation of seller S_i and if it reveals the key to the Hash Y_i then it will mean it is betting for the reputation of seller S_i.
5) A buyer who has betted against the reputation of a seller will win the bet if the majority of buyers have placed bets against the reputation of the same seller at the same betting house otherwise it will lose.
6) A buyer who has betted for the reputation of a seller will win the bet if the majority of buyers have placed

bets for the reputation of the same seller at the same betting house otherwise it will lose.

7) A buyer can place bets of amounts multiples of $1/D-1$ where D is the depth of the Merkle tree from the buyer to the betting house. As shown in Fig. 3(a), the buyer A created the modified unidirectional channel with betting house B.
8) After sharing the set of hashes $\{N_i\}$ and $\{Y_i\}$ with B, A will place the bet for any seller $\{S_i\}$ who has a channel with B.
9) B will inform A about the betting odds of the reputation of a seller S_i. A will reveal its bid by revealing the key to either N_i or Y_i. As shown in Fig. 3(a), buyer A is betting for the reputation of the seller S_i.
10) Next, A will record its bet by creating an HTLC which states the following:
    a) A will get 1 token after time T (equivalent to the creation of x new blocks from the current head of the blockchain) if B does not claim $1-d/D$ of these tokens by presenting the key to H_A^c of the Merkle tree created by which is at the depth d and by presenting the 'proof of bet' which will show that A lost its bet. In this example, Fig. 3(a) A betted for the reputation of seller S_i. Thus to prove that A has lost its bet, B needs to prove that majority of buyers have betted against the reputation of S_i. The remaining tokens will be given to A if it can reveal the key to H_B^d.
11) After creating the above HTLC A will sign it and share it with B. They will exchange keys to hash H_B^d and $H_A^1, \ldots, H_A^p$ (which can reveal the key to H_A^c in the Merkle tree).
12) This will complete A's bet against seller S_i at betting house B. This bet will be settled after time T (after x new blocks) when the betting house closes its channels with the buyers.

Next, the betting house will open a complementary unidirectional channel from itself to the buyer. The description of this channel is similar to the channel from the buyer to the betting house except, in this case, the betting house (shown in Fig. 3(b)) will send an HTLC to the buyer. If the buyer has betted for the reputation of the seller then the HTLC will be as follows:

1) The buyer will get d/D tokens after time T if the betting house does not claim these tokens by proving that the buyer has lost the bet by presenting keys to a negative feedbacks ($\{N_j^i\}$), which is a majority (in terms of the number of buyers who have channels with this betting house).
2) If the buyer had betted against the reputation of the seller then this HTLC will require proof of bet which should show that majority of buyers have placed bets against the seller's reputation at this betting house.

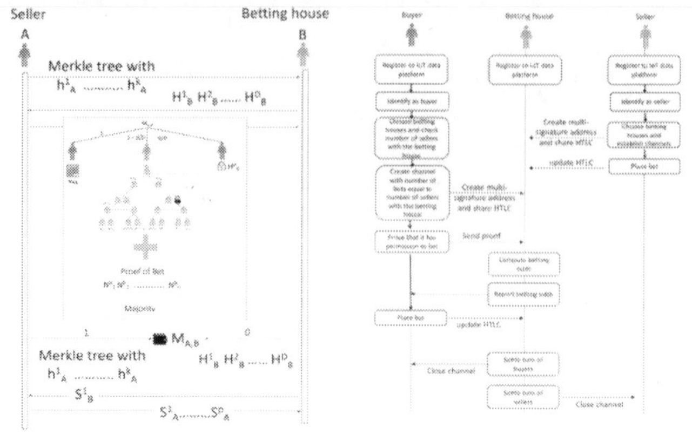

(a) (b)

Fig. 4: (a) channel creation between a seller and a betting house, (b) sequence of events in the decentralised reputation management systems.

E. Channel between a seller and a betting house

The procedure to create a channel between a seller A and a betting house B (shown in Fig. 4(a)) is as follows: It is the same as the creation of a uni-directional offline channel except in the HTLC from A to B, B can claim the tokens betted by A if it can prove that A have lost the bet. In this case, the seller A can only bet for its own reputation. Hence to prove that A has lost the bet, B needs to prove that majority of buyers have betted against S_i's reputation. It can do so by presenting a set of keys corresponding to a subset of the set $N_i^1, \ldots, N_i^m$, which is a majority, i.e., more size of this subset is more than 50%. The betting house will close the channels with the seller will be closed after all channels among the buyers and the betting house is closed. Similar to the channel from a betting house to a buyer, a complementary channel will be opened from the betting house to the seller. Its description is similar to the channel shown in Fig. 3(b).

F. Computing betting odds

A betting house needs to compute the betting odds about the reputation of a seller. It can deploy various algorithms to do so including machine learning-based algorithms to predict betting odds. A simple betting odd algorithm will use the history of bets on a seller's reputation. At any time, there are x bets for the reputation of the seller and y bets against the reputation of the seller. If $x > y$ then betting odds are $0:1$ (indicating that the betting house considers the seller as a reputable seller) and it will present proof of bet as a collection of bets for the seller. Otherwise betting odd will be $1:0$ indicating that the betting house considers the seller a less reputable seller and it will present proof of bet as a collection of bets against the seller.

G. Decentralised reputation management

In the IoT data marketplace, each actor (buyers or sellers) will identify itself either as a buyer or as a seller as it participates in the data marketplace. Each actor can open channels with a fixed total value. A seller or a buyer may have channels with multiple betting houses (one channel with one betting house). A seller may place its bet (that it has a good reputation and buyers will not bet against its reputation) by creating channels with the betting houses mentioned in the section III-E. A buyer may place its bet for or against any seller at any betting house with whom both the seller and the buyer have channels. The buyer may choose one such betting house and ask it for the betting odds. If it prefers the betting odds then it may place its bet for or against the seller. The reputation of a seller is its betting odds and the reputation of buyers is the value of its bets. Fig. 2 shows the workflow of the reputation management system, it is as follows:

1) All buyers, sellers, and betting houses will register to the IoT data marketplace by creating an account in the blockchain network used in the IoT data marketplace. All such actors will be identified by their public keys.
2) Betting on the seller's reputation occurs in cycles where each betting cycle is executed for time x (number of new blocks in the blockchain).
3) At the start of each betting cycle, all sellers create or updates their channels with betting houses within a fixed time deadline (marked with the number of new blocks in the blockchain). By creating the channels, the sellers place bets on their reputations.
4) Next, a buyer can create a channel with a betting house to place bets on the reputation of the sellers.
5) A buyer must prove to a betting house that it has permission to place a bet for/against the reputation of a seller. The buyer should prove that it has purchased/used the service of a seller. It can do so by presenting the key to a Hash of a random string created by the seller. The buyer can present the key / Hash pair to a betting house and the betting house can check with the seller about the authenticity of the key/hash pair presented by the buyer.
6) Next, the betting house will reveal its betting odds for the seller and the buyer can place its bet by revealing keys in the set $\{N_i, Y_i\}$ (N_i indicates that it bets against the reputation of the seller i, Y_i indicates that it bets for the reputation of the seller).
7) This process continues for a fixed number of new blocks as buyers place their bets.
8) A betting cycle is closed after x new blocks as the betting houses will reveal the HTLC and proof of bets in the blockchain network to claim tokens from the bets.

IV. Analysis

Theorem 1. *The decentralised reputation management system is secure.*

Proof. There are two ways HTLCs are published as channels are closed after every betting cycle. If a buyer (seller) loses the bet then the betting house will publish the HTLC sent by the buyer (seller) to the betting house with proof of bets. If a buyer (seller) wins a bet then it will publish the HTLC sent by the betting house to the buyer (seller). We have the following security problems:

1) A buyer (seller) may lose the bet and publish the HTLC from the betting house to claim tokens.
2) A betting house may lose the bet and publish the HTLC from the buyer (seller) to claim the tokens.

In the first case, the buyer (seller) will not immediately receive the tokens as it has to wait for time T. By this time the betting will observe the existence of this transaction in the blockchain and claim tokens by presenting correct proof of bets. In the second case, the betting house will not be able to create false proof of bets. This is because:

1) The set of Hashes ($\{N_j^i, Y_j^i\}$) indicating the bets to be placed by the buyers is visible by all peers of the blockchain as it is included in the transaction used to create the channel from the buyer to the betting house. Thus the betting house can not claim correct proof of bet with false pairs of keys and Hashes.
2) A buyer does not reveal its bet for all sellers and the betting house can not know the key to the Hashes ($\{N_j^i, Y_j^i\}$). Thus the betting house can not construct a false but correct proof of bet.

□

Theorem 2. *The decentralised reputation management system is correct if*

$$\frac{k}{k-1} < \frac{1}{(y_1-1)(y_2-1)} \quad (1)$$

where k is the number of buyers, y_1 is the number of rational buyers and y_2 is the number of irrational buyers.

Proof. The reputation management system is correct if reputation (betting odds) of low quality data sellers becomes low, revenue of irrational buyers who provide false feedback (places wrong bets intentionally) becomes low, and revenue of irrational betting houses who provide false betting odds becomes low. Let the demography of this marketplace is as follows:

- Rational betting houses always announce correct betting odds of the sellers. Irrational betting houses announce incorrect betting odds. Initial budget of each betting house is θ_1.
- Rational Buyers place place bets against incorrect data sellers and bets for correct data sellers. Budget of each buyer is θ_2.
- Correct Sellers provide correct data. Budget of each seller is θ_3.

Let there are y_1 rational buyers and y_2 irrational buyers. As mentioned in section 4.3, all sellers arrive before the beginning of each betting cycle and buyers arrive one at a time uniformly at random. Let k buyers arrive in a betting cycle. We assume that each seller has channels with all betting houses and each buyer has channels with all betting houses. The change in funds of a rational betting house is as follows: The probability that a buyer will place a bet at a betting house is $\frac{1}{x}$ where x is the number of betting houses. The probability that the buyer is rational is $\frac{1}{y_1}$ and irrational is $\frac{1}{y_2}$. The probability that the buyer is placing bets on an incorrect seller is $\frac{1}{z_2}$ and on a correct seller is $\frac{1}{z_1}$.

The rational betting house will lose fund if majority of k buyers $(1+\frac{k}{2}=k_1)$ are are irrational buyers. The probability that there is 1 irrational buyer among a set of k buyers is $\frac{k}{y_2}$. The probability that there are 2 irrational buyers among a set of k buyers is

$$
\begin{aligned}
p_2 = {} & \overbrace{\frac{1}{y_2}}^{\text{First occurrence}} \times \overbrace{\frac{1}{y_2}+\cdots+\frac{1}{y_2}}^{k-1} \\
& + \frac{1}{y_1} \overbrace{\frac{1}{y_2}}^{\text{First occurrence}} \times \overbrace{\frac{1}{y_2}+\cdots+\frac{1}{y_2}}^{k-2} \\
& + \frac{1}{y_1}^2 \frac{1}{y_2} \times \overbrace{\frac{1}{y_2}+\cdots+\frac{1}{y_2}}^{k-3} \\
& + \ldots \\
& + \frac{1}{y_1}^{k-2} \frac{1}{y_2} \times \overbrace{\frac{1}{y_2}+\cdots+\frac{1}{y_2}}^{1} \\
= {} & \frac{1}{y_2}^2 \left[\frac{1}{y_1}\frac{k}{k-1} + \frac{1}{y_1}^2\frac{k-1}{k-2} + \cdots + \frac{1}{y_1}^{k-2}\right]
\end{aligned}
$$

The probability that there are 3 irrational buyers among a set of k buyers is

$$
\begin{aligned}
p_3 = {} & \overbrace{\frac{1}{y_2}}^{\text{First occurrence}} \times \overbrace{p_2}^{\text{occurs 2 times in next k-1}} \\
& + \frac{1}{y_1} \overbrace{\frac{1}{y_2}}^{\text{first occurrence}} \times \overbrace{p_2}^{\text{occurs 2 times in next k-2}} \\
& + \ldots \\
& + \frac{1}{y_1}^{k-2} \frac{1}{y_2} \times \overbrace{p_2}^{\text{occurs 2 times in next 2}}
\end{aligned}
$$

Thus the probability that there are k/2 irrational buyers among a set of k buyers is

$$
\begin{aligned}
p_{k/2} = {} & \overbrace{\frac{1}{y_2}}^{\text{first occurrence}} \times \overbrace{p_{k/2-1}}^{\text{occurs k/2 -1 times in next k-1}} \\
& + \frac{1}{y_1} \overbrace{\frac{1}{y_2}}^{\text{first occurrence}} \times \overbrace{p_2}^{\text{occurs k/2 -1 times in next k-2}} \\
& + \ldots \\
& + \frac{1}{y_1}^{k/2-1} \overbrace{\frac{1}{y_2}}^{\text{first occurrence}} \times \overbrace{p_{k/2-1}}^{\text{occurs k/2 -1 times in next k/2-1}}
\end{aligned}
$$

Similarly, the probability that there are 2 rational buyers among a set of k buyers is

$$
p_2' = \frac{1}{y_1}^2 \left[\frac{1}{y_2}\frac{k}{k-1} + \frac{1}{y_2}^2\frac{k-1}{k-2} + \cdots + \frac{1}{y_2}^{k-2}\right]
$$

The probability that there are k/2 rational buyers among a set of k buyers is

$$
\begin{aligned}
p_{k/2}' = {} & \overbrace{\frac{1}{y_1}}^{\text{first occurrence}} \times \overbrace{p_{k/2-1}'}^{\text{occurs k/2 -1 times in next k-1}} \\
& + \frac{1}{y_2} \overbrace{\frac{1}{y_1}}^{\text{first occurrence}} \times \overbrace{p_{k/2-1}'}^{\text{occurs k/2 -1 times in next k-2}} \\
& + \ldots \\
& + \frac{1}{y_2}^{k/2-1} \overbrace{\frac{1}{y_1}}^{\text{first occurrence}} \times \overbrace{p_{k/2-1}'}^{\text{occurs k/2 -1 times in next k/2-1}}
\end{aligned}
$$

Following should not hold (we will find the conditions so that it does not hold):

$$
\begin{aligned}
& p_2 > p_2' \\
& [y_1\frac{k}{k-1} + \sum(\frac{1}{y_1}^i) + \sum(\frac{1}{y_1}^i\frac{1}{k-i})] \\
& > \\
& [y_2\frac{k}{k-1} + \sum(\frac{1}{y_2}^i) + \sum(\frac{1}{y_2}^i\frac{1}{k-i})]
\end{aligned}
$$

As $y_1 > y_2$ the above equation is a contradiction if

$$
\begin{aligned}
y_1\frac{k}{k-1} + \sum(\frac{1}{y_1}^i) &< y_2\frac{k}{k-1} + \sum(\frac{1}{y_2}^i) \\
\frac{k}{k-1}(y_1 - y_2) &< \frac{y_1 - y_2}{(y_1-1)(y_2-1)} \\
\frac{k}{k-1} &< \frac{1}{(y_1-1)(y_2-1)} \qquad (2)
\end{aligned}
$$

If $p_2' > p_2$ then $p_3' > p_3$ because $y_1 > y_2$. Following this process we conclude that $p_{k/2}' > p_{k/2}$. As the probability of having a majority of rational buyers in each betting cycle is higher than the opposite, the rational betting houses will lose fewer bets than irrational betting houses. As all actors start with a constant budget irrational betting houses will eventually lose all of their funds. As rational betting houses will persist in this betting system, betting odds for all sellers will be correct. □

We note the following:

- In the proposed reputation management system for data marketplace, betting houses keep the reputation records and the rational betting house will gain revenue from it. This will encourage them to invest and build the reputation management platform by joining the blockchain network.
- As the reputation management operations are executed in the offline channels by exchanging HTLCs, it records

very few transactions in the blockchain. Thus the proposed solution is scalable.
- As very few transactions are recorded in the blockchain the cost of running blockchain operations in terms of blockchain transaction fees is very low.
- Betting houses can develop their own algorithm for predicting betting odds. More precise these algorithms, the more accurate the betting odds. With better algorithms betting houses will have more revenue from bets. This will allow further development of the proposed reputation management solution and its integration with data analytics solutions to predict more accurate betting odds.

V. Evaluation

We evaluate the proposed decentralised reputation management with a simulation of the data marketplace using agent-based modelling of the marketplace and blockchain. We use the blockchain simulator used in [19]. In this evaluation, we use two types of buyers, rational buyers (who bet as per the performance of the data seller) and irrational buyers (who do the opposite of rational buyers). There are two types of data sellers, good data sellers provide correct data and bad data seller sales incorrect data. The buyers arrive (places bet) one at a time and a buyer is chosen uniformly at random. We want to show that, the decentralised reputation management system is correct despite the random arrival of the buyers. We use a set of 10000 buyers with 40% irrational buyers chosen uniformly at random. There are 100 sellers with 40% bad sellers. We used two betting houses one rational and another one irrational. A betting house uses historical betting data to determine the betting odds of a seller. If the majority of bets are against the seller then the betting odd is $0:1$, i.e., if a buyer places a bet for the reputation of the seller and it wins then it will get double the betting amount. Otherwise, the betting house will get double the betting amount. In each bet, a buyer and seller bet the same amount of fund the winner gets all such betted funds. However, it is possible to place different betting odds. As the betting odds are $0:1$ in this example, the reputation of the sellers is either 0 or 1. We use the following model of data marketplace simulation (shown in Fig. 5(a)):

- At the start of each betting cycle channels are established among the actors of the marketplace. We use proof of work-based blockchain and offline channel simulator [19] to simulate such events. The blockchain simulator is built with asynchronous event simulation in Python.
- Next, a betting house determines the current betting odds of each seller and announces it.
- Buyers place their bets by exchanging HTLCs with betting houses.
- At the end of each betting cycle, all bets are settled as each betting house or buyer claims tokens by publishing HTLCs to the blockchain network. This closes or updates their channels.

The results of the simulated execution of the data marketplace are shown in the figures below. As shown in the Fig. 5(b) funds of irrational buyers becomes low as they lose bets on the seller's reputation. Fig. 6(a) shows that the reputation (betting odds) of good sellers remains higher than the bad seller. Fig. 6(b) shows that funds of rational betting houses increase over time.

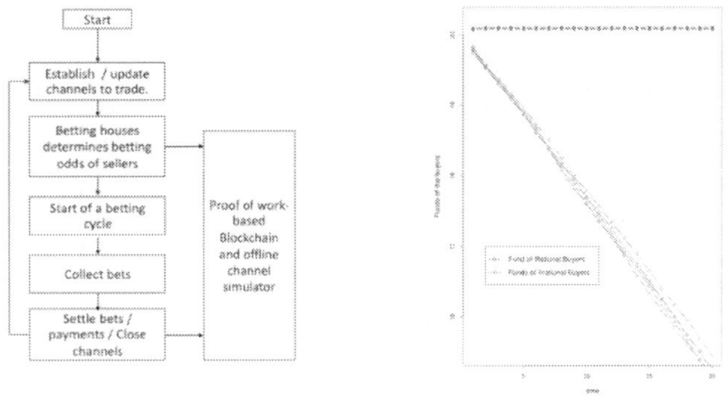

(a) (b)

Fig. 5: (a)Data marketplace simulator, (b) Funds of the buyers after 20 rounds of betting on the seller's reputation. It shows that funds of rational buyers remain higher than irrational buyers.

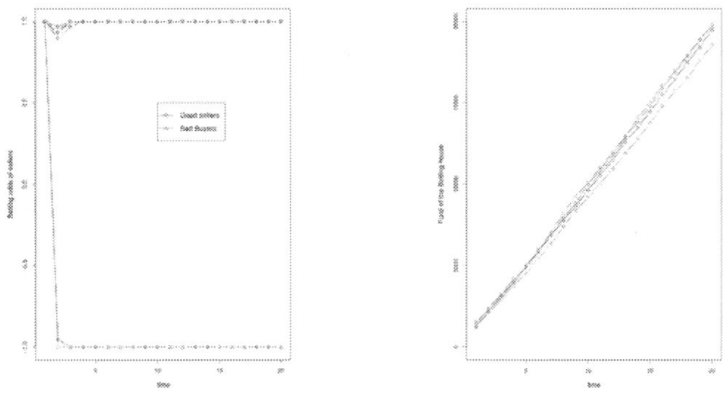

(a) (b)

Fig. 6: (a) Betting odds of the data sellers. It shows that betting odds of good sellers remain higher than bad sellers, (b) Funds of rational betting houses increase.

VI. Conclusion

In this paper, we developed a decentralised reputation management system for IoT data marketplace. The proposed reputation management system is secure and correct as it will prevent biased feedbacks and incorrect aggregation of feedbacks to calculate reputation.

References

[1] G. Dólera Tormo, F. Gómez Mármol, and G. Martínez Pérez, "Dynamic and flexible selection of a reputation mechanism for heterogeneous environments," *Future Generation Computer Systems*, vol. 49, pp. 113–124, 2015. [Online]. Available: https://www.sciencedirect.com/science/article/pii/S0167739X14001289

[2] A. Selcuk, E. Uzun, and M. Pariente, "A reputation-based trust management system for p2p networks," in *IEEE International Symposium on Cluster Computing and the Grid, 2004. CCGrid 2004.*, 2004, pp. 251–258.

[3] I. Psaras, "Decentralised edge-computing and iot through distributed trust," in *Proceedings of the 16th Annual International Conference on Mobile Systems, Applications, and Services*, ser. MobiSys '18. New York, NY, USA: Association for Computing Machinery, 2018, p. 505–507. [Online]. Available: https://doi.org/10.1145/3210240.3226062

[4] G. Fortino, F. Messina, D. Rosaci, and G. M. L. Sarné, "Using blockchain in a reputation-based model for grouping agents in the internet of things," *IEEE Transactions on Engineering Management*, vol. 67, no. 4, pp. 1231–1243, 2020.

[5] M. D. Alshehri and F. K. Hussain, "A centralized trust management mechanism for the internet of things (ctm-iot)," in *Advances on Broad-Band Wireless Computing, Communication and Applications*, L. Barolli, F. Xhafa, and J. Conesa, Eds. Cham: Springer International Publishing, 2018, pp. 533–543.

[6] O. Ben Abderrahim, M. H. Elhdhili, and L. Saidane, "Tmcoi-siot: A trust management system based on communities of interest for the social internet of things," in *2017 13th International Wireless Communications and Mobile Computing Conference (IWCMC)*, 2017, pp. 747–752.

[7] N. S. Nizamkari, "A graph-based trust-enhanced recommender system for service selection in iot," in *2017 International Conference on Inventive Systems and Control (ICISC)*, 2017, pp. 1–5.

[8] L. Atzori, A. Iera, and G. Morabito, "Siot: Giving a social structure to the internet of things," *IEEE Communications Letters*, vol. 15, no. 11, pp. 1193–1195, 2011.

[9] H. Son, N. Kang, B. Gwak, and D. Lee, "An adaptive iot trust estimation scheme combining interaction history and stereotypical reputation," in *2017 14th IEEE Annual Consumer Communications Networking Conference (CCNC)*, 2017, pp. 349–352.

[10] A. Javaid, M. Zahid, I. Ali, R. J. U. H. Khan, Z. Noshad, and N. Javaid, "Reputation system for iot data monetization using blockchain," in *Advances on Broad-Band Wireless Computing, Communication and Applications*, L. Barolli, P. Hellinckx, and T. Enokido, Eds. Cham: Springer International Publishing, 2020, pp. 173–184.

[11] J.-S. Park, T.-Y. Youn, H.-B. Kim, K. Rhee, and S.-U. Shin, "Smart contract-based review system for an iot data marketplace," *Sensors (Basel, Switzerland)*, vol. 18, 2018.

[12] P. Gupta, S. Kanhere, and R. Jurdak, "A decentralized iot data marketplace," 2019.

[13] S. Bajoudah, C. Dong, and P. Missier, "Toward a decentralized, trustless marketplace for brokered iot data trading using blockchain," in *2019 IEEE International Conference on Blockchain (Blockchain)*, 2019, pp. 339–346.

[14] W. Lin, X. Yin, S. Wang, and M. Khosravi, "A blockchain-enabled decentralized settlement model for iot data exchange services," *Wireless Networks*, 2020.

[15] S. Nakamoto, "Bitcoin: A peer-to-peer electronic cash system," *www.bitcoin.org*, 2008.

[16] J. Poon and T. Dryja, "The Bitcoin Lightning Network:Scalable Off-Chain Instant Payments." [Online]. Available: https://lightning.network/lightning-network-paper.pdf

[17] "Raiden network," http://raiden.network/, accessed 01/06.2022.

[18] G. Malavolta, P. Moreno-Sanchez, A. Kate, and M. Maffei, "Silentwhispers: Enforcing security and privacy in decentralized credit networks," *IACR Cryptology ePrint Archive*, vol. 2016, p. 1054, 2016.

[19] B. Hayes, S. Thakur, and J. Breslin, "Co-simulation of electricity distribution networks and peer to peer energy trading platforms," *International Journal of Electrical Power & Energy Systems*, vol. 115, p. 105419, 2020. [Online]. Available: http://www.sciencedirect.com/science/article/pii/S0142061519302972

Newsjam: A Multilingual Summarization Tool for News Articles

Shane Kaszefski-Yaschuk
LORIA
Université de Lorraine
Nancy, France
Email: kaszefsk1u@etu.univ-lorraine.fr

Joseph Keenan
LORIA
Université de Lorraine
Nancy, France
Email: joseph-alexander.keenan@loria.fr

Adelia Khasanova
LORIA
Université de Lorraine
Nancy, France
Email: adelia.khasanova9@etu.univ-lorraine.fr

Maxime Méloux
Bureau d'Économie Théorique et Appliquée
Université de Lorraine
Nancy, France
Email: maxime.meloux4@etu.univ-lorraine.fr

***Abstract*—This paper introduces *Newsjam*, a multilingual summarization tool for COVID-19 news articles. To this purpose, two extractive summarization methods were implemented: Latent Semantic Indexing and K-means clustering on contextual word embeddings on French and English data. This tool was then evaluated using three evaluation metrics and four different corpora; two existing ones as well as two custom-built ones. Finally, the best performing methods were implemented into a complete pipeline, going from text scraping and classification to summarization, and ultimately posting the summaries to Twitter automatically.**

Keywords*—*summarization; twitter; covid-19; news.

I. INTRODUCTION

The ongoing COVID-19 pandemic has caused people from around the world to feel fatigued from the overload of pandemic-related news articles being released every day [1]. One study collecting data from 11 different countries found that more than 26 million coronavirus related articles have been posted since the beginning of the pandemic [2].

These observations have prompted us to create *Newsjam*, a COVID-19 news summarization tool aimed at reducing news fatigue by keeping only the main points of pandemic-related articles and aggregating them in a single place, therefore reducing the amount of time and effort it takes to stay informed about the pandemic.

Newsjam consists of four interconnected parts:

- A web scraper to locate and scrape relevant COVID-19 articles from multiple French and English news websites
- An article classification model to separate these articles into four possible regions of interest
- A summarization model able to generate short summaries for selected articles
- A pipeline automating those steps by regularly fetching new articles, classifying and summarizing them, and then posting the summary as a single tweet to Twitter

In particular, the last part implies that our generated summaries must abide by the maximum tweet length of 280 characters.

The paper is organized as follows. Section II briefly surveys tools that are pertaining to *Newsjam*. Methodology is described in Section III, which details the different corpora used, a brief overview of annotation guidelines, as well as the classification and annotation approaches employed. Section IV concerns the experimental setup and evaluation protocol, and contains our empirical results. In Section VI, we provide a qualitative analysis of the results and conclude with perspectives of future work in Section VII.

II. LITERATURE REVIEW

This section briefly presents text summarization and classification methods and tools encountered in the literature.

A. *Text Summarization*

There are two main methods of automatic text summarization in the literature [3]. Extractive summarization centers around identifying key sentences in the text and putting them together verbatim, whereas abstractive summarization involves generating novel text. Extractive approaches include assigning importance scores to sentences using topic modeling, k-means clustering, and latent semantic indexing [4]. Primary approaches seen in abstractive text summarization include the use of deep learning, Recurrent Neural Network encoder-decoders, Gated Recurrent Units, and Long Short-Term Memory [5].

Text summarization comes with a few key challenges. During the testing stage, reference summaries are needed for evaluation. However, datasets often contain poor reference summaries or do not contain them at all, making evaluation unreliable or impossible [5]. Other challenges include the occurrence of Out-Of-Vocabulary (OOV) words that are absent from the training dataset but are central to understanding a document, and finding metrics able to evaluate a summarized or paraphrased fragment on both a syntactic and semantic level [6].

Given the multiple challenges encountered in text summarization, the question arises of how to validate the results. The most commonly used metric is Recall-Oriented Understudy for Gisting Evaluation (ROUGE), which compares a generated summary to a reference one (typically created by a human) and calculates the number of overlapping units [7]. ROUGE is however far from ideal: Dorr, Monz, President, Schwartz, and Zajic [8] found that the metric was sensitive to the type of summarization. ROUGE scores also tend to be higher for summaries that are longer or generated by using supervised learning approaches [9].

B. Text Classification

Text classification methods include Decision Trees, Logistic Regression (LR), Naive Bayes (NB) and Support Vector Machine (SVM) [10]. NB is one of the oldest methods of text classification, which is based on Bayes' Theorem and determines the probability that each document belongs to a given class [11]. It can operate using several probability distributions, such as the normal (Gaussian), Bernoulli and multinomial distributions. LR is a simple but effective binary classifier for text classification, which calculates the probability of a document belonging to two different classes. SVM is a supervised learning model that was also originally built as a binary classifier, but was later extended to support multiple classes [11]. Lastly, Decision Trees calculate the probability of different 'children' belonging to the 'parent' of a tree [12].

III. METHODOLOGY

This section describes how corpora acquisition and annotation were performed in our pipeline, followed by the chosen implementation of text classification and summarization.

A. Corpora

When discussing the coronavirus pandemic, many words such as *pandemic* and *vaccine* occur much more frequently than in regular news articles. Thus, after careful consideration, it was decided that new corpora should be created in order to provide better accuracy for summarizing novel articles about the pandemic compared to a more general news-based corpus.

For French, articles were scraped from the online version of the newspaper *Actu* and *L'Est Républicain*. Articles were retrieved along with reference summaries which were extracted from the highlights section or title of the article.

For English, articles were similarly extracted from the online version of *The Guardian*. This website was chosen in particular due to the fact that it hosts several versions of *The Guardian*: A USA-based version covering news from the USA and Canada, a UK-based version covering the British Isles, and an Australian one covering both Australia and New Zealand.

In both cases, articles were retrieved on an extended time frame ranging from September 2020 to March 2022.

In addition, two large corpora were selected for evaluation of our models. The French version of the MultiLingual SUMmarization corpus (MLSUM) [13], made up of news articles and summaries from *Le Monde*, was selected for French. For English, the *CNN/Daily Mail* corpus was used [14].

B. Annotation

In order to provide news articles that are relevant to readers, the scope of the tool was limited to 4 distinct geographical regions: France, English-speaking North America, the British Isles, and Australia/New Zealand. To achieve this, a classifier was implemented to determine whether or not a given news article is relevant to a particular region. To this purpose, annotation guidelines for tagging articles as local (relevant) or global (irrelevant) for each region were created. The latter category includes not only news about other countries, but also global events, such as decisions made by the World Health Organization.

Four annotators, labeled A, B, C and D, were selected for the task of annotating our custom-built corpora. For each corpus, two to three annotators tagged the entire dataset. Articles are tagged with "local" or "global" for the *Actu/L'Est Républicain* corpus, and with one of the four possible tags for the *Guardian* corpus (North America, British Isles, Oceania or Global). For each pair of annotators, the *Ao*, *S*, Scott's π and Cohen's κ inter-annotator agreement coefficients were then computed. The results are summarized in Table I.

TABLE I
INTER-ANNOTATOR AGREEMENT FOR EACH PAIR OF ANNOTATORS.

Dataset	*Actu*	*Guardian*			*L'Est Républicain*		
Metric	**A-B**	**A-B**	**A-C**	**B-C**	**A-B**	**A-D**	**B-D**
A_o	0.995	0.987	0.917	0.913	0.966	0.976	0.978
S	0.990	0.974	0.834	0.827	0.958	0.952	0.955
π	0.956	0.961	0.761	0.747	0.949	0.879	0.888
κ	0.956	0.961	0.761	0.748	0.949	0.879	0.888

We observe high agreement between all pairs of annotators, for all coefficients and datasets. Furthermore, we observe the highest agreement between annotators A and B, reaching approximately 0.95 in all situations. After careful review of the results, we compute reference tags for our corpora by taking the majority vote between annotators. In case of disagreement, the priority was given to the native speaker of the language in which the article is written.

The resulting datasets, to be used for classification training and testing, proved to be rather imbalanced. The French language dataset, containing articles from *L'Est Républicain* and *Actu*, has more articles about France (58%) than about the rest of the world (42%). The makeup of the English language dataset (Guardian articles) is as follows: 48% about North America, 24% about the British Isles, 16% about Oceania, and 11% about the rest of the world.

C. Article Classification

The pre-processing of the corpus for classification begins with noise removal (punctuation and irrelevant special characters), stopword removal, and lemmatization. Three different methods for classification were implemented: Multinomial Naive Bayes (MNB), Logistic Regression (LR), and Support

Vector Machine (SVM). All three methods were used for both binary and multi-class classification. These methods are inherently probabilistic, so we decided to test several of them to see which one gives the most accurate results in our case. Two classifiers were ultimately created: one for distinguishing between French and non-French articles, and the other one for tagging English articles with the appropriate geographical region as described in Section III-B.

For model-specific issues, one way to improve the performance is hyper-parameter tuning, which can be done by exhaustive search over the parameter space. MNB may benefit from tuning the α parameter, which represents Laplace smoothing, and helps tackle the issue of zero probabilities. For the LR model, we searched for the best C parameter. Regarding the SVM model, we tuned the C parameter as well to find a balance between the minimum margin and accounting for outliers in the data.

D. Summarization

Two extraction approaches for summarization were chosen: Latent Semantic Indexing and K-means clustering on contextual word embeddings.

1) Latent Semantic Indexing: Latent Semantic Indexing (LSI) is a technique initially introduced for automatic document classification [15] and information retrieval [16], but it was later found to be efficient for automatic text summarization [17][18] and its evaluation [19][20]. LSI typically applies a matrix factorization algorithm called Singular Value Decomposition (SVD) to the Term Frequency-Inverse Document Frequency (TF-IDF) matrix of the document. Our algorithm replicates that of Gong and Liu [17], including for sentence selection. For each article, the optimal number of topics n_{topics} was chosen by measuring C_v topic coherence [21]. We then chose $n_{topics} = \arg\max_{k \in [\![2,10]\!]} C_v(k)$. 2 and 10 were arbitrarily picked as initial bounds, and further analysis would be required to determine the optimal bounds.

Sentences are then categorized by topic, and the output summary is generated by looping through the topics and choosing the best-scoring sentence for each topic until the aforementioned maximum summary length of 280 characters is reached. In practice, this length restriction allows for very few sentences in a summary. Highly-ranked sentences are therefore skipped in favor of lower-ranked ones if the former would make the summary go over the character limit and the latter would not.

We apply LSI to the TF-IDF of a list of keywords generated by removing punctuation and stopwords from the article and lemmatizing the remaining words. Our intent in using keywords rather than the raw text is to eliminate noise that could be caused by stopwords, and to apply topic modeling only to the most important words in a document.

2) Word Embeddings and K-means Clustering: K-means clustering is an alternative way to model topics within a document, which has been successfully applied to text summarization before [22].

Our implementation uses contextual word embeddings as the raw input of k-means clustering, which are generated on a sentence basis using the pre-trained models FlauBERT [23] and CamemBERT [24] for French and RoBERTa [25] for English. Embeddings were chosen with the intuition that they capture semantic information. Specifically, contextual embeddings were used with the hope that they would perform better than a bag-of-words model such as TF-IDF. We arbitrarily choose $n_{clusters} = 5$ for k-means clustering, and further research is necessary to determine the optimal value.

Output scores are generated on a word basis (and not a sentence one) by computing the cosine similarity between a word's embedding and the centroids of the article's topics. For each cluster, the top words are picked and mapped back to the original sentence that contains them. The subsequent sentence selection and summary building process is then the same as for the LSI model.

Fig. 1. LSI model.

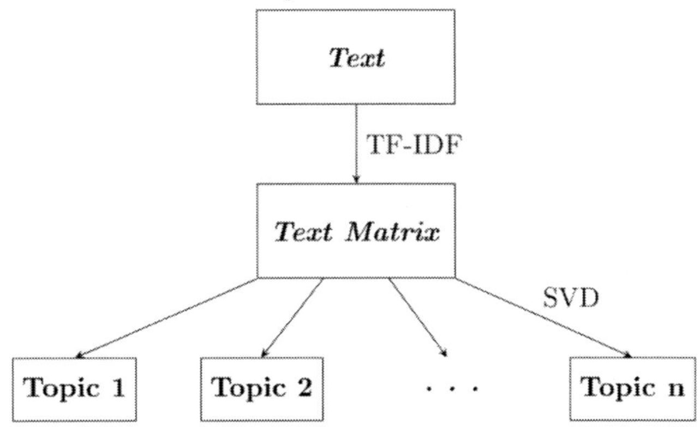

Fig. 2. K-means clustering model.

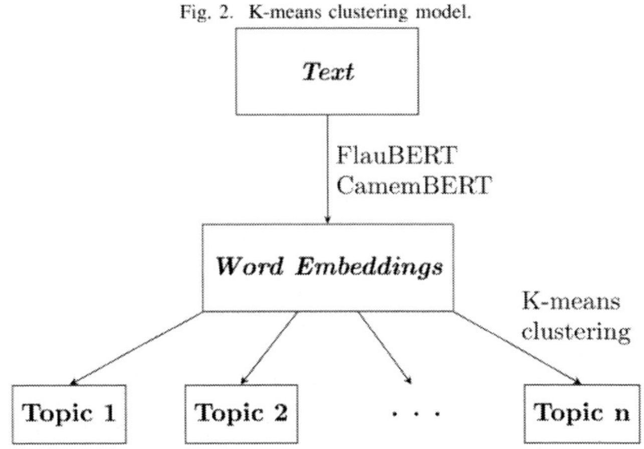

IV. Experimental Setup

This section contains quantitative information about our corpora, as well as the chosen methods of evaluation of the article classification and summarization methods.

A. Datasets

Our French corpus contains 787 articles from *Actu* and 1,803 from *L'Est Républicain*, adding up to a total of 2,503 articles along with their summaries. Our English corpus contains 2,010 articles from *The Guardian* with summaries.

The French version of the MLSUM corpus contains over 400,000 news articles. For evaluation, we restricted ourselves to the test set of that corpus, which contains 15,828 articles. Similarly, a test set of 11,490 articles was selected from the CNN/Daily Mail corpus.

B. Article Classification Evaluation

In a machine learning process, it is often insufficient to split the dataset into training and testing subsets and assume that the model will always perform well on unseen data. For this reason, k-fold cross-validation was used to further evaluate the classifier. This method divides data into a chosen number k of sets, of which $k-1$ are used for training and the remaining one for testing. The choice of the testing set changes with each execution. A five-fold validation on all models was run and the values of all four metrics were collected: accuracy, precision, recall, and F1-score. The MNB, LR and SVM models were evaluated both before and after tuning.

C. Summarization Evaluation

To evaluate the summarization models, three different metrics were selected: the well-known ROUGE-L [26], as well as the much more recent, state-of-the-art metrics BERTScore [27] and Word Mover's Distance (WMD) [28]. These metrics calculate output scores via three different means: ROUGE-L, following a surface-level approach, attempts to align sequences of words in the generated and reference summaries. BERTScore evaluates texts on a deeper level by using contextual BERT embeddings to compute cosine similarity between two texts. Both of these metrics output three values per summary: precision, recall, and F1-score. Those are proportions ranging from zero to one, where a higher score indicates higher performance. Lastly, WMD computes a single score per summary, representing its semantic distance to the corresponding reference summary, modeled as a transportation problem. Its values range from 0 up to the size of the vocabulary in words, with a lower score indicating a higher quality summary.

We compute our metrics on two different forms of our data:

- The *standard score* is computed on pairs consisting of the generated summary and the reference summary.
- The *keyword score* is computed on pairs consisting of stemmed, keyword-only (see III-D1) versions of the generated and reference summaries.

To our knowledge, it is not common practice for text summarization models to evaluate keyword versions of summaries. The purpose behind adding this evaluation is to reduce the risk of score inflation due to stopword similarity. We also expect stemming to increase the opportunity for matching word subsequences in ROUGE-L between our generated summaries and the reference ones, which is the same motivation that led to the inclusion of a Porter stemmer module in the METEOR evaluation metric [29]. We do not expect this keyword score to be significantly different for BERTScore or WMD, as those rely on semantics through the use of embeddings.

All summarization and evaluation experiments were performed on the Grid'5000 testbed [30].

V. Results

Experimental results are split into two parts: one pertaining to article classification, and one concerning summarization.

A. Article Classification Results

Our article classification results are in Tables II and III. For the English classifier, results are expressed in terms of macro-averaged scores.

Even after tuning, the MNB consistently showed underwhelming performance compared to LR and SVM. Its performance was especially poor when it came to multi-class classification: the model barely classified any samples in the categories with lower support correctly. In contrast, LR and SVM showed comparably adequate results. They both performed slightly better on the French corpus; and the metrics for the multi-class corpus came close behind. Tuning LR and SVM using GridSearch improved their performance by approximately 1%.

For LR, the optimal value for C appeared to be a low value ($C = 100$). Lower values tend to be more fit for imbalanced datasets as they require more regularization and more weight to the complexity penalty to avoid overfitting. For SVM, we found that a larger C value ($C = 100$), which creates a smaller-margin hyperplane, improved the performance of our model.

B. Summarization Results

Our summarization results are shown in Tables IV and V.

We find that the LSI model outperforms the k-means clustering implementations for all scores and all datasets except for MLSUM. This is most noticeable for the ROUGE-L score. On MLSUM, k-means clustering performs slightly better depending on the chosen metric. We also observe that

TABLE II
CLASSIFICATION RESULTS FOR FRENCH.

Method	Accuracy	Precision	Recall	F1
Multinomial Naive Bayes	0.842	0.711	0.842	0.775
MNB (tuned)	0.845	0.732	0.845	0.781
Logistic Regression	0.934	0.934	0.934	0.934
LR (tuned)	0.943	0.943	0.943	0.934
Support Vector Machine	0.934	0.934	0.934	0.921
SVM (tuned)	0.943	0.943	0.943	0.934

TABLE III
CLASSIFICATION RESULTS FOR ENGLISH.

Method	Accuracy	Precision	Recall	F1
Multinomial Naive Bayes	0.610	0.505	0.610	0.505
MNB (tuned)	0.628	0.505	0.628	0.505
Logistic Regression	0.934	0.934	0.934	0.934
LR (tuned)	0.935	0.935	0.935	0.935
Support Vector Machine	0.921	0.921	0.921	0.918
SVM (tuned)	0.932	0.932	0.932	0.932

TABLE IV
SUMMARIZATION EVALUATION FOR FRENCH (AVERAGE SCORES FOR WMD, AVERAGE F1-SCORES FOR OTHER METRICS).

Method	ROUGE-L	Keyword ROUGE-L	BERTScore	Keyword BERTScore	WMD	Keyword WMD
MLSUM corpus, test set (15,828 articles)						
LSI	**0.0652**	**0.0627**	0.5894	0.5885	**0.2517**	0.2652
FlauBERT + k-means	0.0564	0.0571	0.5905	**0.5909**	0.2558	0.2629
CamemBERT + k-means	0.0591	0.0598	**0.5907**	0.5904	0.2528	**0.2602**
Built corpus (787 + 1,803 = 2,560 articles)						
LSI	**0.1536**	**0.1538**	**0.6267**	**0.6238**	**0.2355**	**0.1959**
FlauBERT + k-means	0.1040	0.1075	0.6137	0.6134	0.2471	0.2080
CamemBERT + k-means	0.1093	0.1123	0.6153	0.6143	0.2452	0.2057

TABLE V
SUMMARIZATION EVALUATION FOR ENGLISH (AVERAGE SCORES FOR WMD, AVERAGE F1-SCORES FOR OTHER METRICS).

Method	ROUGE-L	Keyword ROUGE-L	BERTScore	Keyword BERTScore	WMD	Keyword WMD
CNN/Daily Mail corpus, test set (11,490 articles)						
LSI	**0.1207**	**0.1894**	**0.4947**	**0.4807**	**0.2178**	**0.1709**
RoBERTa + k-means	0.0839	0.1513	0.4680	0.4640	0.2342	0.1807
Built corpus (2,010 articles)						
LSI	**0.0748**	**0.1162**	**0.4822**	**0.4663**	**0.2297**	**0.2241**
RoBERTa + k-means	0.0533	0.0953	0.4702	0.4650	0.2390	0.2331

the keyword-only version of the various score is significantly better for ROUGE-L on both English corpora and for Word Mover's Distance on our French corpus and on the CNN/Daily Mail one, but that it produces either no improvement or a regression for other metrics and corpora. Finally, we observe that our English model performs significantly better on the CNN/Daily Mail corpus than on our custom one, while the opposite is true for French.

VI. DISCUSSION

Since there is no one metric that performs high and above all the others for article classification, we focus on one metric that we deem to be the most important. Therefore, we focus on the F1-score. We justify this choice with our goal to maximize the amount of true positives while minimizing the amount of false positives and false negatives, which translates to minimizing the misidentification of local and global articles in the model. Given this choice, both the tuned LR and tuned SVM methods are the best options for article classification. In the full pipeline, the tuned LR model was chosen for the classifier due to its slightly higher evaluation results.

In terms of summarization, we notice that LSI outperforms k-means clustering in nearly all metrics and situations. Although k-means clustering performs better with respect to BERTScore and Word Mover's Distance on the MLSUM dataset, the gain is of half a percentage point or less, whereas LSI can give a ROUGE-L score up to 5% higher on our French corpus. LSI has therefore been chosen as the default summarization method in the full summarization pipeline.

Our evaluation shows poor ROUGE-L scores for all datasets and summarization methods. This is easily explainable by the fact that ROUGE-L scores are computed on a purely surface level; in our case, as summaries often contain one to two sentences, it is unlikely to find large subsequences overlapping with the reference text. This coincides with the findings in [31], according to which ROUGE-L scores usually have very low correlation with human judgments.

On the other hand, the BERTScore reaches acceptable levels for English and good results for French. We observe similarly good results for Word Mover's Distance.

For French, the scores typically indicate a higher performance of the models on our corpus by several percentage points. We hypothesize that this could be due to different writing styles in the source newspapers causing changes such as different ratios of stopwords in both corpora. This may have led to articles in the MLSUM corpus being more strongly affected by the keyword scores.

For English, the opposite effect occurs: there is a significant decrease in performance across the board when switching from the CNN/Daily Mail corpus to our corpus. This could be due to a number of factors, such as our corpus containing a larger language diversity through inclusion of multiple varieties of English, and having longer average article length.

Using the keyword score seems to make little difference with respect to the BERTScore, which could be due to BERTScore's reliance on embeddings, the content of which may be more significant for keywords. The discrepancy between ROUGE-L scores for English are harder to account for, but may arise from a larger list of stopwords or more efficient stemming. It is unclear why the keyword-only version of Word Mover's Distance is significantly lower on the CNN/Daily Mail corpus and on our French corpus, while being nearly unchanged for the remaining two datasets.

We would like to draw attention to two important points. The first is that working with a maximum length of 280 characters severely restricts our models' ability to output a high-quality summary. When combined with the sentence selection algorithm, which is designed to minimize the amount of unused characters in the output tweet, it often happens that output summaries are not necessarily optimal with regard to our models. This is further reinforced by the fact that our models are extractive and typically have to work with articles consisting of a couple dozen sentences.

The second is that while looking deeper into samples of the generated summaries, we found that the summaries chosen by our model often outlined the articles well and matched a quality reference summary. For example, in the MLSUM LSI summaries, we notice a recurring issue where we feel that our model's summary matches the article, but receives a low ROUGE-L score due to a poor reference summary. This seems inevitable when working with a corpus of this magnitude, but it is important to note because it exhibits a way in which the scores may not always reflect the quality of a generated summary. To further exhibit this matter, a quick look at the generated summaries seems to show that BERTScore better represents the quality of our models. The following example, drawn from Article 54 of the French MLSUM testset, shows an instance of a quality summary given a poor score. It demonstrates that our model is able to select high-quality summaries, but that they will not always be evaluated as such since some of the reference summaries are low-quality.

- **Generated summary:** "Douze personnes ont été abattues vendredi 31 mai par un tireur dans un bâtiment municipal de Virginia Beach (Etat de Virginie), station balnéaire de la côte est américaine."
  [*On Friday, May 31st, twelve people were killed by a shooter in a municipal building in Virginia Beach (Virginia), a seaside resort on the east coast of the USA.*]
- **Reference summary:** "Le suspect principal, un employé des services de la ville, a tiré « à l'aveugle ». Il est lui aussi décédé."
  [*The main suspect, a city worker, fired "blindly". He also died.*]
- **Scores:**
  - ROUGE-L F1: **0.151** (standard), **0.066** (keyword)
  - BERTScore F1: **0.157** (standard), **0.119** (keyword)
  - WMD: **0.316** (standard), **0.348** (keyword)

To further evaluate the relevance of computed scores compared to human evaluation, one would need one or several native speakers to manually annotate each generated summary as good or bad, and to assess how those scores relate to our chosen metrics.

Finally, one issue that has affected all datasets is poor summary selection, which may be due to the performance of the summarization methods themselves.

As for the classification part of our task, we limited ourselves to traditional, supervised methods, such as Multinomial Naive Bayes, Support Vector Machine, and Logistic Regression. We are well aware that the state-of-art approaches now revolve mainly around deep learning (DL). It has also been established in scientific reviews that unsupervised models do demonstrate superior performance: XLNet-Large and XLNet showed consistently good classification results on multiple 'classic' datasets, such as IMDB and Yelp reviews [32]. For instance, for the SST-2 dataset, the best result yielded by a traditional model (Naive Bayes) was 81.8, while the best result yielded by a DL model (XLNet) was 97.0.

Even with the success of DL models today, there are a few key reasons simpler statistical models were chosen. DL models come with a handful of unique challenges that traditional supervised models do not have. For instance, most DL models cannot easily be interpreted, and poor interpretability makes it difficult to pinpoint exactly why one DL model outperforms another one [32]. Furthermore, it can be hard to decipher what a model has learned to achieve a desirable benchmark in order to use this insight later. Lastly, our custom corpora were not big enough to effectively train a DL model.

VII. Conclusion and Future Work

A web scraper was built and dynamic COVID-19 corpora covering French and English news articles were created and manually annotated for local relevance. Then, text classification and summarization models for news articles were created.

The classifier evaluation results are satisfactory, with a maximum F1-score of 93.4% (French corpus) and 93.5% (English corpus) in the tuned LR and SVM models. On the other hand, the summarization results are mixed, but we observe satisfying accuracy, especially after accounting for the restrictions put on the summarization model.

Lastly, a full pipeline was implemented that automatically selects and classifies news articles pertaining to COVID-19, summarizes them, and finally posts them to Twitter. In the future, the overall performance and usefulness of our tool could be improved by adding more news sources, and optimizing our summarization models or relaxing their constraints, such as the 280 character limit. Moreover, the framework and workflow can be easily adapted and deployed on other use-cases, such as different news topics.

All tweets produced by our pipeline can be found on the Newsjam Twitter account. The entirety of *Newsjam*'s code and results can also be found on GitHub [https://github.com/pie3636/newsjam].

Acknowledgments

The authors thank Miguel Couceiro and Maxime Amblard for their valuable guidance and time. This work was financially supported by Antoine Tabbone and the Institut des sciences du Digital, Management and Cognition, Nancy, France (IDMC).

References

[1] M. Savage, *Coronavirus: How much news is too much?* en, 2020. [Online]. Available: https://www.bbc.com/worklife/article/20200505-coronavirus-how-much-news-is-too-much Retrieved on 2022-05-10.

[2] K. Krawczyk *et al.*, "Quantifying Online News Media Coverage of the COVID-19 Pandemic: Text Mining Study and Resource," en, *JMIR*, vol. 23, no. 6, e28253, Jun. 2021, ISSN: 1438-8871. DOI: 10.2196/28253. [Online]. Available: https://www.jmir.org/2021/6/e28253 Retrieved on 2022-05-10.

[3] H. Saggion and T. Poibeau, "Automatic text summarization: Past, present and future," in *Multi-Source, Multilingual Information Extraction and Summarization*, Berlin, Heidelberg: Springer, 2013, pp. 3–21.
[4] M. Allahyari *et al.*, "Text summarization techniques: A brief survey," *CoRR*, vol. abs/1707.02268, 2017. arXiv: 1707.02268.
[5] D. Suleiman and A. Awajan, "Deep learning based abstractive text summarization: Approaches, datasets, evaluation measures, and challenges," *Mathematical Problems in Engineering*, vol. 2020, pp. 1–29, 2020. DOI: 10.1155/2020/9365340.
[6] W. Soto, "X-pareval: A multilingual metric for paraphrase evaluation," M.S. thesis, Université de Lorraine, 2021.
[7] C.-Y. Lin, "Looking for a few good metrics: Rouge and its evaluation," in *NTCIR Workshop*, 2004.
[8] B. J. Dorr, C. Monz, S. President, R. Schwartz, and D. Zajic, "A methodology for extrinsic evaluation of text summarization: Does rouge correlate?" In *Proceedings of the ACL Workshop on Intrinsic and Extrinsic Evaluation Measures for Machine Translation and/or Summarization*, 2005, pp. 1–8.
[9] N. Shulter, "The limits of automatic summarisation according to rouge," in *Proceedings of the 15th Conference of the EACL: Volume 2, Short Papers*, 2017, pp. 41–45.
[10] M. K. Dalal and M. A. Zaveri, "Automatic text classification: A technical review," *IJCA*, vol. 28, no. 2, pp. 37–40, 2011.
[11] K. Kowsari *et al.*, "Text classification algorithms: A survey," *Information*, vol. 10, no. 4, p. 150, 2019.
[12] D. M. Magerman, *Statistical decision-tree models for parsing*, 1995. arXiv: cmp-lg/9504030 [cmp-lg].
[13] T. Scialom, P.-A. Dray, S. Lamprier, B. Piwowarski, and J. Staiano, "Mlsum: The multilingual summarization corpus," *arXiv preprint arXiv:2004.14900*, 2020.
[14] K. M. Hermann *et al.*, "Teaching machines to read and comprehend," *Advances in neural information processing systems*, vol. 28, 2015.
[15] H. Borko and M. Bernick, "Automatic document classification," *JACM*, vol. 10, no. 2, pp. 151–162, 1963. DOI: 10.1145/321160.321165.
[16] S. C. Deerwester, S. T. Dumais, T. K. Landauer, G. W. Furnas, and R. A. Harshman, "Indexing by latent semantic analysis," *J. Am. Soc. Inf. Sci.*, vol. 41, pp. 391–407, 1990.
[17] Y. Gong and X. Liu, "Creating generic text summaries," in *Proceedings of Sixth ICDAR*, 2001, pp. 903–907. DOI: 10.1109/ICDAR.2001.953917.
[18] M. Ozsoy, F. Alpaslan, and I. Cicekli, "Text summarization using latent semantic analysis," *J. Information Science*, vol. 37, pp. 405–417, Aug. 2011. DOI: 10.1177/0165551511408848.
[19] J. Steinberger, K. Jezek, *et al.*, "Using latent semantic analysis in text summarization and summary evaluation," *Proc. ISIM*, vol. 4, pp. 93–100, 2004.
[20] J. Steinberger and K. Jezek, "Evaluation measures for text summarization.," *Computing and Informatics*, vol. 28, pp. 251–275, Jan. 2009.
[21] M. Röder, A. Both, and A. Hinneburg, "Exploring the space of topic coherence measures," *WSDM 2015 - Proceedings of the 8th ACM International WSDM Conference*, pp. 399–408, Feb. 2015. DOI: 10.1145/2684822.2685324.
[22] K. Shetty and J. S. Kallimani, "Automatic extractive text summarization using k-means clustering," in *2017 ICEECCOT*, 2017, pp. 1–9. DOI: 10.1109/ICEECCOT.2017.8284627.
[23] H. Le *et al.*, "Flaubert: Unsupervised language model pre-training for french," *CoRR*, vol. abs/1912.05372, 2019. arXiv: 1912.05372.
[24] L. Martin *et al.*, "CamemBERT: A tasty French language model," in *Proceedings of the 58th Annual Meeting of the ACL*, Online: ACL, Jul. 2020, pp. 7203–7219. DOI: 10.18653/v1/2020.acl-main.645. [Online]. Available: https://aclanthology.org/2020.acl-main.645.
[25] Y. Liu *et al.*, "Roberta: A robustly optimized BERT pretraining approach," *CoRR*, vol. abs/1907.11692, 2019. arXiv: 1907.11692.
[26] C.-Y. Lin, "Rouge: A package for automatic evaluation of summaries," in *ACL 2004*, 2004.
[27] T. Zhang, V. Kishore, F. Wu, K. Q. Weinberger, and Y. Artzi, *Bertscore: Evaluating text generation with bert*, 2020. arXiv: 1904.09675 [cs.CL].
[28] M. J. Kusner, Y. Sun, N. I. Kolkin, and K. Q. Weinberger, "From word embeddings to document distances," in *Proceedings of the 32nd ICML - Volume 37*, ser. ICML'15, Lille, France: JMLR.org, 2015, 957–966.
[29] A. Lavie and A. Agarwal, "METEOR: An automatic metric for MT evaluation with high levels of correlation with human judgments," in *Proceedings of the Second WMT*, Prague, Czech Republic: ACL, Jun. 2007, pp. 228–231. [Online]. Available: https://aclanthology.org/W07-0734.
[30] D. Balouek *et al.*, "Adding virtualization capabilities to the Grid'5000 testbed," in *Cloud Computing and Services Science*, ser. Communications in Computer and Information Science, I. I. Ivanov, M. van Sinderen, F. Leymann, and T. Shan, Eds., vol. 367, Springer International Publishing, 2013, pp. 3–20, ISBN: 978-3-319-04518-4. DOI: 10.1007/978-3-319-04519-1_1.
[31] F. Liu and Y. Liu, "Correlation between rouge and human evaluation of extractive meeting summaries," in *ACL*, 2008.
[32] S. Minaee *et al.*, "Deep learning–based text classification: A comprehensive review," *ACM Comput. Surv.*, vol. 54, no. 3, Apr. 2021, ISSN: 0360-0300. DOI: 10.1145/3439726.

Decision Support System for Controlling Home Automation Appliances with Resource Constraints

Agnieszka Betkowska Cavalcante
Gido Labs sp. z o.o.
Poznań, Poland
email: a.b.cavalcante@gidolabs.eu

Monika Grajzer
Gido Labs sp. z o.o.
Poznań, Poland
email: m.grajzer@gidolabs.eu

Michał Raszewski
LARS Andrzej Szymański
Niepruszewo, Poland
email: michal.raszewski@lars.pl

***Abstract*—We introduce a Decision Support System (DSS) for controlling access to embedded home automation devices working fully offline and with limited resources. To provide a hands-free and safe interface to its users, the system combines the following technologies: keyword spotting, speaker verification, automatic speech recognition and understanding, dialog management, and speech synthesis. The proposed system was implemented on an embedded device and tested in home and office environments for the English and Polish languages. In experiments, end-users gave a score of 8.4 out of 10 with respect to a subjective figure-of-merit we have proposed.**

Keywords–Access Control; voice-controlled home automation; Decision Support System; natural language communication; voice biometrics verification.

I. INTRODUCTION

Speech-based interfaces are recently becoming one of the key components of home automation systems. In this kind of setting, they are used to command many home appliances such as thermostats and lights [1]. One of the core elements of those interfaces is Automatic Speech Recognition (ASR) and the related Conversational Agent (CA) that manages the speech-based interactions with a user. The CA is responsible for identifying user commands and intentions based on which changes are made to the parameters of the devices (such as the temperature of thermostats). The entire dialog system can be, thus, considered as a Decision Support System (DSS) that analyses incoming audio signals, detects speech commands, and performs actions based on the collected input data. The ASR and CA modules perform sophisticated, resource-consuming operations, which may use a significant amount of device resources, especially in home automation systems implemented on custom-built embedded devices. This implies that DSSs need to be equipped with an access control module, which activates the core ASR/CA functionalities based on its acoustic-based knowledge [2] only if necessary. The access control module is composed primarily of (i) Voice Activity Detection (VAD), which switches the device to a listening mode after speech is detected; and (ii) a Keyword Spotting (KWS) module, which detects if the particular pass-phrase (keyword) has been spoken [3]. Other methods of access control for home automation devices may also include Speaker Recognition (SR) technology, which is based on voice biometrics and allows only authorized users to access system resources [2][3].

Owing to the complexity of speech processing, many components of contemporary DSS systems of similar functionality are often performed in the cloud. This, however, requires sending and, potentially, storing audio data at external premises, which may raise privacy concerns [4]. Therefore, there is a strong need for solutions working locally, fully offline.

Developing such systems for embedded devices is challenging because of their hardware limitations, especially those related to a CPU speed and a battery consumption. As a result, DSS components should offer their expected functionality with a possibly small resource aquisition, and with the ability to process audio input in real-time. In addition, DSS systems and, in particular, the access control modules, should be characterized by a low False Positive Rate (FPR) to avoid raising false alarms and granting unauthorised access to the core home automation system. Moreover, limiting the number of unnecessary system activations helps to increase the performance of the ASR/CA module.

Current solutions, proposed for DSS system components, are typically cloud-based, or require a significant amount of resources. Customisation is necessary for both, the ASR engine and the CA system, in order to limit the system's scope and, as a consequence, also diminish the required computational power. Additionally, in case of some components, such as the KWS module, even though the system performance reported in the recent research results is very promising, the reported FPR levels are still not sufficient for commercial application, when applied without any supporting intelligence [3][5]–[7]. Moreover, the commercially available ASR, AC and KWS systems are mostly aimed at recognising English speech/speakers [5]–[7]. Implementing them for a less common language (such as Polish), typically requires gathering a training database of audio samples, which is both time-consuming and financially expensive. Hence, providing a well-performing system with only a small-size database is very challenging [3].

To address the above challenges, we propose a DSS that would work on an embedded device and allow to efficiently make decisions on granting access to the voice-controlled home automation system and on user intentions, regarding the device set-up. The custom-designed decision-making engine exploits the knowledge extracted from the audio signals – collected by the device microphone with the support of KWS and SR modules for the access control system and ASR together with CA for further information processing and retrieval. In this paper, we present the research results related to design and implementation of all necessary components of such a DSS system, which was targeting the small-scale embedded device based on the Yocto Linux distribution [8] and the STM core hardware platform [9]. The proposed solution has been tested with a number of end-users in real-world scenarios. The research results presented in this paper constitute a follow-up to our previous work on the access control system design which was presented at the eKNOW2020 [3]. In this paper, we focus on the performance results obtained during the final field trials and describe the DSS system as a whole, focusing on the performance of making the final decision about the identified user intent and the executed home automation device functionality.

The rest of the paper is organised as follows: in Section II, we present a short overview of related work, followed by the description of the proposed DSS system and the methodology taken to implement its components for embedded devices in Section III. In Section IV, we discuss the test environment and the obtained test results and follow with conclusion in Section V.

II. RELATED WORK

Voice-controlled home automation systems are equipped with voice interfaces that identify user's commands and provide an access to the core system functionality [10]–[12]. They can use a dialog system that exploits elements of Natural Language Processing (NLP) techniques to extract user intent from potentially incomplete input information [13][14]. Although technical solutions exist, which implement the necessary components of a DSS system for the voice-based interfaces, their usage is often envisioned for the devices with higher computational power (such as, e.g., mobile phones). Hence, they use complex NLP techniques, which cannot be handled by a small, resource-constrained devices that we were targeting [14]. In particular, most of the best-performing ASR and AC components are based on the complex neural networks [12][14][15]. In addition, the top-performing solutions available today, including the ones that are capable of controlling home automation devices, such as, e.g., Amazon Alexa [16], Apple's Siri [17] and Google Home [18], are available only in the cloud-based set-up. This way, resource-consuming techniques are implemented in the cloud and made available to mobile devices via API calls over Internet connection. However, for systems targeting strictly offline environments, similar to the one presented in this paper, such solutions are inaccessable and must be replaced by small-size, robust, custom-made local implementation. Moreover, the popular cloud-based solutions [16]–[18], offer full NLP-based functionality only to a set of languages, typically limited to the most common ones.

Referring to the Access Control system, the most straightforward solution is using VAD/KWS module [6]. The KWS system, which has been trained on silence or background noise samples, can also take on a role of a VAD solution. The recent research on implementing KWS systems focuses on applying neural networks, particularly Residual Neural Networks architectures (ResNet) [6][19]. ResNets are characterised by a lower complexity and faster training phase and were proved to obtain very good performance even for relatively small-sized networks – reaching the accuracy of 95% [6]. While such results are impressive, they are far from being industrially applicable: assuming that FPR is 2% [6] and the system makes a prediction every second, there will be 72 false alarms in one hour — a number inacceptable from the point of view of an end-user [3]. However, since their complexity is not that high as for the NNs used in, e.g., the ASR systems, they are a good candidate technology for the target devices investigated in this paper.

Similarly, the recent approaches to the Speaker Recognition also use lightweight neural networks, which offer good performance with limited resource requirements [19]. These are also promising candidate solutions to support a biometric-based DSS, which can identify speakers and grant them proper permissions [20]. However, additional actions should be usually taken to improve FPR of such systems in practical set-ups. Hence, a challenge in the design of a targeted DSS still remains in improving the FPR of a combined KWS and SR technologies for the Access Control module. Some approaches to address this problem introduce pushing a button [11], detecting the audio louder then a certain threshold [10] or rely on more advanced features – such as, e.g., in [12], where KWS is followed by additional reasoning [3]. The latter kind of solutions are often very complex and, likely, too resource-consuming for small embedded devices.

Although computational complexity of possible approaches to construct the DSS system for the voice-controlled devices remains a challenge, the access control approaches and their FPR in practical set-ups also calls for new solutions, while many related works on voice interfaces neglect this aspect, regardless of the fact that it has significant impact on the practical implementation of such solutions [21][22]. This calls for new approaches that would offer required effectiveness on embedded devices.

III. SYSTEM ARCHITECTURE

We have designed a DSS system to control devices, such as air conditioners, thermostats, and heating furnace, among others. To increase the security of the system, it works locally and with access to neither the Internet nor cloud-based resources. All communication takes place via speech interfaces where users' utterances are decoded into technical commands and where users are verified by a biometric voice system. The proposed system architecture is depicted in Figure 1.

The DSS system operates on embedded devices, such as intercoms in the continuous listening mode. It consists of many modules, including keyword spotting, speaker recognition, automatic speech recognition, dialog system / conversational agent, and speech synthesis (Text To Speech – TTS). The decision taken by the DSS is sent to a middleware and later to a backend, which executes the commands on a desired device.

The access control DSS constantly analyses the signal from the microphone and searches for a specific keyword with a access control system that has been proposed in [3]. Once that keyword is spotted, the core ASR-based dialog system is activated. The command spoken by the user (e.g., "set the temperature in the living room to 5 degrees") is converted to text by the ASR system. The transcribed utterance is processed by the CA, which tries to understand the user's intent ("set the temperature") and assesses whether the input contains enough information related to that intent. If so, the DSS decides the type of command, its parameters, and its recipient (one of the devices of the backend). The constructed technical command is sent to backend via a dedicated middleware. If the provided user's input is not sufficient to define such command, the Dialog System will continue the conversation and ask the user for the missing information.

In parallel, the DSS authorizes a user with the SR module and the stored voice biometric patterns. The system executes commands only if the user voice is successfully recognized. The speaker recognition processing can take a few seconds because of the limited computation capabilities of the targeted devices. Therefore, this step is performed in the background

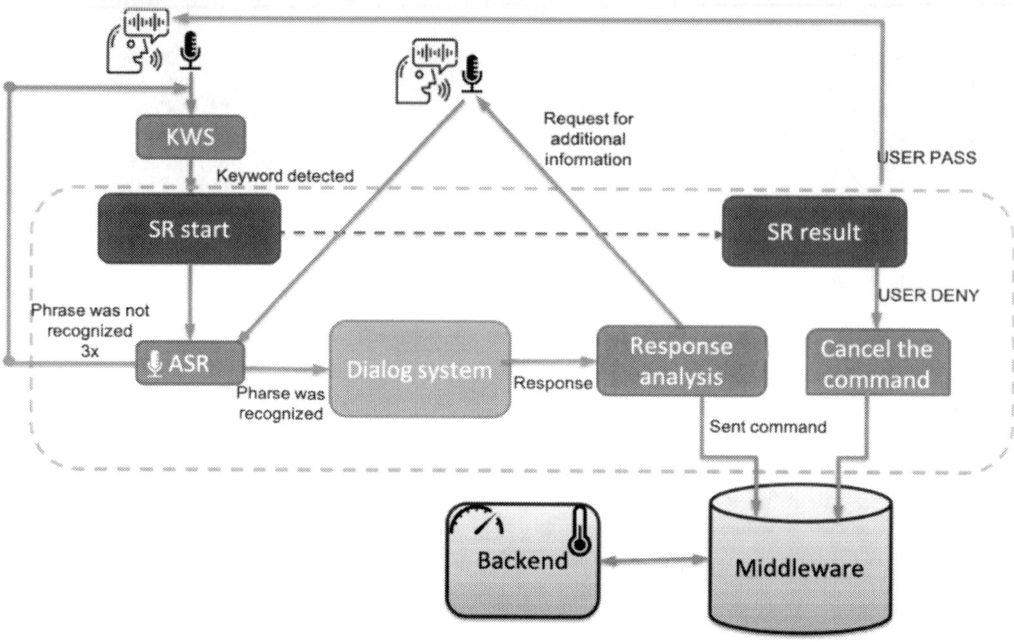

Figure 1. The Access Control DSS System design.

while the user speaks with the dialog system. By doing so, the user has the impression that the DSS operates in real-time.

These decision-making subsystems form a DSS, where at each step decisions are made based on the knowledge collected on the previous steps. A detailed description of each element is presented in the following subsections.

A. Access control module

The KWS system – a core component of the access control module – is based on a neural network with the ResNet architecture “res8” [6], and it contains a relatively small number of network parameters (approx. 110K). More specifically, we have based our solution on the system described in [6], which was trained on the Google Speech Commands Dataset (GSCD) – we have then performed a transfer learning procedure and used solution [6] as a feature extractor. For this purpose, a dataset of 698 positive examples of the selected keyword from 36 people has been collected. Together with a larger database of phonetically representative Polish speech (taken as negative examples), it was used for training the KWS classifier layer with 2 outputs (keyword vs. non-keyword). In addition, for the training phase 80% of examples were augmented with background noises of variable loudness, originating from the GSCD dataset. These background noises were also used to create negative examples of silence (i.e., the lack of speech) [3].

The designed system works in real-time, with a sliding window of $1s$ that moves by $0.2s$ [3]. Those parameters were established experimentally, as a compromise between satisfactory spotting of utterances and computational overhead. 40 Mel-Frequency Cepstral Coefficients acoustic features are used, normalised, and fed into the ResNet, which acts as a binary classifier returning a numerical score. Typically, if the score is higher than a certain threshold, it is assumed that the keyword was uttered. In our case, a threshold corresponding to the Equal Error Rate (EER) was taken [3].

The access control module also consists of many other submodules that are described in [3]. The first one – "Loudness Checker" – requires the incoming audio to have a certain minimum level of loudness. The second one, called "Timer", limits the time duration of an audio buffer that is being processed to $1.2s$ – if the triggering word is not observed shortly after that, the audio can be considered as background noise, and further processing of that signal can be skipped. Such a design also allows to lower the resource consumption. The third submodule – “Score Smoothing” – smooths the results obtained from KWS by calculating the mean of the last n predictions. The usage of these submodules allowed to reduce significantly the FPR of the Access Control system [3].

The proposed solution was primary implemented and tested on a Raspberry Pi 3B (CPU: 1,2 GHz quad-core ARM-8 Cortex-A53 (64-bit); 1 GB RAM). The device was equipped with a custom-made microphone matrix with 5 independent microphones. The experiments were conducted as field trials, where real hardware was used. 13 users were asked to utter the correct keyword 30 times. In addition, they spoke two words very similar to the keyword and eight other words three times each. The access control DSS evaluated each sample and the results were averaged. The proposed module, with the Score Smoothing submodule, using the last three predictions achieved an accuracy of 90.77% with TPR of 86.41% and FPR of 4.87% [3].

B. Speaker recognition module

The input to the SR module is strongly correlated with the KWS scores. Only a single frame processed by the KWS module, with the strongest trigger, is used to perform user authorisation. This process, hence, uses the utterance containing the system keyword. During authorization, the collected voice sample is compared to the user voice footprints (speaker embeddings), which store biometric information representative for the person's voice. These were computed earlier based on sample recordings, being the repetition of the custom keyword (10 repetitions have been collected, approx. 1s each). As a result, the created SR system can be considered as text-dependent, which allowed to increase its performance.

The SR system is based on ResNet neural network similar to the one presented in [19]. The related model was further trained by us with a low learning rate using a dataset with voices of 100 polish speakers in a transfer learning procedure that improved the performance for the Polish language. The accuracy of the trained SR module was tested on the database of 36 polish speakers (III-A), which contained the samples of a custom keyword and several sentences recorded by each speaker. The new model, together with the proposed new system design using a text-dependent approach, allowed to improve the performance (expressed as an EER) for the identification of a single speaker from 9.83% to 1.7%. The reference value of 9.83% has been obtained for the basic model from [19] in the test performed on the database of 100 polish speakers, by using random enrollment samples and random test samples of length similar to the ones used in the experiments on the database of 36 speakers (evaluating the new system design). For the experiment comparing the same SR system set-ups (i.e., enrollment on the recordings containing 5 repetitions of a custom keyword and test on the single recording containing this keyword), the newly created model with the EER of 1.7% outperformed the basic model, which resulted in the EER of 2.27%. The SR solution is able to recognize both – English and Polish speakers.

C. Automatic speech recognition

The choice of a suitable speech recognition platform for the communication between the DDS system and users (speech to text) is influenced by two requirements: (1) the need to operate with limited resources; and (2) the need to train acoustic models with a relatively small amount of training data. Taking that into account, a CMU open source vocabulary, speaker-independent continuous speech recognition engine [23] for embedded devices was chosen.

For English, an acoustic model and phonetic dictionary provided with pocketsphinx library [23] were selected. The grammar in Java Speech Grammar Format (JSGF) were custom-prepared to enable voice control of home automation systems.

For the Polish language, a dedicated acoustic model was trained with recordings collected with the mPass platform [24]. Each of 100 people, 49 males and 51 females, recorded the following: (i) a phonetically balanced text consisting of 322 sentences, and (ii) approximately 300 commands for controlling home devices. Each phoneme was represented by a three-state HMM model with eight mixtures per state – the number of mixtures were selected experimentally based on the size of the training material. Mel Frequency Cepstral Coefficients (MFCC) with delta-delta were chosen as a signal representation. A phonetic dictionary with 234 words and the JSGF Grammar were prepared in a similar manner for the English language.

The evaluation of the Polish speech recognition system was done with the cross-validation method. The data of one user were removed from the training set, and the set of commands for that user was recognised by the ASR. The results were averaged, and the system achieved the accuracy of 96.2%.

In addition, the experiments were conducted as field trials with a Raspberry Pi platform (with the configuration described in section III-A). In office and home environments, 10 Polish speakers spoke 41 sentences/commands in Polish to a ASR installed on an embedded device. Four native English speakers, five native Polish speakers, and one Brazilian did the same in English. The results were averaged. The word accuracy of the system was 97.98% for Polish and 94.77% for English.

D. Dialog system / conversational agent

The proposed dialog system uses openDial [25] – a lightweight, Java based, domain-independent toolkit that was originally designed to perform dialog management tasks. It combines logical and statistical approaches to dialogue modeling. More specifically, it consists of many modules with a shared memory represented by a Bayesian network. The domain models are specified via probabilistic rules encoded in XML.

We have created a natural language understanding model, which recognizes the user's intended actions from the text provided by the ASR system (such as 'increase the temperature', 'set the time', 'decrease the temperature', 'turn on device' ,'get the date', 'get battery level', among others). In addition, the model needs to update slots (required parameters) to the chosen action. For instance, in case of 'set the holiday mode', the required information consists of: (i) the number of days and hours, (ii) the temperature value, and (iii) the room identifier. If any of the slots are not filled, the system asks the user to provide the missing pieces of information.

In addition, the dialog management module was designed to make decisions regarding dialog states and flow – such as asking user to repeat the sentence, ask the user about missing information, finish the dialog, among others.

The final module of the dialog system is the natural language generation module, which specifies the mapping between the current dialog state and the system response. The output has a twofold form: (i) the text addressed to the user via speech synthesis, and (ii) a technical command for the device.

For instance, a dialog could have the following form:

- **user**: Increase the temperature in the living room
- **system**: By how many degrees?
- **user**: By 3 degrees.
- **system**: Temperature in the living room has been increased by 3 degrees.

E. Middleware

The software implementation on an embedded device contains also the middleware, which is responsible for handling communication between the voice-controlled DSS and the hardware of the embedded device (i.e., sensors/actuators). This way, the commands identified by the logic of the DSS system can be aquired and stored in a dedicated database and communicated to the actuators with a proper timing and order. The RabbitMQ broker is used for handling communication between the DSS system and a middleware. After middleware receives a RabbitMQ command, it sends an appropriate request on the internal REST (HTTPS) server. The REST server then converts that request to a message in format understandable by the Aura module on the hardware-related backend and then sends it to the selected actuator module via a serial port. The Aura module itself is an STM32 microcontrolller with a 868MHz transceiver (Spirit1), it communicates with the main board using UART. The microcontroller's firmware allows it to communicate with other home automation devices wirelessly through the Aura Radio Protocol, which may be usefull for more complex set-ups. The Aura protocol is a proprietary solution developed specifically for the Auraton Smart devices.

F. The voice control hardware

Figure 2. Voice control embedded device – exterior view.

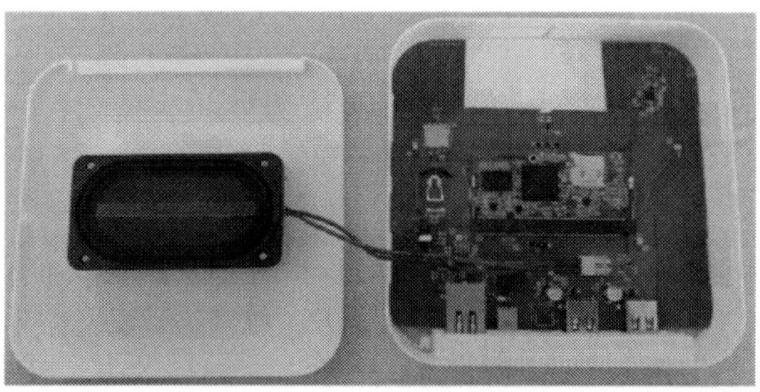

Figure 3. Voice control hardware platform – interior.

The voice control application worked on an STM32MP157 microprocessor, which is based on an ARM-A7 architecture, running two cores at 650 MHz. The developed platform is equipped with 1GB RAM, a Wi-Fi module, Ethernet, and a 868 MHz radio to communicate with peripheral devices. The application runs on an Embedded Linux based on OpenSTLinux and customised with the Yocto framework. Voice is recorded and streamed using a 5 digital MEMS microphones placed on the PCB in a semicircle. The user gets feedback after each command via a mono loudspeaker. Audio samples from each microphone are formed into one stream using the ALSA framework, and they are passed to the DSS module that runs in a Docker container. The identified user command (from the DSS output) is send to a message broker(RabbitMQ). Next, the message is received by a middleware, and it is passed to the REST API server, which saves each request in a dedicated SQLite database.

In addition, the device can also be controlled with a mobile application. It communicates with the device using the same RabbitMQ server, which is also responsible for sending data to the RF 868 MHz module and further on to the peripheral devices. An overview of the embedded device is presented in Figure 2 and Figure 3.

IV. EVALUATION

The evaluation of the proposed DSS system was performed in real-life scenarios. The testers had to perform 27 assignments using the targeted device. More specifically, each of the users has been given a task to set a desired configuration to the chosen home automation system or to collect data from it. The exact information regarding, for example, the choice of the rooms, the temperature, the dates, and the time was not provided, so that the creation of a final command was left to the user. All testers were only informed that the system understands voice communication and what are its general capabilities, but no further details were provided.

The accuracy of the whole DSS was evaluated based on the number of positively completed tasks. In particular, the following items were taken into account:

1) the number of successfully completed tasks in the first attempt (i.e., the user's command was understood correctly and voice biometric verification was positive)
2) the number of successfully completed tasks in the second or third attempt (for instance, in the first or second attempt, the DDS did not understand the user and asked to repeat the command, the user was understood wrongly and canceled the execution of the command, or the user did not pass the voice authorization).
3) the number of unsuccessful task executions in three attempts.

The results are shown in Table I. In this test case, 8 users, male and female, were providing commands to the system in Polish. The average accuracy of task completion in the first attempt was 82.2% – that includes keyword spotting, the successful understanding of the dialog with the user, and correct user's voice verification. The percentage of correctly performed tasks in at most three attempts increased to 97.1%.

TABLE I. TASK COMPLETION ACCURACY FOR ACCESS CONTROL DEVICE – POLISH NATIVE SPEAKERS

User	Acc. of successfully completed tasks		Acc. of [%]	
	1st attempt	*2nd/3rd attempt*	*SR verification*	*failure*
user1	77.8%	14.8%	100%	7.4%
user2	88.9%	7.4%	90.5%	3.7%
user3	70.4%	29.6%	100%	0.0%
user4	85.2%	14.8%	81.8%	0.0%
user5	85.2%	14.8%	68.2%	0.0%
user6	96.3%	3.7%	100%	0.0%
user7	74.1%	22.2%	95.2%	3.7%
user8	80.0%	12.0%	84.2%	8.0%

In addition, a survey of the level of user satisfaction has been performed. The user was evaluating intuitiveness of the system and its subjective effectiveness. The results are shown in Table II. On average, the testers evaluated the intuitiveness as 8.8, and the effectiveness as 8.4 out of 10. Similar experiments were carried out for the second group of users with the commands spoken in English. Due to the situation with COVID-19, we had only six testers and none of them was a native speaker. The average accuracy of task completion in a first attempt was 78.7%, and the performance of 94.3% was obtained in at most three attempts. On average, the testers evaluated intuitiveness of a DSS system as 8.5, and the effectiveness as 7.8 out of 10.

TABLE II. SURVEY OF THE LEVEL OF USER SATISFACTION WITH ACCESS CONTROL DSS

user	Effectiveness	Intuitiveness
user1	9.5	9.0
user2	8.0	9.0
user3	8.0	10
user4	9.0	9.0
user5	7.0	6.0
user6	10	10
user7	9.0	8.0
user8	7.0	9.0

There were mainly three types of errors that lowered the prototype performance:

- the testers were using grammatically incorrect commands (as it happens in colloquial speech), or they were making mistakes and correcting themselves
- the sequence of words spoken by the testers was not predicted and provided in the dialog system
- the ASR system had problems with correctly recognizing numbers when they were not spoken clearly. This is due to the fact that numbers are recognized mostly based on acoustic models. For instance, in the sentence 'set the temperature to X degrees', the grammar does not provide additional information and occurrence of any number has the same probability.
- the command was understood correctly by the DSS, but the user verification was not successful

In addition, if the system did not understand the command in the beginning of the test, the users frequently got frustrated, and it adversely affected further performance of the DSS. If the error occurred in the middle of the test, such effect was not observed. To counteract this phenomenon, problems related to user experience should be further studied.

The above-mentioned errors cannot be completely removed, if a voice command format is not imposed. However, the ASR and dialog system can be adapted to a specific user. When using a system of this type, the user also tends to learn how to speak to increase the probability of being understood. As a result, the overall system performance should increase with time.

Although one cannot expect flawless operation of any voice interface, we have shown that with a tailored design it can achieve performance levels, which are sufficient to properly control the home automation device. Moreover, it could be very useful when combined with other multi-modal interfaces.

V. CONCLUSION AND FUTURE WORK

We have described the DSS system for voice-controlled home automation devices running on embedded platforms with limited resources. The system grants access to the home automation devices and enables to collect information necessary for their control. The proposed solution combines many technologies, such as keyword spotting, speaker verification, automatic speech recognition and understanding, dialog management, and speech synthesis to provide a safe and natural interaction with the user.

The voice control prototype device that was presented in this article, was tested in real scenarios of home and office environments. The testers freely used natural language to convey their commands. The experiments proved the usefulness of this solution.

As a part of future work, we plan to focus on improving the user experience. This can be done by developing more flexible dialog schemes, and by combining the existing voice-based DSS system with multi-modal interfaces to further reduce the probability of a task completion failure.

ACKNOWLEDGMENT

The research was supported by the National Centre for Research and Development in Poland under the grant no. POIR.01.01.01-00-0044/17.

REFERENCES

[1] C. J. Baby, F. Khan, and J. N. Swathi, "Home automation using web application and speech recognition," in 2017 International conference on Microelectronic Devices, Circuits and Systems (ICMDCS), 2017, pp. 1–6.

[2] A. Kaklauskas, Intelligent Decision Support Systems. Springer International Publishing, Cham, 2015, ch. 2, pp. 31–85, in Biometric and Intelligent Decision Making Support, ISBN: 978-3-319-13659-2.

[3] M. Pabiszkak, M. Grajzer, and L. Sawicki, "Access control method for the offline home automation system," in eKNOW:2020: The Twelfth International Conference on Information, Process, and Knowledge Management. IARIA, 2020, pp. 97–101.

[4] A. Cuthbertson. Google defends listening to private conversations on google home: But what intimate moments are recorded? [Online]. Available: https://www.independent.co.uk/life-style/gadgets-and-tech/news/google-home-recordings-listen-privacy-amazon-alexa-hack-a9002096.html [retrieved: 05, 2022]

[5] T. N. Sainath and C. Parada, "Convolutional Neural Networks for Small-footprint Keyword Spotting," Proc. 16th Annu. Conf. Int. Speech Commun. Assoc. INTERSPEECH 2015, 2015, pp. 1478–1482.

[6] R. Tang and J. Lin, "Deep residual learning for small-footprint keyword spotting," in 2018 IEEE International Conference on Acoustics, Speech and Signal Processing (ICASSP). IEEE, 2018, pp. 5484–5488.

[7] C. Lengerich and A. Hannun, "An end-to-end architecture for keyword spotting and voice activity detection," arXiv preprint arXiv:1611.09405, 2016.

[8] Yocto Project. Getting started: The yocto project® overview. [Online]. Available: https://www.yoctoproject.org/software-overview [retrieved: 05, 2022]

[9] STMicroelectronics. Secure Hardware Platforms. [Online]. Available: https://www.st.com/en/secure-mcus/secure-hardware-platforms.html [retrieved: 05, 2022]

[10] C. Sidhartha, S. Siddharth, S. S. Narayanan, and J. H. Prasath, "Voice activated home automation system," in National Conference on Man Machine Interaction 2014, vol. 1. ASDF, India, 2014, pp. 69–72.

[11] K. A. Lee, A. Larcher, B. Thai, B. Ma, and H. Li, "Joint application of speech and speaker recognition for automation and security in smart home," in INTERSPEECH 2011, 12th Annual Conference of the International Speech Communication Association, Florence, Italy, 01 2011, pp. 3317–3318.

[12] Siri Team. Hey siri: An on-device dnn-powered voice trigger for apple's personal assistant. [Online]. Available: https://machinelearning.apple.com/research/hey-siri [retrieved: 05, 2022]

[13] R. Justo et al., "Improving dialogue systems in a home automation environment," in AMBI-SYS, 02 2008, p. 2.

[14] A. M. Bashir, A. Hassan, B. Rosman, D. Duma, and M. Ahmed, "Implementation of a neural natural language understanding component for arabic dialogue systems," Procedia Computer Science, vol. 142, 2018, pp. 222–229, arabic Computational Linguistics. [Online]. Available: https://www.sciencedirect.com/science/article/pii/S1877050918321835

[15] A. S. Tulshan and S. N. Dhage, "Survey on virtual assistant: Google assistant, siri, cortana, alexa," in International symposium on signal processing and intelligent recognition systems. Springer, 2018, pp. 190–201.

[16] Amazon Alexa. [Online]. Available: https://developer.amazon.com/en-US/alexa [retrieved: 05, 2022]

[17] Apple. Control your home with Siri. [Online]. Available: https://support.apple.com/en-us/HT208280 [retrieved: 05, 2022]

[18] Google Home. [Online]. Available: https://home.google.com/welcome/ [retrieved: 05, 2022]

[19] W. Xie, A. Nagrani, J. S. Chung, and A. Zisserman, "Utterance-level aggregation for speaker recognition in the wild," in ICASSP 2019-2019 IEEE International Conference on Acoustics, Speech and Signal Processing (ICASSP). IEEE, 2019, pp. 5791–5795.

[20] M. Vacher et al., "Speech and speaker recognition for home automation: Preliminary results," in 2015 International Conference on Speech Technology and Human-Computer Dialogue (SpeD). IEEE, 2015, pp. 1–10.

[21] Y. Mittal, P. Toshniwal, S. Sharma, and D. Singhal, "A voice-controlled multi-functional smart home automation system," in 2015 Annual IEEE India Conference (INDICON), 10 2015, pp. 1–6.

[22] G. López, V. Peláez, R. González, and V. Lobato, "Voice control in smart homes using distant microphones: A voicexml-based approach," in Ambient Intelligence, D. V. Keyson et al., Eds. Berlin, Heidelberg: Springer Berlin Heidelberg, 2011, pp. 172–181.

[23] D. Huggins-Daines et al., "Pocketsphinx: A free, real-time continuous speech recognition system for hand-held devices," in 2006 IEEE International Conference on Acoustics Speech and Signal Processing Proceedings, vol. 1. IEEE, 2006, pp. I–I.

[24] A. Cavalcante and M. Grajzer, "Proof-of-concept evaluation of the mobile and personal speech assistant for the recognition of disordered speech," International Journal on Advances in Intelligent Systems, vol. 9, 12 2016, p. 589.

[25] P. Lison and C. Kennington, "Opendial: A toolkit for developing spoken dialogue systems with probabilistic rules," in Proceedings of ACL-2016 system demonstrations, 2016, pp. 67–72.

The Social Accumulator (SOAC)

An explanation model for digital interaction among human actors

Karsten Böhm
FH Kufstein Tirol University of Applied Sciences
WEBTA Institute
Kufstein, Austria
email: karsten.boehm@fh-kufstein.ac.at

Abstract—**This contribution is addressing current issues in the increasing intensity of digital supported interaction and the perception and experiences made by human actors. Special attention is being put on the more than two years of due to the precautions in relation to the pandemic caused by the COVID19-virus. As a result, the concept of the Social Accumulator (SOAC) is introduced in this paper for the first time. It builds on the experiences from the intensified digital interactions both in academia and business life and should serve as an explanation model for the effects of digital interaction, that is easy to understand and to apply. The SOAC should help to understand the processes of Knowledge Creation and Knowledge Sharing when being driven by digital tools, which becomes increasingly important in a world that transforms education and businesses towards a highly digitized world.**

Keywords: Digital Transformation; Social Interaction; Higher Education; Digital Interaction; Communication; Collaboration; CSCW.

I. Introduction

Digitization and the digital transformation of our economy and out society has been an important topic in the recent years. The last two years under the influence of the global COVID19 pandemic acted like a catalyst for an almost instant digital transformation in many economies. In countries like Austria and Germany that period could be seen as the first large scale and real-life application of fully digital work experience, whereas other countries in Europe like Sweden, Denmark or Estonia already had substantial experience with the digital transformation at scale.

From a knowledge management perspective this situation was unique and interesting, as the use of information technology was always considered an important part of developing knowledge intensive businesses and activities. Thus, it is interesting to reflect back on the experience from a Knowledge Management perspective considering the interaction among human users (mostly) using digital channels.

In the beginning of the pandemic technical challenges and the improvement of the infrastructure, the availability of software systems and the building of the necessary skills were dominating the agendas in many organizations, in business and academia alike. However, much to everybody's surprise those challenges that were considered major showstoppers for technology adoption in the Knowledge Management community were resolved rather quickly. The collaboration in the digital world became the new norm and soon felt like the "new normal".

As the duration the of the pandemic extended in the second year, it became much more obvious that the mode of digital interaction had its own properties, which lead to advantages and disadvantages at the same time. Connections between colleagues and peers could be established quickly and communication and collaboration between individuals and groups of all sizes was facilitated by a number of useful tools that developed quickly to fit to the demand. Geographic distance was no impediment anymore, travel times virtually did not exist anymore. The transition from paper to digital in office became a reality at last and implemented easier ways of knowledge sharing among the users. On the other side the differentiation between working time and free time became much more blurred, the amount and the duration of digital meetings increased for most users very significantly and the time slots for concentrated work shrunk. Despite the massive use of digital communication tools, the individual feeling of loneliness or being isolated increased and informal conversation or communication did not happen that easily. This hampered informal knowledge exchange and affected the human well-being in the long run.

The long-term effects led to a kind of tiredness and exhaustion and became the label "Zoom fatigue" [1] and recent research validated the effect in a study carried out in Germany [2].

The channel reduction theory (from German: „Kanalreduktionstheorie") [3] assumes that remote communication generally has deficits. Newer studies identify a shift of the relation between the communication partners. At the same time, new phenomenon seems to take place: 1) Intimacy between communication partners can be even higher in an online setting, because the situation leads to a higher readiness of self-revelation (phenomenon: "Talking to a Stranger") and 2) digital setting often focus on the factual level. This is being perceived in a positive way as communication is more efficient and less status oriented and refers to the Disentrainment Hyperpersonal Model of computer mediated communication [4].

The situation described above, "This rapid and large-scale switch from in-person to remote interactions", had been described earlier as Remote Living or "Telelife" [5], which puts emphasis on the fact that we will collaborate more remotely. It seems to be the case, that the massive application of technology mediated communication and collaboration does not only have benefits and positive effects, but also drawback – which is a common observation in massive use of any technology. Therefore, the right balance between digital interaction and direct interaction of human actors seem to be important in the author's opinion.

Since the perception that direct interaction between human and digital interaction in which technical means are used for the communication (e.g., a phone call, a chat or a video conference call) are perceived differently in terms of richness and cognitive load, as well as towards trust building and perceived interactivity. This might be due to the fact that the channels are less rich [6], [7], we will use both channels. In essence direct interactions are perceived as more attractive and easier than digital interactions by most users. This became especially obvious during COVID19-pandemic when everything switched to solely digital interaction for a rather long period of time.

Here the question on when to use which channel and how to interleave those to channels arises.

Within this contribution we will introduce the concept of the Social Accumulator (SOAC) as an explanation model for the digital interaction of human actors, that focuses on the beneficial and the negative effects of computer supported collaboration (CSCW). By emphasizing on the different factors in a simple conceptual model, the SOAC should support the interleaving of digital and personal channels during communication and collaboration activities.

The paper is structures as follows: in section 2 the concept of SOAC is introduced which is followed by an illustration of positive and negative characteristics that effect the SOAC of human actors in section 3. After that in section 4 some application areas of the model and challenges in the application are described. the paper concludes in section 5 with a summary and the outlook for future research.

II. The Concept of the Social Accumulator

The main contribution of this paper is the concept of the SOAC, which should serve as an explanation model for the characteristics of (intensified) digital interaction. The author perceives a need for grasping the positive and negative effects of digital interaction in a simplified form in order to plan, to facilitate and to execute digital communication and other forms of direct communication in the most effective way without the need to be an expert in that research field. This might be also important in the discussion about the future workplace [8] and post pandemic education models [9].

SOAC builds on the analogy of an electric accumulator that stores electric energy, transformed to the aspect of interaction between human actors. Refueling activities are providing an energizing element and feel good for the humans interacting with each other. But there are also draining activities which are perceived by the human actors as taking energy from them. Figure 1 illustrates our concept of an SOAC.

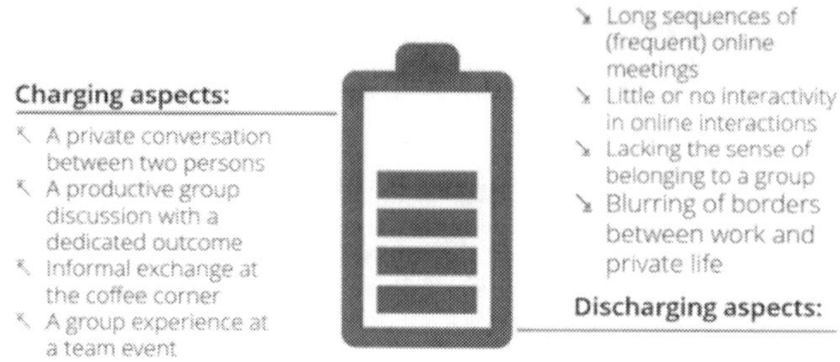

Figure 1. The concept of the Social Accumulator (SOAC) with some charging and discharging aspects as examples.

The term Social Accumulator is currently not used, although it is briefly mentioned in [10], but in the different context of social status of the youth generation. Therefore, in the opinion of the author, the metaphor of an accumulator that charges or discharges the perception of a communication or collaboration activities might be intuitive. With the focus of digital interaction in mind, we can consider the general observation that a direct conversation between human actors ("face-to-face") is generally being perceived as richer and more satisfying than a digital interaction. Thus, we consider those types of interactions as *positive* or *charging activities* with respect to the SOAC, while we consider extensive digital interactions generally as *negative* or *discharging activities*, following the concept of the zoom fatigue.

Based on the observations the (mental) concept of a SOAC is being 'charged' in direct interactions of human users and 'discharged' in digital interactions. When balanced correctly viable amount of 'social energy' is available for the human user and the interaction is perceived as sufficient. If the level drops below a certain level, this becomes a (perceived) problem and affects the well-being of the user, if the situation continues to last longer – that's the observation from the longer COVID19 periods. If the level exceeds the average energy level substantially the interaction is perceived as an especially valuable interaction – users call this a good chat, that was inspirational, for example. If this situation occurs more often, the context of the interaction is perceived in a positive way, e.g. as an inspirational workplace or motivating group. Figure 2 illustrates the process on at a schematic level.

It should be noted, however, that the digital and direct interaction do not have a negative effect (discharging) or positive effect per se, but that the right balance or orchestration of charging and discharging effects are important for a working communication relation between the participants.

The level of *Social Energy* (SE) available to the human actors is having a strong influence on his or her ability to create and share knowledge and might also influence his or her level of creativeness and innovation [11]. The term social energy is often used in the connection of energy supply and use within a nation or society.

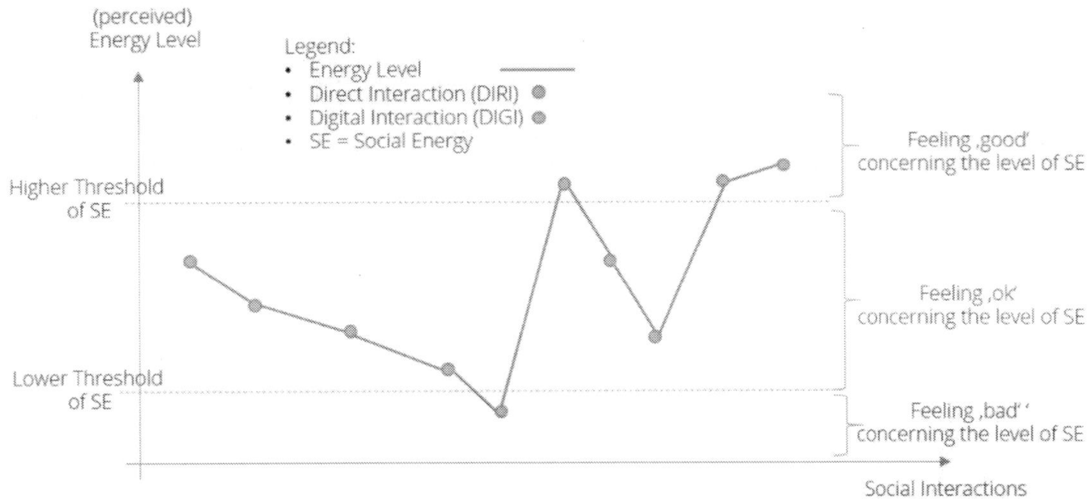

Figure 2. Illustration of the changing SOAC charging stage influenced by direct interactions and digital interactions over time.

Another definition can be found in the context of a societal force that aims at the wellbeing of its members by "doing good".

The relation between SE and the context of communication is less well defined in research literature and more informally described, see [12]. In the context of this contribution the term social energy is being defined as an individual and subjectively perceived energy level of a human actor with respect to his or her capability or willingness to enter into or contribute to a physical or digital conversation. As an immediate result, SE has a strong impact on knowledge related activities like knowledge creation, knowledge sharing, knowledge use and knowledge transfer. SE is changing over time and even during a conversation.

The *awareness* created by the SOAC model first of all serves as a way to reflect on one's own communication and collaboration situation, which puts the actor in a position to act on it.

Simply assessing the current situation might be a start and a result of the reflection could be a change of the communication mode (e.g. from digital interaction to direct interaction). As a next step a human actor could also track the SE over time to learn more about positive and negative aspects on digital interaction from his or her individual perspective.

It should be noted, that the authors would like to focus with this model at the dichotomy of direct vs. digital communication. With this respect the focus is being put on the channel and its methods and properties. It is clear that the human interaction is also largely influenced by the topic of the communication and the opinions and general feelings of the human actors. Those aspects can also have positive and negative aspects and require actions like a conflict resolution. These aspects are, however, not topic of this contribution.

III. Charging and Discharging the SOAC

The aspects and characteristics of the digital and the direct communication channel can be considered towards their charging effects (adding social energy to the SOAC) and the discharging effects (taking social energy from the SOAC) and will be a subject for detailed future research. In order to illustrate the effect, examples of both categories will be described in the following subsections.

A. *Positive aspects charging the SOAC*

To illustrate the aspects that are draining social energy some of those discharging aspects are being described in more detail below:

1. *A fruitful conversation*: between two human actors that evolves interesting and sometimes unexpected results is a good example of a fueling activity. Very often it is not only the exchange of information but the overall situation, gestures and mutual empathy that makes a difference here. As an important side effect psychological safety is created in such situations.
2. *An informal talk*: at a coffee corner or similar place is a form of latent communication that happens as a by-product of another activity (e.g. taking a coffee). This often leads to the exchange of interesting information, knowledge sharing and even the creation of new knowledge stimulated by the situation. The main characteristic is that it is unplanned, but not unlikely. Those events happen much less likely in digital interactions. One of the reasons might be the less frequent and less natively incurred interactions in digital settings.
3. *A team experience*: almost always requires a presence setting to allow for the emergence of a team spirit while working on a common goal or being submerged in a joint activity, very often these

activities serve as trust building entities for new groups or are reassessing mutual trust level for existing team that fuels the SOACs of the participants. Such settings can create transparency within the group as an important side-effect that fuels the positive perception of the group-members.

B. Negative aspects discharging the SOAC

To illustrate the aspects that are draining social energy some of those discharging aspects are being described in more detail below:

1. *A high frequency and/or long duration of digital interactions*: might be considered as tiring to the human actors. This fact had been reported in a number of studies and it is important to clarify that this could also occur in situations in which only one of the human actors is under such a high load of digital interactions leading to a communication setting which is perceived very different by the participants (e.g. a team lead that is connecting to its peers in 1:1 session).
2. *Few interactions during a digital interaction:* are another impact factor that is adding cognitive load to the human user, especially if the video setting is static and thus requires additional effort for the human brain to remain focused. When presentation settings are transferred 1:1 from a presence setting, they are often perceived more demanding in the digital communication and take less time or include more interactions to retain the attention of the audience.
3. *The perception of constant availability*: for human actors might add to the perceived stress level as well. The lowered barrier of getting in contact with the other participant in a synchronous interaction might inflict his or her current working process and a cultural assumption within the organization that everyone is expected to be available almost always and instantly can lead to less efficiency in the working tasks and a high level of engagement at the same time.

IV. Potential Application areas of SOAC

In this section some application areas for the SOAC will be explained in detail and it's interesting to note that the SOAC can serve for different purposes in different application areas. From a Knowledge Management perspective, the charging and discharging aspects of the SOAC could be helpful to identify barriers in the fields of those Knowledge (Co)-creation, Knowledge Sharing and Knowledge Use among the different actors in the application settings that are described below.

A. The context of Higher Education (HEI)

The effects of the COVID19 pandemic and the intensified use of distant teaching just changed the way how Higher Education of the future is seen by students and lecturers alike. Due to those experiences Higher Education Institutions (HEI) will have to reflect on how to modernize the education in post-pandemic age with a mixture of presence and distant teaching activities. It is very likely, that even education programs that relied on presence teaching only will include some form of e-learning elements into their curricula. Even hybrid settings in which presence teaching and distant teaching occur simultaneously might be a valid scenario for the future. It is obvious, that some topics are more suitable for distant teaching than others (e.g. labs and exercises) but on the other hand also some students will favor digital interactions while others prefer a more direct interaction. Balancing those two forms of interaction between lecturer and students in the right way (in terms of didactic requirements and individual preferences), will retain a competitive advantage for a HEI in a market that constantly becomes more competitive and globalized due to the extension into the digital domain by market participants (e.g. Coursera, Udacity). The SOAC will help lecturers and to derive a measurement system during planning and execution of their lecturers to find the right mix between direct and digital interaction while planning and during execution of their lectures. For students SOAC could work as a tool to reflect on the own learning preferences with respect to their preferred form of communication and they could adapt accordingly by becoming aware of the advantages and drawbacks of digital interaction.

B. The context of professional trainings

For the professional training in the workplace setting and as part of the lifelong learning the results of the COVID19 pandemic showed to companies and trainers that digital training can be effective and efficient. The requirement of traveling to a training became less of a demand and the integration in the everyday work schedule was much easier for digital training, leading to a higher acceptance rate for training in general and budget saving aspects (no travel and accommodation costs). On the other side, the focus on the training itself in a presence training and the direct and valuable exchange between participants and towards the trainer had been assigned a new value due to the drawbacks of digital trainings. Overall, it can be expected, that the market for professional training's will be changed due to the results of the pandemic, yet it is still to be shown what the long-term effects will be.

The SOAC can help trainers design the interaction with the participants in an effective way by mixing direct and digital interactions in such a way that participants benefit in an optimal way from the training. Being aware of the characteristics of the charging and discharging effects will help to establish a level of social interaction that is common in a presence training also in a digital setting. SOAC helps to incorporate education in the professional job setting to fit to the individual requirements and thus provide a framework for the trainer to derive and monitor the charging state of the participants in his or her training. The concepts of SOAC might be combined with more agile approaches in delivering the teaching practices, too.

C. The context of virtual companies

The third application area that the author would like to shed light on in terms of SOAC is the digitization process within companies, that had been accelerated by the pandemic, too. Here, the concept of "New Work" [13], [14] became a reality in the perception and evolving work models of many organizations that resisted such changes before. This significant and ongoing change on the organization of companies often leads to more distributed or virtualized companies, especially in the IT-domain. While being common pattern in northern European countries, this is relatively new in the DACH area. From a managerial point of view this change creates new challenges for managing teams and project due to the fact of (perceived) fewer social interactions. The SOAC will help managers and team leaders as a managerial concept to understand the needs of their colleagues and team mates better and to act according to their (individual) needs, since they are able to sense and classify the charging and discharging activities during the digital and direct interactions. For the employees the SOAC can act like a model that helps them to become aware and to voice their needs in terms of communication and interaction over the various channels.

Monitoring the social energy of the members of a group always had been an important task for leaders. However, in a hybrid working environment with a large amount of digital interaction it will be more important to monitor the SE of the team members and to recharge their SOACs early enough to prevent "outages" that might affect team motivation and performance. The concept of SOAC could help to manage team-SE more actively.

D. Challenges for the application of SOAC

Applying the mental model of a SOAC will have its challenges, which are a subject to future research. Some of the foreseen challenges are briefly mentioned in this section in order to provide some hints for the application in the settings described above.

It will be important to keep the simplicity of the concept and to stick as close to the accumulator metaphor as possible in order to make application simple and intuitive for the human actors in the communication process.

Likewise, it will be important and challenging to make the current SE visible for the individual and for the group in order to create awareness and the opportunity to act on critical states of the SOAC appropriately. A promising approach for teams could be the use of retrospectives as a method from the agile software development for groups [15]. An adapted and simplified version might even work for the individual as a form of self-retrospective that can be mapped to the communication events in the recent period to plot the SE-levels over time.

Finally, charging and discharging factors will overlay each other and communication setting (presence or digital) might not be directly related to the SE level or being conscious for the human users in every situation. Therefore, the identification of relevant communication events and their contribution to the SE-level in a precise way is going to be another challenge.

V. Conclusion & Future Research

The main contribution of the paper is the introduction of the SOAC as a mental concept that might serve as a simple explanation model for the social energy level of an individual or a group and the perceived differences of direct and digital interactions. This might help to understand the interplay between the different forms of interaction and thus support the improvement of the overall interaction between human users as both forms are and will be present in our daily professional life. Further, the paper contributes in terms of working out different individual aspects that have to be considered when planning and orchestrating the different forms of interaction. This is being exemplified using application examples from three different fields.

Being currently on the conceptual level, this contribution is missing the empirical data, whose gathering is subject to further research in the different usage scenarios mentioned above. This next step will also be used to collect responses from the human stakeholders in the interaction process concerning the understanding and usefulness of the mental model of a SOAC.

Acknowledgment

The author would like to thank the Tyrolean Science Fund ("Tiroler Wissenschaftsförderung"), which supported this research under grant number F.33280/6-2021 and the feedback provided by the reviewers of this contribution and colleagues which helped to improve it.

References

[1] G. Fauville, M. Luo, A. C. Muller Queiroz, J. N. Bailenson, and J. Hancock, 'Zoom Exhaustion & Fatigue Scale', Social Science Research Network, Rochester, NY, SSRN Scholarly Paper ID 3786329, Feb. 2021. doi: 10.2139/ssrn.3786329.

[2] 'Zoom-Fatigue – Instituts for Employment and Employability'. https://www.ibe-ludwigshafen.de/zoom_fatigue/ (accessed Mar. 27, 2022).

[3] N. Döring, *Social Psychology of the Internet. The importance of the Internet for communication processes, identities, social relations and groups.*, 2nd ed. Göttingen Bern: Hogrefe Verlag, 2003.

[4] J. Walther, 'The Effect of Feedback on Identity Shift', *Comput.-Mediat. Commun. Media Psychol.*, vol. Vol. 14, no. Issue 1, pp. 1–26, 2011.

[5] J. Orlosky *et al.*, 'Telelife: The Future of Remote Living', *ArXiv210702965 Cs*, Jul. 2021, Accessed: Jul. 10, 2021. [Online]. Available: http://arxiv.org/abs/2107.02965

[6] A. M. Johnson and A. L. Lederer, 'The Effect of Communication Frequency and Channel Richness on the Convergence Between Chief Executive and Chief Information Officers', *J. Manag. Inf. Syst.*, vol. 22, no. 2, pp. 227–252, Nov. 2005, doi: 10.1080/07421222.2005.11045842.

[7] K. Ishii, M. M. Lyons, and S. A. Carr, 'Revisiting media richness theory for today and future', *Hum. Behav. Emerg. Technol.*, vol. 1, no. 2, pp. 124–131, 2019, doi: 10.1002/hbe2.138.

[8] D. Smite, N. B. Moe, J. Hildrum, J. G. Huerta, and D. Mendez, 'Work-From-Home is Here to Stay: Call for Flexibility in Post-Pandemic Work Policies',

ArXiv220311136 Cs, Mar. 2022, Accessed: Apr. 29, 2022. [Online]. Available: http://arxiv.org/abs/2203.11136

[9] L. Bayerlein, M. T. Hora, B. A. Dean, and S. Perkiss, 'Developing skills in higher education for post-pandemic work', *Labour Ind.*, vol. 31, no. 4, pp. 418–429, Oct. 2021, doi: 10.1080/10301763.2021.1966292.

[10] D. V. Lepeshev and A. N. Teslenko, 'Social status of scientific activity in the minds of the youth of Kazakhstani', *Eur. Sci. J. ESJ*, vol. 10, no. 17, Art. no. 17, Jun. 2014, doi: 10.19044/esj.2014.v10n17p%p.

[11] '7 Ways to Recharge When You're Feeling Drained of Social Energy', *Andy Mort*, Feb. 16, 2015. https://www.andymort.com/social-energy/ (accessed Apr. 29, 2022).

[12] 'Understanding Social Energy & Communication Styles – Evergreen Planner'. https://www.evergreenplanner.com/2021/03/17/understanding-social-energy-communication-styles/ (accessed Apr. 29, 2022).

[13] R. C. Barnett, 'A New Work-Life Model for the Twenty-First Century', *Ann. Am. Acad. Pol. Soc. Sci.*, vol. 562, no. 1, pp. 143–158, Mar. 1999, doi: 10.1177/000271629956200110.

[14] M. Helmold, 'Culture Change Towards New Work Concepts', in *New Work, Transformational and Virtual Leadership: Lessons from COVID-19 and Other Crises*, M. Helmold, Ed. Cham: Springer International Publishing, 2021, pp. 45–54. doi: 10.1007/978-3-030-63315-8_4.

[15] Y. Andriyani, R. Hoda, and R. Amor, 'Reflection in Agile Retrospectives', in *Agile Processes in Software Engineering and Extreme Programming*, Cham, 2017, pp. 3–19. doi: 10.1007/978-3-319-57633-6_1.

VR-ProcessMine: Immersive Process Mining Visualization and Analysis in Virtual Reality

Roy Oberhauser[0000-0002-7606-8226]
Computer Science Dept.
Aalen University
Aalen, Germany
e-mail: roy.oberhauser@hs-aalen.de

Abstract—**Repeatable processes are fundamental for describing how enterprises and organizations operate, for production, for Industry 4.0, etc. As digitalization and automation progresses across all organizations and industries, including enterprises, business, government, manufacturing, and IT, evidence-based comprehension and analysis of the processes involved, including their variations, anomalies, and performance, becomes vital for an increasing set of stakeholders. Process Mining (PM) relies on logs or processes (as such evidence-based) to provide process-centric analysis data, yet insights are not necessarily visually accessible for a larger set of stakeholders (who may not be process or data analysts). Towards addressing certain challenges described in the Process Mining Manifesto, this paper contributes VR-ProcessMine, a solution for visualizing and interacting with PM results in Virtual Reality (VR). Our realization shows its feasibility, and a case-based evaluation provides insights into its capabilities.**

Keywords-virtual reality; process mining; process analysis; business process mining; business process management.

I. Introduction

The digital transformation sweeping through society affects businesses and organizations everywhere, resulting in an increased emphasis on business agility and automation. Business Processes (BPs) or workflows are one significant automation area, as evidenced by the Business Process Management (BPM) market, which is forecast to grow from $8.8B in 2020 to $14.4B by 2025 [1]. Each execution of such a process leaves a digital footprint of process-related events and the timepoint of execution, typically contained in various log files across the various IT systems (business, manufacturing, etc.) involved in an enterprise. BPs are a way for ordering the activities involved in and executed in an enterprise, be they automated, semi-automated, or human-driven, and thus BPM is where much of the value generated by an enterprise is achieved.

Process Mining (PM) is a sub-field of data science specifically focused on analyzing event data generated when (business) processes are executed [2]. Because PM relies on event logs of actual process executions, it is evidence-based (or fact-based). This analysis can provide essential insights for understanding and optimizing (business) process execution. When referring to processes we assume BPs to be a subset of the more abstract term and will use both terms interchangeably. One process variant represents a set of process instances that resulted in the same sequence of events.

The Process Mining Manifesto [3] describes eleven challenges for PM. Two of these, *C10: Improving Usability for Non-experts*, and *C11: Improving Understandability for Non-experts*, are a primary motivation for our work. A secondary effect is to address *C9: Combining Process Mining with other Types of Analysis*.

In general, visualization remains a challenge when dealing with large data sets that involve relations and different variation sets. As data and processes become more relevant to the digital enterprise and stakeholders more digitally savvy, it is all the more relevant and challenging to include non-expert enterprise stakeholders in process analysis. By leveraging Virtual Reality (VR), BP analysis can be made more accessible to a wider set of stakeholders, such that not just process modeling specialists, but also those directly involved in executing a BP or observing an automated BP can view und gain insights to various issues regarding a BP of interest, including the combination with other relevant enterprise models.

In prior work, we developed VR-BPMN [4] to visualize business processes in VR based on the BPMN notation. Our VR-EA [5] contributed a VR solution for visualizing, navigating, annotating, and interacting with ArchiMate EA models. And VR-EAT [6] presented our VR-based solution for visualizing dynamically-generated EA diagrams from EA tools. This paper contributes VR-ProcessMine, a solution for visualizing and interacting with PM results in Virtual Reality (VR). Our prototype realization shows its feasibility, and a case-based evaluation provides insights into its capabilities for addressing the aforementioned challenges.

The remainder of this paper is structured as follows: Section 2 discusses related work. In Section 3, the solution is described. Section 4 provides details about the realization. The evaluation is described in Section 5 and is followed by a conclusion.

II. Related Work

PM is supported by various tools. Open source tools includes the ProM Framework [7], Apromore [8], and PM4Py [9]; commercial options include products from over 35 vendors, including Celonis, Disco, UiPath, ARIS, and PAFnow. These tools typically provide a 2D user interface with some being Web-based interfaces (e.g., Celonis, UiPath, Apromore), whereas we provide a VR-based solution.

Work involving PM with VR include Vogel & Thomas [10] show groundwork and an architecture concept, yet no prototype is described nor are VR screenshots provided. Other work combining PM with VR is often specialized to processes in certain sectors, such as training for factory or manufacturing, logistics, safety, or education and learning, or the health sector. For instance, Roldán et al. [11] describe a complex assembly training system for Industry 4.0 operators.

III. Solution

VR is defined as a "real or simulated environment in which the perceiver experiences telepresence" (Steuer 1992), a mediated visual environment, which is created and then experienced. VR provides an unlimited space for visualizing a growing and complex set of enterprise models and processes and their interrelationships simultaneously in a spatial structure. As enterprise models grow in complexity and reflect the deeper integration of both the business and IT reality, an immersive digital enterprise environment provides an additional visualization capability to comprehend the "big picture" for structurally and hierarchically complex and interconnected diagrams and digital elements, while providing an immersive experience for digital process model visualization and analysis in a 3D space viewable from different perspectives.

As to benefits of an immersive VR experience vs. 2D for an analysis task, [12] investigated a software analysis task that used a Famix metamodel of Apache Tomcat source code dependencies in a force-directed graph. They found that VR does not significantly decrease comprehension and analysis time nor significantly improve correctness (although fewer errors were made). While interaction time was less efficient, VR improved the UX (user experience), being more motivating, less demanding, more inventive/innovative, and more clearly structured.

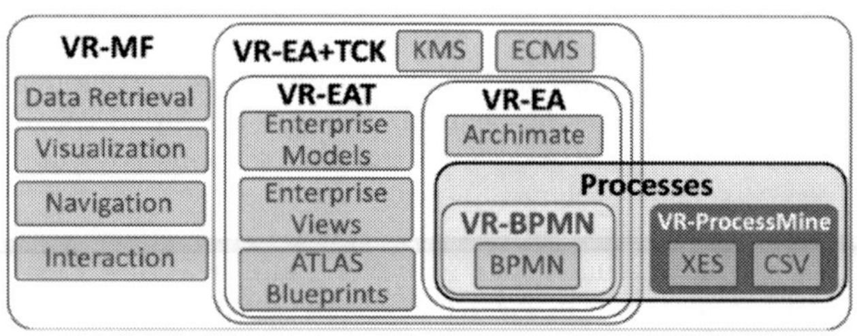

Figure 1. The VR-ProcessMine solution concept (blue) in relation to our prior VR solution concepts.

Our generalized solution concept for VR-ProcessMine is shown in Figure 1. VR-ProcessMine utilizes our generalized VR Modeling Framework (VR-MF) [5], which provides a VR-based domain-independent hypermodeling framework, which addresses four primary aspects that require special attention when modeling in VR: visualization, navigation, interaction, and data retrieval. VR-EA [5] provides specialized direct support and mapping for EA models in VR, including both ArchiMate as well as BPMN via VR-BPMN [4]. VR-EAT [6] extends this further with integration of EA tools for accessing dynamically generated diagrams and models from an EA tool in VR. VR-EA+TCK extends these capabilities by integrating further enterprise knowledge, information, and content repositories such as a Knowledge Managemement System (KMS) and/or an Enterprise Content Management System (ECMS).

In order to support PM and visual analysis, the VR-ProcessMine solution should exhibit the following capabilities:

- *Log file import*: event logs in different event log formats can be imported and processed;
- *Multiple analyses*: multiple event logs can be loaded in order to compare them directly;
- *3D visualization*: elements should be depicted in 3D to support an immersive observation experience;
- *Free element placement*: an individual analysis should be movable in VR space so that they can be compared in locality with another analysis of interest;
- *Hide/show analyses*: to minimize visual clutter, analyses can be hidden and then seen again;
- *Trace detection*: relations between events should be clearly visible; and
- *Colored hot spots*: events are colored to indicate their relative frequency.

A. Visualization in VR

In order to differentiate process variants (depending on the analysis being done), our visualization concept for VR depicts each of these on separate vertical plates standing on a common hyperplane representing a single process. This permits any plate to be selected, moved, and compared with others of interest. Furthermore, since the number of process variants can be very large, it leverages the unlimited space in VR, allowing the hyperplane to depict many process variants at once. All process variants are initially equally spaced on the hyperplane and can be compared with each other.

B. Navigation in VR

The immersion afforded by VR requires addressing how to navigate the space while reducing the likelihood of potential VR sickness symptoms. Thus, two navigation modes are included in the solution: the default uses gliding controls, enabling users to fly through the VR space and view objects from any angle they wish. Alternatively, teleporting permits a user to select a destination and be instantly placed there (i.e., by instantly moving the camera to that position); while this can be disconcerting, it may reduce the susceptibility to VR sickness for those prone to it that can occur when moving through a virtual space.

C. Interaction in VR

Since interaction with VR elements has not yet become standardized or intuitive, in our VR concept, user-element interaction is handled primarily via the VR controllers and a virtual tablet. Our VR-Tablet provides detailed context-specific element information, and can provide a virtual keyboard for text entry fields (via laser pointer key selection) when needed.

IV. Realization

Our solution prototype is partitioned into the Data Hub, a backend for data processing and PM, and the front end responsible for VR visualization (see Figure 2).

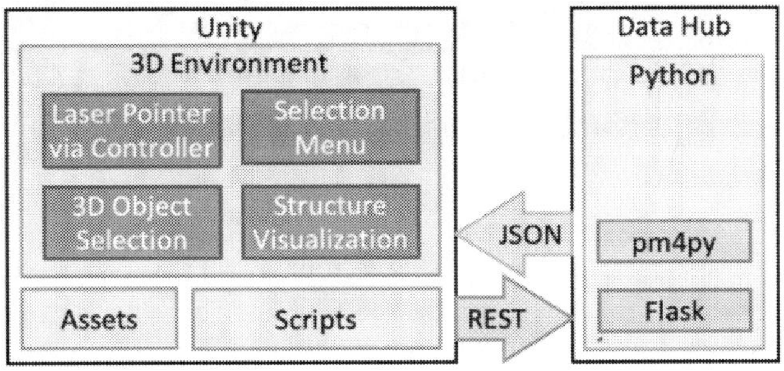

Figure 2. VR-ProcessMine logical architecture.

A. Process Mining

The Data Hub, based on Python 3.9, prepares datasets for visualization. Flask was used to provide REST APIs with JSON for frontend integration. The python library pm4py (Process Mining for Python) [9] is used to convert imported log files into data objects and data frames. The result depends on the type of graph desired. A Directly-Follows Graph (DFG) algorithm provides a summary of all process event transitions and variants and how often each process variant was executed. Listing 1 shows the result of the parsed dataset providing the number of transitions occurring between two events.

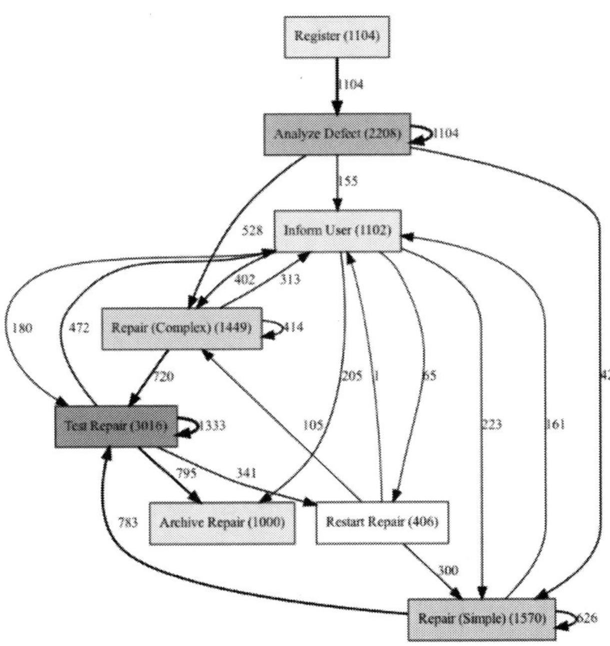

Figure 3. Example DFG-based process map result from pm4py.

Figure 3 shows a DFG-based process map visualization result using pm4py. A node represents an event. A graph consists of a set of transitions between a set of nodes.

Data is converted to a dictionary, whereby all duplicates are removed so that each node exists only once in the graph. The recursive list of fan-in relations (nodes reaching this node) together with their occurrence frequency provides the basis for a weighted directed graph as shown in Listing 2. Aggregating the total occurrences across all incoming transitions of a node (event) provides a total frequency of that event across all process instances.

```
Counter({
    ('Test Repair', 'Test Repair'): 1333,
    ('Register', 'Analyze Defect'): 1104,
    ('Analyze Defect', 'Analyze Defect'): 1104,
    ('Test Repair', 'Archive Repair'): 795,
    ('Repair (Simple)', 'Test Repair'): 783,
    ('Repair (Complex)', 'Test Repair'): 720,
    ('Analyze Defect', 'Repair (Complex)'): 528,
    ...
})
```

Listing 1. Snippet of a parsed DFG dataset.

```
{
  "Register": {
    "start":
  },

  "Analyze Defect": {
    "Register": 1104,
    "Analyze Defect": 1104
  },

  "Repair (Complex)": {
    "Analyze Defect": 528,
    "Repair (Complex)": 414,
    "Inform User": 402,
    "Restart Repair": 105
  },
    ...
}
```

Listing 2. Recursive list of fan-in relations.

B. Virtual Reality

VR realization is handled by the frontend, based on Unity 2021 using Steam VR and implemented in C#. VR hardware consisted of an HTC Vive. Via our VR-Tablet concept, a user can specify a log file to be processed. Currently CSV and XES formats are supported. Once loaded, the first plate shows a DFG with entire set of nodes and transition frequency (see Figure 4), with the plates behind it showing the different process variants (if any).

To support interaction, an affordance in the form of an anchor (sphere) is provided on a corner of each vertical plate or hyperplane, which if selected can be used to reduce visual clutter by collapsing (hide) or expanding (show) that object, or the anchor can be used to place the object elsewhere.

The total number of input transitions to a node represent the total number of times that event occurred. Thus, the higher this number, the higher the frequency. To represent this visually, a ten-step color scale was used to map the frequency between low activity (blue) and high activity (red), analogous to mapping temperature (see Figure 5). This can be used to quickly identify frequently occurring events in a process and help focus analysis and potential optimizations.

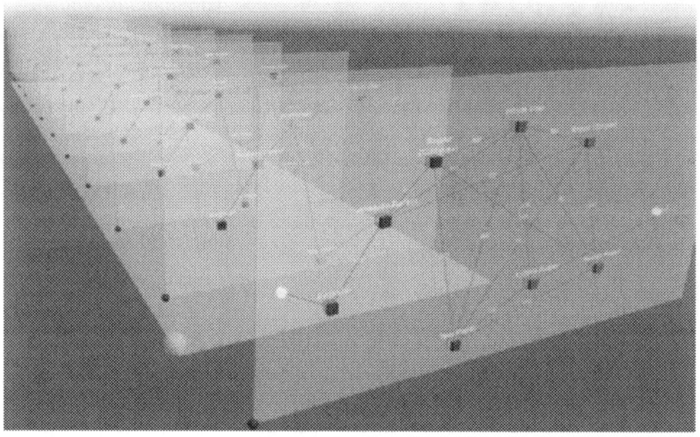

Figure 4. Initial plate shows DFG with entire set of nodes and transition frequency. Each plate thereafter represents one process variant.

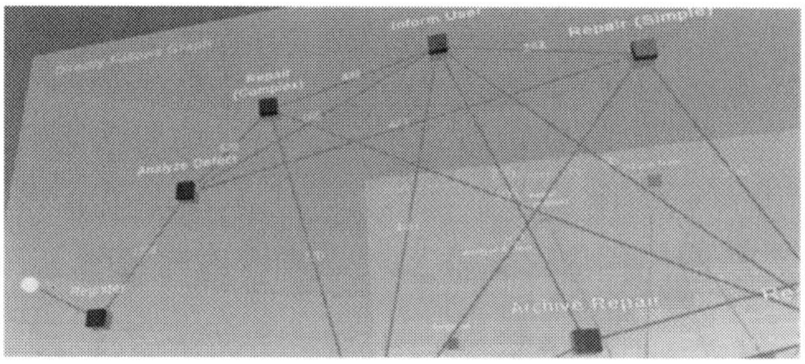

Figure 5. Node color and edges in a DFG.

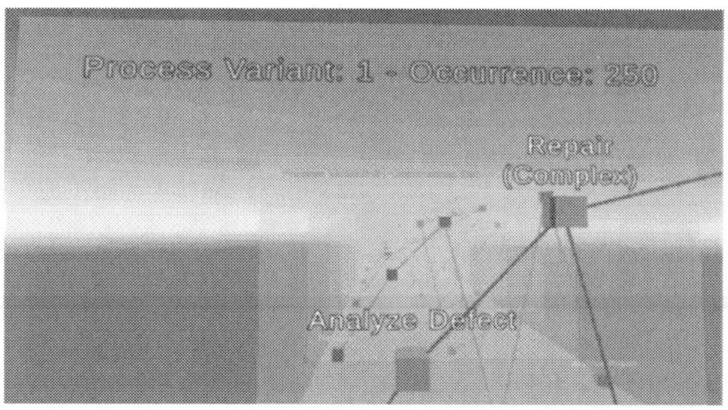

Figure 6. Partial process variant showing occurence frequency.

Process variants with only the relevant nodes (events) that occurred are shown uniquely in separate planes. The variants are assigned a default ID with their occurrence frequency indicated on top (see Figure 6). To support analysis and differentiation, placement of all nodes follows the initial placement in the DFG so that variants can be placed to overlap across the z-axis with the nodes in the same position, or when placed side-by-side the equivalent node locations are placed in the same relative position on each plate.

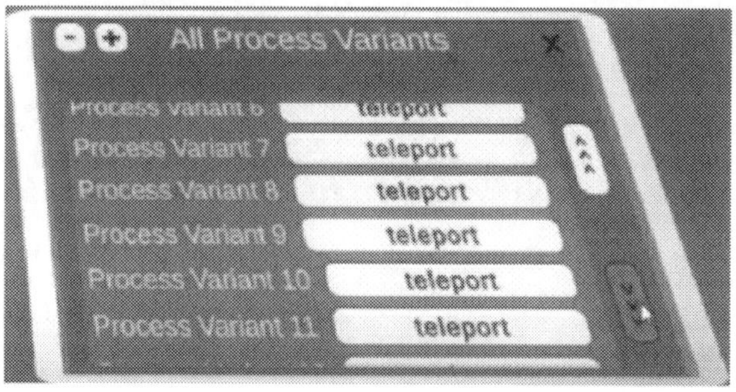

Figure 7. VR-Tablet showing scrollable variant list with a teleport option.

Besides the fly-through ability in VR using the controllers, navigation support includes the ability to quickly teleport to a specific variant by using the VR-Tablet and choosing a variant of interest as shown in Figure 7.

V. EVALUATION

To evaluate the solution, we utilize a case study focusing on three challenges identified in the Process Mining Manifesto [3]. These are:

C10: Improving Usability for Non-experts and

C11: Improving Understandability for Non-experts.

C9: Combining Process Mining with other Types of Analysis.

Our dataset consisted of randomly generated process variants based on a software defect repair process (a snippet is shown in Listing 3). A process variant represents multiple process instances that exhibited the same sequence (or node transition) order.


```
{
"variant": "Register,Analyze Defect,Analyze Defect,Inform User,Repair (Complex),Repair
(Complex),Test Repair,Test Repair,Archive Repair",
"case:concept:name": 78
},
{
"variant": "Register,Analyze Defect,Analyze Defect,Repair (Simple),Inform User,Repair (Simple),
Test Repair,Test Repair,Archive Repair",
"case:concept:name": 75
},
{
"variant": "Register,Analyze Defect,Analyze Defect,Repair (Simple),Repair (Simple),Test Repair,
Test Repair,Inform User,Archive Repair",
"case:concept:name": 67
},
{
"variant": "Register,Analyze Defect,Analyze Defect,Repair (Complex),Repair (Complex),Test
Repair,Inform User,Test Repair,Archive Repair",
"case:concept:name": 64
},
{
"variant": "Register,Analyze Defect,Analyze Defect,Repair (Simple),Repair (Simple),Test Repair,
Inform User,Test Repair,Archive Repair",
"case:concept:name": 41
},
{
"variant": "Register,Analyze Defect,Analyze Defect,Repair (Simple),Repair (Simple),Test Repair,
Test Repair,Restart Repair,Repair (Simple),Inform User,Repair (Simple),Test Repair,Test Repair,
Archive Repair",
"case:concept:name": 29
},
{
"variant": "Register,Analyze Defect,Analyze Defect,Inform User,Repair (Simple),Repair (Simple),
Test Repair,Test Repair,Archive Repair",
"case:concept:name": 28
},
{
"variant": "Register,Analyze Defect,Analyze Defect,Repair (Simple),Repair (Simple),Test Repair,
Test Repair,Inform User,Restart Repair,Repair (Simple),Repair (Simple),Test Repair,Test Repair,
Archive Repair",
"case:concept:name": 21
},
```


Listing 3. Dataset snippet of randomized process variants (in JSON).

A. Improving Usability and Understandability for Non-experts

One aspect that these challenges intend to address is that PM results are made accessible to end-users, and that they can intuitively interact with these, and understand these in their daily work routines. As such, they require intuitive user interfaces (UIs) to support usability as detailed in C10.

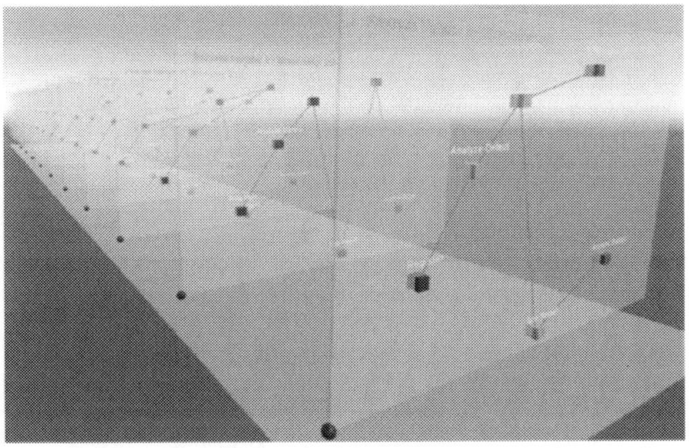

Figure 8. All process variants displayed on a hyperplane.

To support user-friendly UIs, our solution provides an immersive VR experience addressing visualization, navigation, interaction, and data retrieval. With regard to visualization, each process variant is visualized on a 2D plate (Figure 8), leveraging the third dimension for scaling to display all process variants, providing an overview of how many variants exist. Via fly-through navigation, differences can be observed. Furthermore, via our VR-Tablet concept (Figure 7), the user can instantly teleport to a specific one. For interaction, the VR-Tablet can provide details of an event or object.

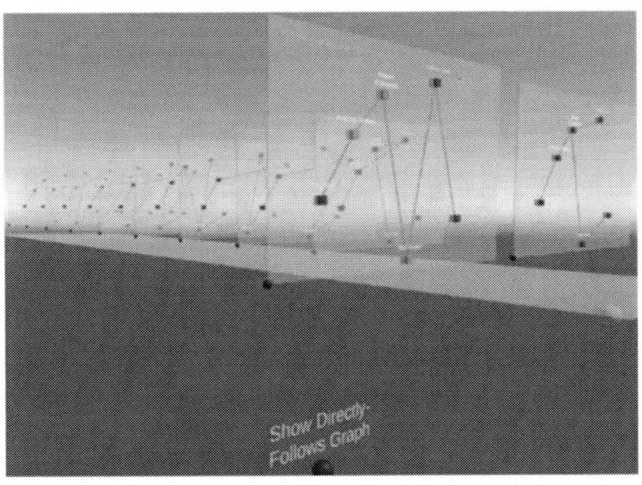

Figure 9. Anchor control for variant comparison or collapsing/expanding.

Plate anchors provide an affordance for flexibly collapsing or moving plates (Figure 9). Via data retrieval from our data hub concept, the VR-Tablet hides the sophisticated PM algorithms within a PM service, making suitable types of PM analysis accessible via the integration of the pm4py library as a service.

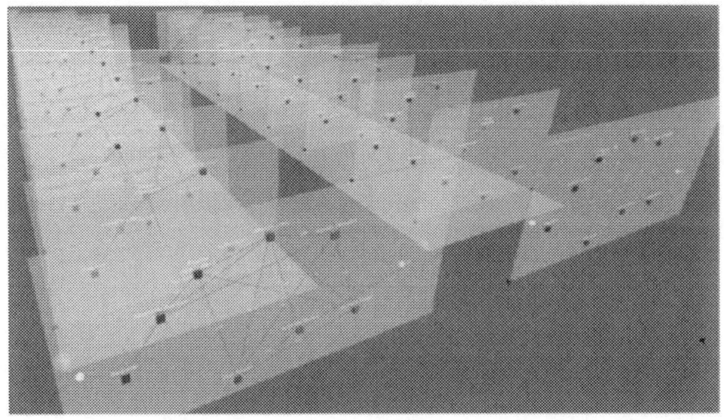

Figure 10. Different processes can be displayed via different hyperplanes.

Furthermore, via the hyperplane concept, our solution can scale to depict a large set of different processes (and their variants) simultaneously, supporting larger cross-process analysis scenarios as seen in Figure 10.

B. Combining PM with other Types of Analysis

Although PM and analysis does provide operational insights, any resulting outcomes typically hinge on some comparison with the original process model (or schema) and potentially other enterprise-relevant knowledge or data. Furthermore, a result of a comparison to a process model may require adjustments to the process model to remove errors or for effectiveness improvements or efficiency optimizations. One advantage of VR's unlimited space is the ability to represent multiple heterogenous models simultaneously and for non-experts to immersively discover and navigate these models.

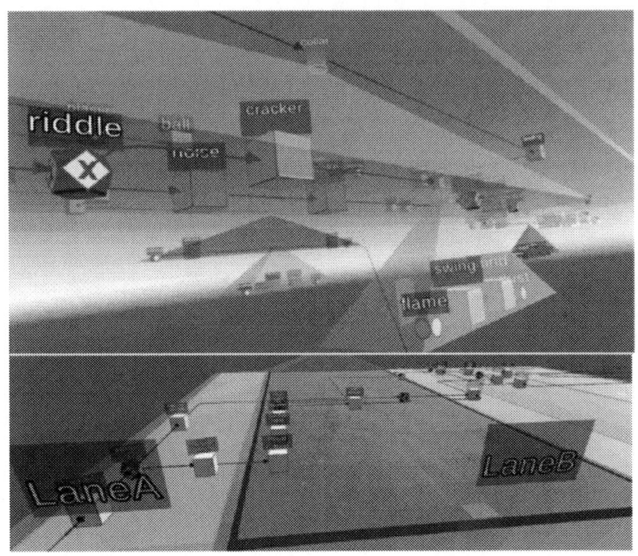

Figure 11. VR-BPMN [4]: subprocesses (top) and swimlanes (bottom) in VR.

Towards combining PM with other analysis types, where BPMN models are available, VR-ProcessMine results can be displayed side-by-side with a VR-BPMN model (Figure 11), allowing non-experts to immersively comprehend various process aspects not necessarily evident via PM, such as subprocesses and swimlanes.

Figure 12. VR-EAT: Enterprise hypermodeling and analysis in VR.

Furthermore, as exemplified with VR-EAT [6], our VR-based heterogeneous hypermodeling capability shown in Figure 12, PM results could be visualized next to other enterprise models, making deeper cross-model and cross-domain analysis readily accessible and allowing operational insights to guide such an analysis.

VI. Conclusion

Increasing digitalization in enterprises and organizations implies that the business and operational processes executed will increasingly also become digitally accessible, offering a significant opportunity. While current PM tools and techniques can provide valuable insights for optimizing (business) processes, these benefits can be hindered when possible insights are not readily accessible to a larger (non-expert) stakeholder set, including those directly involved in performing these processes. VR-ProcessMine contributes an immersive solution concept for visualizing and interacting with PM results in VR. Our realization shows its feasibility, and the case-based evaluation provides insights into its capabilities towards addressing certain challenges described in the Process Mining Manifesto, in particular improving usability, understandability, and the potential to combine PM with other types of analysis.

Future work includes more comprehensive PM analyses, deeper integration with our enterprise hypermodeling VR-EA-TCK and VR-BPMN solution concept, automatic filtering of process variants by a node or transition of interest, collaboration support, and a comprehensive empirical study.

Acknowledgment

The authors would like to thank Laura Berroth for her assistance with the design, implementation, evaluation, and diagrams.

References

[1] Business Process Management Market by Component, Deployment Type, Organization Size, Business Function, Industry, and Region - Global Forecast to 2025. [Online]. Available from: https://www.marketsandmarkets.com/Market-Reports/business-process-management-market-157890056.html 2022.05.10

[2] W. van der Aalst, Process Mining - Data Science in Action, Second Edition. Springer, 2016.

[3] W. V. D. Aalst, et al., "Process Mining Manifesto," In: International Conference on Business Process Management. Springer, Berlin, Heidelberg, 2011, pp. 169-194.

[4] R. Oberhauser, C. Pogolski, and A. Matic, "VR-BPMN: Visualizing BPMN models in Virtual Reality," In: Shishkov, B. (ed.) BMSD 2018. LNBIP, vol. 319, Springer, Cham, 2018, pp. 83–97. https://doi.org/10.1007/978-3-319-94214-8_6

[5] R. Oberhauser and C. Pogolski, "VR-EA: Virtual Reality Visualization of Enterprise Architecture Models with ArchiMate and BPMN," In: Shishkov, B. (ed.) BMSD 2019. LNBIP, vol. 356, Springer, Cham, 2019, pp. 170–187. https://doi.org/10.1007/978-3-030-24854-3_11

[6] R. Oberhauser, P. Sousa, and F. Michel, "VR-EAT: Visualization of Enterprise Architecture Tool Diagrams in Virtual Reality," In: Shishkov B. (eds) Business Modeling and Software Design. BMSD 2020. LNBIP, vol 391, Springer, Cham, 2020, pp. 221-239. https://doi.org/10.1007/978-3-030-52306-0_14

[7] B. F. Van Dongen, A. K. A. de Medeiros, H. Verbeek, A. Weijters, and W. van der Aalst, "The ProM Framework: A new era in Process Mining Tool Support," In: International Conference on Application and Theory of Petri Nets, Springer, 2005, pp. 444–454.

[8] M. La Rosa et al., "APROMORE: An advanced process model repository," Expert Systems with Applications, 38(6), pp.7029-7040, 2011.

[9] A. Berti, S. J. van Zelst, and W. M. P. van der Aalst, "Process Mining for Python (PM4Py): Bridging the Gap Between Process-and Data Science," In: Proceedings of the ICPM Demo Track 2019, co-located with 1st International Conference on Process Mining (ICPM 2019), 2019, pp. 13-16. http://ceur-ws.org/Vol-2374/

[10] J. Vogel and O. Thomas, "Towards a virtual reality-based process elicitation system," 40 Years EMISA 2019. LNI P-304, Gesellschaft für Informatik e.V., 2020, pp. 91-104, ISBN 978-3-88579-698-5

[11] J. J. Roldán, E. Crespo, A. Martín-Barrio, E. Peña-Tapia, and A. Barrientos, "A training system for Industry 4.0 operators in complex assemblies based on virtual reality and process mining," Robotics and computer-integrated manufacturing, 59, 2019, pp.305-316.

[12] R. Müller, P. Kovacs, J. Schilbach, and D. Zeckzer, "How to master challenges in experimental evaluation of 2D versus 3D software visualizations," In: 2014 IEEE VIS International Workshop on 3Dvis (3Dvis), IEEE, 2014, pp. 33-36.

Fake News Identification Using Neural Language Models

Andrew L. Mackey
Computer Science and Computer Engineering
University of Arkansas
Fayetteville, Arkansas, USA
almackey@uark.edu

Susan Gauch
Computer Science and Computer Engineering
University of Arkansas
Fayetteville, Arkansas, USA
sgauch@uark.edu

Jacob Fuller
Computer Science and Computer Engineering
University of Arkansas
Fayetteville, Arkansas, USA
jrf022@uark.edu

Caden Williamson
Computer Science and Computer Engineering
University of Arkansas
Fayetteville, Arkansas, USA
cjw059@uark.edu

Kate Pearce
Bentonville High School
Bentonville, Arkansas, USA
kate.g.pearce@gmail.com

***Abstract*—Given the widespread use of social media and other online platforms for sources of new content, there has been an increased interest in the research community to improve existing methods for automating the detection of fake news content. We present several models for automating the detection of fake news content while utilizing current state-of-the-art neural language models. Our work provides an evaluation of the efficiency of different transformer-based neural language models for the fake news detection task. The evaluation shows that the proposed models are able to maintain high accuracy (98.5%) throughout experimentation tasks. We conclude by discussing the effects of the different neural language models.**

***Index Terms*—Fake news classification; misinformation; neural language models; natural language processing**

I. INTRODUCTION

A growing number of users obtain news from social media platforms and other online sources. According to results from the Pew Research Center, approximately 68% of American adults obtain their information from social media platforms occasionally [23]. There are multiple reasons for why many users prefer these methods of delivery, among which we will find ease of access and discussion-oriented interactions as possible reasons. The growing dependence of these platforms as sources for news has prompted many organizations to take steps increase the reliability of various postings on their sites.

The low barriers to entry with digital platforms facilitate the introduction of fake, deceptive, misleading, or malicious news content to users with relative ease with widespread societal impacts if left unabated. In one case, a single malicious posting to a social media site caused a significant fluctuation in stock market activity [27]. Another major implication has been in election interference where authors post blatantly falsified information to favor a particular political candidate [28]. It should also be noted that not all news information has sinister underlying motivations. Some sources of online news are published with the intent of misleading the reader for entertainment purposes. The consequence of this scenario is some readers may be inadvertently misled to believe it is real.

The task of classifying fake news is often not a binary decision due to the varying degrees in correctness and underlying motivation or intent of deception. For example, a single statement can be factually incorrect, or otherwise inaccurate, thus prompting a discussion for how the document should be classified. Granular-level techniques could be employed to evaluate the truthfulness of statements on a scale rather than using binary levels. An example of this can be found in how PolitiFact ranks comments on a scale [9]. There are many challenges in this task given how minor changes in wording can lead to differences in how correct a statement is.

In this work, we propose a model that leverages state-of-the-art neural language models to automate the detection of fake news to curtail the spread of misinformation. We present an analytic study of advancements in neural language models and their impact on the fake news detection task. Furthermore, we provide empirical evidence that demonstrates how our proposed model leads to improvements in the fake news detection performance. We discuss the efficiency of our proposed model relative to other models with similar goals.

In Section 2, we begin by reviewing previous work conducted over fake news, neural networks, and neural language models. Section 3 presents information over the fake news detection task, the data set used, and our proposed models. Section 4 details the experiments and results described in this work. Section 5 concludes by discussing the significance of the experiments.

II. Related Work

In the following, we consider previous work in the areas of fake news detection and word embeddings.

A. Fake News Detection

Fake news has been an active research area for the past several years across multiple disciplines. We first start by defining fake news as content whereby the authors intend to deceive, or otherwise mislead, readers. Content labeled as fake news can be further divided in different categories: satire, hoax, propaganda, and clickbait. Satirical work is fake news content with some purpose of entertainment, generally through sarcasm or other misinformation [9]. Hoaxes are content whereby the author passes deceptive content as truthful, also with the goal of deception for humor. Propaganda are deceptive content with the goal of causing harm to a specific entity or party. Clickbait is content that attracts users through misleading content.

Fake news detection has a variety of tasks that have been reviewed, such as rumor detection [25], spam detection [26], and emotion analysis of news articles [20]. Fake news detection can also involve text, images, or a combination of both. Automated fake news detection methods usually target biases in the linguistic style of writing and word usage [9]. This typically involves the content of the article, user reactions or responses, or source fo the article [6].

Some authors have also studied the effects of social media, disinformation, and political polarization with public policy-making and quality of democracies [22]. Social media has enabled misleading and/or fake news content to propagate throughout social networks with limited restrictions [10]. It has also been demonstrated the users can have problems differentiating between real and fake content [1] [3]. Furthermore, it may also be difficult to label an article as being real or fake due to nuances in the writing [8].

B. Word Embeddings

Word embeddings [29] are neural language models where words are represented as continuous vector-representations in a dimensional space that is typically reduced in size in comparison to other techniques, such as bag of words methods where feature vectors are often of $|V|$ width, or the size of the lexicon. In the work presented in [21], the authors introduced the Continuous Bag-Of-Words (CBOW) and continuous Skip-gram models as methods for learning distributed vector representations that reflect both syntactic and semantic relationships between words in a language. The CBOW model seeks to predict a word based on the context words. The Skip-gram model was developed to find different word representations that can be used for establishing adjacent words for a given document by maximizing the average log probability where c denotes the size of the window and w_t represents the centralized word:

$$\frac{1}{T}\sum_{t=1}^{T}\sum_{-c<j\leq c,j\neq 0}\log \Pr(w_{t+j} \mid w_t) \tag{1}$$

One major problem identified in the work for the full softmax is its lack of efficiency. The authors in Mikolov et al. [29] thus proposed other techniques that are computationally efficient approximations to the full softmax, such as negative sampling, Noise Contrastive Estimation (NCE), negative sampling, and subsampling.

In subsequent work, the authors in Pennington et al. [5] presented improvements to word embedding representations by constructing a global log-bilinear regression model that combined global matrix factorization and local context windowing techniques. The work from [19] presented bidirectional language models computed over the entire input sentence while jointly maximizing the log likelihood of both the forward and backward directions:

$$\Pr(t_1, t_2, ..., t_N) = \prod_{k=1}^{N} \Pr(t_k \mid t_1, t_2, ..., t_{k-1}) \tag{2}$$

$$\Pr(t_1, t_2, ..., t_N) = \prod_{k=1}^{N} \Pr(t_k \mid t_{k+1}, t_{k+2}, ..., t_N) \tag{3}$$

(4)

The log likelihood of the forward and backward passes is defined by the following where Θ_x is the token representation parameters, Θ_s is the softmax layer parameters, and $\overrightarrow{\Theta}_{\text{LSTM}}$ and $\overleftarrow{\Theta}_{\text{LSTM}}$ are the parameters for the long short-term (LSTM) layers for the forward and backward directions:

$$\sum_{k=1}^{N}\Big[\log\big(\Pr(t_k \mid t_1, ..., t_{k-1} \ ; \ \Theta_x, \overrightarrow{\Theta}_{\text{LSTM}}, \Theta_s\big) \tag{5}$$

$$+\log\big(\Pr(t_k \mid t_{k+1}, ..., t_N \ ; \ \Theta_x, \overleftarrow{\Theta}_{\text{LSTM}}, \Theta_s\big)\Big] \tag{6}$$

Authors from Devlin et al. [13] presented the Bidirectional Encoder Representations from Transformers (BERT) where their approach focuses on bidirectional pre-training while achieving a fine-tuned representation model to reduce or eliminate dependencies on task-specific architectures. The authors also contend that their work improves the work from [19] as prior work concatenated independently trained forward and backward language models whereas BERT implemented deep bidirectional representations.

DeBERTa, which improves upon BERT and RoBERTa models, uses a disentangled attention mechanism [16]. This allows each word to be represented by utilizing two vectors that encode both the content and position. The attention parameters for the tokens are calculated by using disentangled matrices for both the content and relative positions. In addition, DeBERTa incorporates an enhancement to the mask decoder as a substitute for the output softmax layer that allows it to predict the masked tokens for the purpose of pretraining. XLNet, an extension of the Transformer-XL model, is an autoregressive method that learns bidirectional contexts through the maximization of expected likelihood over all permutations of the input sequence factorization order [15]. GPT-J is a neural language model with 6 billion parameters that is an open-source alternative to the GPT-3 model [17] [18].

C. Recurrent Neural Networks

LSTM and Gated Recurrent Unit (GRU) networks are both forms of recurrent neural networks that are capable of processing temporal sequences of data. Both networks are capable of managing the vanishing gradient problem that is commonly found when processing long sequences in traditional recurrent neural networks.

An LSTM cell contains three major gates that attempt to control how information passes into and out of the cell: input gate i, output gate o, and a forget gate f. Let t represent the time step of a sequence such that $t \in [0 \ldots \tau]$. The input gate $\mathbf{i}_t$ at time step t determines what information is relevant and can be added from the previous hidden state $\mathbf{h}_{t-1}$ and the current input $\mathbf{x}_t$. The forget gate $\mathbf{f}_t$ is used to decide which information will be be utilized and which information will be forgotten (or ignored) at time step t. Lastly, the output gate $\mathbf{o}_t$ is used for determining the values of the next hidden state $\mathbf{h}_t$. An LSTM maintains cell state for both the short-term and long-term. The short-term is denoted as h and the long-term is denoted as c, noting that $\mathbf{c}_{t=0} = \begin{bmatrix}0 & 0 & \cdots & 0\end{bmatrix}$ and $\mathbf{h}_{t=0} = \begin{bmatrix}0 & 0 & \cdots & 0\end{bmatrix}$.

$$\mathbf{f}_t = \sigma(\mathbf{W}_f \mathbf{x}_t + \mathbf{U}_f \mathbf{h}_{t-1} + \mathbf{b}_f) \tag{7}$$
$$\mathbf{i}_t = \sigma(\mathbf{W}_i \mathbf{x}_t + \mathbf{U}_i \mathbf{h}_{t-1} + \mathbf{b}_i) \tag{8}$$
$$\mathbf{o}_t = \sigma(\mathbf{W}_o \mathbf{x}_t + \mathbf{U}_o \mathbf{h}_{t-1} + \mathbf{b}_o) \tag{9}$$
$$\widetilde{\mathbf{c}}_t = \tanh(\mathbf{W}_c \mathbf{x}_t + \mathbf{U}_c \mathbf{h}_{t-1} + \mathbf{b}_c) \tag{10}$$
$$\mathbf{c}_t = \mathbf{f}_t \odot \mathbf{c}_{t-1} + \mathbf{i}_t \odot \widetilde{\mathbf{c}}_t \tag{11}$$
$$\mathbf{h}_t = \mathbf{o}_t \odot \tanh(\mathbf{c}_t) \tag{12}$$

The two activation functions used are the sigmoid activation function $\sigma(x)$ and hyperbolic tangent function $\tanh(x)$. The range of values for both activation functions differ with $\sigma(x) \in [0, 1]$ and $\tanh(x) \in [-1, 1]$. The operator $\odot$ denotes the Hadamard product. The input vector $\mathbf{x}_t$ is defined as $\mathbf{x}_t \in \mathbb{R}^d$ where d denotes the number of input features. The hidden state vector $\mathbf{h}_t$ is defined as $\mathbf{h}_t \in (-1, 1)^h$.

GRU cells are similar to LSTM cells, but with simplifications while maintaining comparable performance. There are several notable differences between GRU and LSTM cells. First, an LSTM maintains two state vectors for c and h; a GRU cell maintains a single vector h for state. In addition, a GRU maintains an update gate $\mathbf{z}_t$ that controls for both the forget gate and input gate, and a reset gate $\mathbf{r}_t$ which is responsible for the short-term memory $\mathbf{h}_t$.

Recurrent layers generally look at the previous and current time steps to produce an output without any intuition about future time steps. In some situations, it may be advantageous to gather context for inputs at a given time step. Consider the situation of word embeddings. A token at time step t may require information from previous and future time steps. A simple solution to this is to implement a *bidirectional recurrent layer* which implements two recurrent layers and finally combine the outputs of each layer at each time step t (generally this is performed through concatenation): one recurrent layer that iterates in the order of $\{t = 0, t = 1, t = 2, ..., t = n\}$, and another recurrent layer that iterates in the reverse order of $\{t = n, t = n-1, t = n-2, ..., t = 1\}$. Bidirectional recurrent layers can be applied to standard recurrent units, LSTM units, or GRUs.

D. Attention

Attention mechanisms were introduced by [24] for the task of neural machine translation. Their work extended the basic encoder-decoder models and allowed for decoders to have an attention mechanism so encoders are not required to encode all information into fixed-length vectors. This attention layer, or *alignment model*, is capable of focusing on features at each time step that are important, which is trained jointly with the encoder-decoder model. The following conditional probability was proposed where s_i represents the hidden state of the RNN for time step i, y_i represent the target word, and c_i represents the context vector:

$$p(y_i \mid y_1, ..., y_{i-1}, \mathbf{x}) = g(y_{i-1}, s_i, c_i) \tag{13}$$

$$s_i = f(s_{i-1}, y_{i-1}, c_i) \tag{14}$$

The context vector c_i is computed from a the sequence of annotations h_i as $\langle h_1, h_2, \cdots, h_{T_x} \rangle$ which is produced by an encoder from a given input sentence. The context vector c_i is constructed as a weighted sum between the annotations h_i and the weights of annotation α_{ij}, where e_{ij} represents the alignment model with scores that measure how well the output aligns with the previous hidden state of the decoder (where a represents a feedforward neural network):

$$c_i = \sum_{j=1}^{T_x} \alpha_{ij} h_j \qquad \alpha_{ij} = \frac{\exp(e_{ij})}{\sum_{k=1}^{T_x} \exp(e_{ik})} \tag{15}$$

$$e_{ij} = a(s_{i-1}, h_j) \tag{16}$$

It is important to note that a is jointly trained with the model. In addition, the sum of all weights α_{ij} for a given time step will have a sum of 1. Other work has been proposed to use multiplicative attention with other simplifications that improve on concatenative attention.

III. Fake News Detection

A. Dataset

In our experiments, we used the publicly available dataset from [9]. The dataset contains different news articles obtained from seven different fake, or otherwise unreliable, news sites, including The Onion, The Borowitz Report, Clickhole, American News, DC Gazette, The Natural News, and Activist Report. Each of the news articles are labeled as being *satire*, *hoax*, *propaganda*, or *trusted*. The trusted news articles were obtained from [11]. In the trusted news articles data source, the authors constructed an approach to building a supervised reading comprehension dataset with news articles obtained from convolutional neural networks ($n = 90,266$). Our experiments extracted $n = 10,000$ randomly selected news articles from the set of possible $90,266$ different articles available in the CNN dataset.

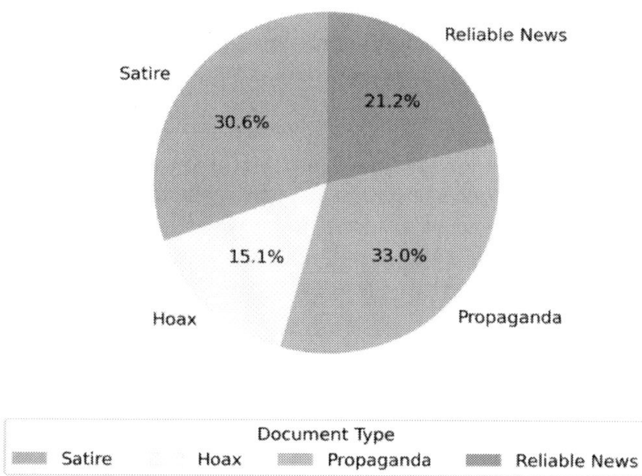

Fig. 1. The distribution of the dataset used for classification is presented by the news article type.

TABLE I
News articles with number of documents, average document lengths, and median document lengths

Doc. Type	# of Docs	Avg. Tokens	Med. Tokens
Satire	$13,942$	206 ± 177	105
Hoax	$6,892$	141 ± 122	109
Propaganda	$15,061$	587 ± 808	458
Trusted	$9,681$	428 ± 205	401

Table I summarizes the type of news articles, document frequencies, mean document lengths and standard deviations, and median document lengths. News articles from the propaganda class have a higher average number of tokens than other classes. When considering the robustness of the statistical measures to control for outliers, the median of the propaganda class is marginally higher than the trusted class. All data is preprocessed using standard natural language preprocessing techniques, including downcasing, stopword removal, tokenization, etc. We utilize the NLTK toolkit [1] for computational linguistic analysis. The overall distribution of the data can be seen in Figure I.

B. Models

Our experiments evaluate different neural network models and word embeddings for the fake news detection task. We construct five baseline models that are developed with an embedding layer, which is a trainable dense vector that can be used to represent each unique word in the lexicon. The first model contains a single embedding layer, two LSTM layers, an attention layer, and a classification segment comprised of two dense layers, and an output layer with a softmax activation function having a number of neurons corresponding to the number of output classes. Dropout is also added to mitigate the possible situation of overfitting. Attention layers are used to determine which parts of the data have greater importance than other parts through a separate alignment model. This alignment model is trained jointly with the other parts of the network.

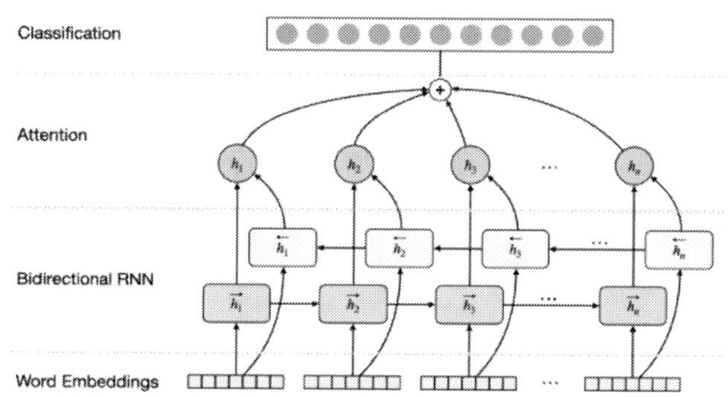

Fig. 2. The proposed recurrent neural network model for our experiments uses a bidirectional network with an attention layer.

The next several models are constructed from the original model with modifications to the sequence processing layers. The second model uses bidirectional LSTM) layers so that both the forward and backward sequences are concatenated and learned during the training phase (see Figure 2). The third model considers the use of GRU in place of LSTM layers. The forth model is constructed from bidirectional GRU layers.

The final model is constructed by using a convolutional neural network (CNN) on the sequences of data. We implement a stack of $1D$-convolutional layers, batch normalization, and ReLU activation layers. The batch normalization layer centers and scales the activation vectors from the hidden layers of the current batch by using the mean and variance. We implement dropout in the model to prevent overfitting. A global max pooling layer is added, which returns the maximum value

[1] https://www.nltk.org/

for each feature channel. Finally, a set of fully connected layers are added followed by a layer with a softmax activation function with the number of units corresponding to the number of $\hat{\mathbf{y}}$ target classes such that $\hat{y} \in \{\text{fake}, \text{real}\}$.

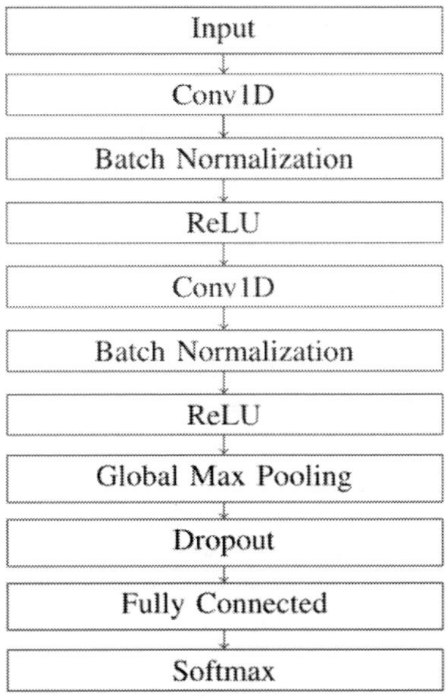

Fig. 3. 1-D convolutional neural network (CNN) model

Each of the documents were converted to sequences of word embeddings. For our baseline model, we assigned a unique integer to each token and implemented a standard word embedding layer with 128 dimensions. To evaluate the performance of various word embedding methods, we compare our baseline model to word embeddings produced by BERT, DeBERTa, XLNet, and GPT-J. The BERT embeddings contained a total of $L = 12$ hidden layers with a hidden size of $H = 128$ and $A = 2$ attention heads. We used the V2-XLarge DeBERTa pre-trained model with a $128,000$ vocabulary, 710 million parameters, hidden size of $H = 1536$, and $L = 24$ hidden layers. XLNet contains $L = 12$ hidden layers, hidden size of $H = 768$, and $A = 12$ attention heads.

For all models, the batch size was set to 64 and we implemented early stopping criteria to limit potential overfitting. We utilize the Adam optimization algorithm and a categorical cross-entropy loss function for this multi-class classification task. A learning rate of 0.001 was used. Each experiment was conducted from training, testing, and validation splits of sizes 0.7, 0.2, and 0.1, respectively. For each of the performance metrics reported, the mean of each experiment is reported from 10 random shuffles of the data.

In our experimentation tasks, we evaluated multiple neural network models, including LSTM, GRU, bidirectional recurrent neural networks (both LSTM and GRU), and 1D convolutional neural networks. Each document is represented in the training set as a set of fixed-length word embeddings formed by utilizing one of the techniques described previously. To ensure that each document contains the same number of features, we padded all documents that where the number of tokens is less than specified sequence length ($|d| < we_{\text{size}}$). Similarly, any document that exceeds the word embedding length ($|d| > we_{\text{size}}$) is right-truncated.

IV. Evaluation

Having presented models for the task of identifying fake news, we present our evaluations of the models using the data described in earlier sections. Our hypothesis is that the fake news detection task can be improved by leveraging state-of-the-art neural language model representations and improved neural network architectures.

Our first task is to establish which neural language model representations work best for the task of automating fake news detection. For this requirement, we used the model architecture as presented previously with LSTM layers, an attention layer, and a classification segment. We compared embedding layers, BERT, XLNet, DeBERTA, and GPT-J for each of the documents in the training and testing sets. Based on our experiments, the BERT neural language model outperforms the other methods with a mean accuracy of 98.1%. While other methods have additional model parameters, attention mechanisms, and other improvements to their models, they do not seem to outperform BERT for this specific task. In addition, the training time for BERT was faster in the amount of training time required when compared to the others. We conclude that BERT achieves both the best results and fastest training time.

TABLE II
Comparison of Neural Language Models

Method	Accuracy	Precision	Recall	F1
WE+LSTM	0.978	0.979	0.977	0.978
BERT+LSTM	**0.981**	**0.981**	**0.981**	**0.981**
XLNet+LSTM	0.956	0.956	0.956	0.956
DeBERTa+LSTM	0.960	0.960	0.959	0.960
GPTJ+LSTM	0.971	0.971	0.971	0.971

In our next experiments, we present our evaluation of the neural network architectures as presented in earlier with the top performing neural language model from the aforementioned experiments. The work presented in [20] achieved a 76.3% accuracy using a feed forward neural network architecture with BERT for document-level embeddings. We establish this as a baseline model for our experiments. Our experimental design evaluates the performance of documents converted to sequences from the neural language models as input to the neural network models that carry out the fake news classification. Previous work emphasized document-level embeddings whereas we focus on sequences of embeddings from transformer architectures.

The results presented in Table III demonstrate the accuracy for each of the models using the BERT neural language model.

TABLE III
COMPARISON OF BASELINE METHODS WITH BERT AND NEURAL NETWORK MODELS

Type	Method	Accuracy	Precision	Recall	F1
BASELINE	BERT+NN	0.763	0.798	0.721	0.757
MODELS	BERT+LSTM	0.981	0.981	0.981	0.981
	BERT+BiLSTM	**0.985**	**0.985**	**0.985**	**0.985**
	BERT+GRU	0.982	0.982	0.982	0.982
	BERT+BiGRU	0.983	0.983	0.983	0.984
	BERT+ConvNet	0.972	0.972	0.972	0.972

The BERT+BiLSTM model achieved the highest accuracy and was constructed by using bidirectional LSTM layers. It should also be noted that the BERT+BiGRU model is relatively comparable to the top performing model while using layers with fewer gates. The BERT+ConvNet model achieved a mean accuracy slightly lower than the LSTM and GRU models. All experimental models outperform the baseline models we defined earlier, which highlights the benefits of using sequences of inputs from neural language models for the fake news detection task.

TABLE IV
EVALUATION OF NEURAL LANGUAGE MODELS AND NETWORK ARCHITECTURES

Model	BERT	XLNet	DeBERTa	GPTJ	Average
LSTM	0.981	0.956	0.960	0.971	0.967
BiLSTM	**0.985**	0.955	0.974	0.970	0.971
GRU	0.982	0.962	0.973	0.973	**0.973**
BiGRU	0.983	0.955	0.962	0.971	0.968
ConvNet	0.972	0.947	0.958	0.959	0.959
Average	**0.981**	0.955	0.965	0.969	0.967

Our final task is to compare the mean performance of model architectures and neural language models. Table IV provides the mean accuracy for each neural network architecture and neural language model. As previously mentioned, the top performing neural language model for our experiments was BERT. However, the top performing model, on average, was obtained from the model that leverages layers using the GRU, which is marginally higher than BiLSTM.

The proposed BERT+BiLSTM model using sequences as input was able to achieve a 22.2% increase over the baseline BERT+NN model, which leverages document-level neural language model outputs as inputs to the model. Similarly, leveraging GRU layers with all neural language models achieves a 21% improvement while requiring less parameters than the BiLSTM layer. The mean performance for all proposed models using BERT and sequences as input achieved 98% accuracy, which is an improvement of 21.8%. Finally, leveraging sequences as inputs for all propose architectures and neural language models had a mean score of 96.7%, which was a 20.4% increase over the baseline.

The experiments presented here demonstrate the ability of recurrent neural networks when combined with state-of-the-art word embeddings to facilitate the classification of fake news. Our results also demonstrate that the additional training time and overhead required for some word embeddings do not necessarily yield better classification results for the fake news classification task as indicated in our experiments. Furthermore, more complex architectures for neural language models may improve semantic and syntactic understandings or relationships between words, but additional training data may be necessary to fully exploit these capabilities.

V. CONCLUSION AND FUTURE WORK

We presented a comparative analysis of various state-of-the-art methods for neural language models and neural network architectures for the fake news detection task. Our proposed BiLSTM+BERT model was able to achieve a 98.5% accuracy, which is an improvement over the baseline model. This demonstrates the effectiveness of bidirectional LSTM layers when combined with BERT for automating the classification of fake news articles. Given that the research continues to improve neural language models, future work will need to evaluate improvements in this space to determine how we can efficiently represent documents with the same model performance or improve upon the current model performance.

REFERENCES

[1] M. Barthel, A. Mitchel, and J. Holcomb, Many americans believe fake news is sowing confusion, *Pew Research Center*, 2016.
[2] R. Collobert, J. Weston, L. Bottou, M. Karlen, K. Kavukcuoglu, and P. Kuksa, "Natural language processing (almost) from scratch," *Journal of machine learning research*, 12(ARTICLE): pp. 2493–2537, 2011.
[3] C. Domonoske, Students have 'dismaying' inability to tell fake news from real, study finds, *National Public Radio*, 23, 2016.
[4] T. Mikolov, K. Chen, G. Corrado, and J. Dean, Efficient estimation of word representations in vector space, *arXiv preprint arXiv:1301.3781*, 2013.
[5] J. Pennington, R. Socher, and C. Manning, "Glove: Global vectors for word representation," In *Proceedings of the 2014 conference on empirical methods in natural language processing (EMNLP)*, pp. 1532–1543, 2014.

[6] N. Ruchansky, S. Seo, and Y. Liu, "Csi: A hybrid deep model for fake news detection," In *Proceedings of the 2017 ACM on Conference on Information and Knowledge Management*, pp. 797–806, 2017.
[7] K. Shu, L. Cui, S. Wang, D. Lee, and H. Liu, "defend: Explainable fake news detection," In *Proceedings of the 25th ACM SIGKDD International Conference on Knowledge Discovery & Data Mining*, pp. 395–405, 2019.
[8] K. Shu, A. Sliva, S. Wang, J. Tang, and H. Liu, "Fake news detection on social media: A data mining perspective," *ACM SIGKDD explorations newsletter*, 19(1): pp. 22–36, 2017.
[9] H. Rashkin, E. Choi, J. Jang, S. Volkova, and Y. Choi, "Truth of varying shades: analyzing language in fake news and political fact-checking," *Proceedings of the 2017 Conference on Empirical Methods in Natural Language Processing*, pp. 2931–2937, 2017.
[10] C. Castillo, M. Mendoza, and B. Poblete, "Information credibility on twitter," *Proceedings of the 20th international conference on World wide web*, pp. 675–684, 2011.
[11] K. Hermann, T. Kocisky, E. Grefenstette, L. Espeholt, W. Kay, M. Suleyman, and P. Blunsom, Teaching machines to read and comprehend, 2015.
[12] Q. Le and T. Mikolov, Distributed representations of sentences and documents, 2014.
[13] J. Devlin, M. Chang, K. Lee, and K. Toutanova, Bert: Pre-training of deep bidirectional transformers for language understanding, *arXiv preprint* 2018.
[14] X. Zhou and R. Zafarani, A survey of fake news: fundamental theories, detection methods, and opportunities, *ACM Comput. Surv* 2020.
[15] Z. Yang, Z. Dai, Y. Yang, J. Carbonell, R. Salakhutdinov, and Q. Le, XLNet: Generalized Autoregressive Pretraining for Language Understanding, arXiv:1906.08237, 2019.
[16] P. He, Z. Liu, J. Gao, and W. Chen, DeBERTa: Decoding-enhanced BERT with Disentangled Attention, arXiv:2006.03654, 2020.
[17] T. Brown et al, Language Models are Few-Shot Learners, arXiv:2005.14165, 2020,
[18] B. Wang and A. Komatsuzaki, GPT-J-6B: A 6 Billion Parameter Autoregressive Language Model, https://github.com/kingoflolz/mesh-transformer-jax, 2021.
[19] M. Peters et al, Deep contextualized word representations, *arXiv* 2014.
[20] A. Mackey, S. Gauch, and K. Labille, "Detecting Fake News Through Emotion Analysis," *eKNOW* 2021.
[21] T. Mikolov, K. Chen, G. Corrado, and J. Dean, Efficient estimation of word representations in vector space, *arXiv preprint arXiv:1301.3781* 2013.
[22] J. Tucker, et al, "Social media, political polarization, and political disinformation: A review of the scientific literature," *Political polarization, and political disinformation: a review of the scientific literature (March 19, 2018)* 2018.
[23] E. Shearer, More than eight-in-ten Americans get news from Digital Devices, *Pew Research Center*, 2021.
[24] D. Bahdanau, K. Cho, and Y. Bengio, Neural machine translation by jointly learning to align and translate, *arXiv preprint arXiv:1409.0473* 2014.
[25] Z. Jin, J. Cao, Y. Jiang, and Y. Zhang, "News credibility evaluation on microblog with a hierarchical propagation model," *2014 IEEE international Conference on Data Mining*, pp. 230–239,2014.
[26] H. Shen, F. Ma, X. Zhang, L. Zong, X. Liu, and W. Liang, "Discovering social spammers from multiple views," *Neurocomputing*, pp. 49–57,2017.
[27] C. Matthews. How does one fake tweet cause a stock market crash?, *Time*, 2013.
[28] H. Parkinson. Click and elect: How fake news helped Donald Trump win a real election, *The Guardian*, 2016.
[29] T. Mikolov, I. Sutskever, K. Chen, G. Corrado, and J. Dean, "Distributed representations of sentences and documents," *Advances in neural information processing systems*, 2013.

TABLE V
FAKE NEWS CLASSIFICATION METHODS WITH EACH OF THE PROPOSED MODELS

Type	Method	Accuracy	Precision	Recall	F1
BASELINE	WE+LSTM	0.978	0.979	0.977	0.978
	WE+BiLSTM	0.979	0.979	0.979	0.979
	WE+GRU	0.977	0.977	0.977	0.977
	WE+BiGRU	0.976	0.976	0.976	0.977
	WE+ConvNet	0.966	0.968	0.965	0.967
LSTM	BERT+LSTM	0.981	0.981	0.981	0.981
	XLNet+LSTM	0.956	0.956	0.956	0.956
	DeBERTa+LSTM	0.960	0.960	0.959	0.960
	GPTJ+LSTM	0.971	0.971	0.971	0.971
BILSTM	BERT+BiLSTM	0.985	0.985	0.985	0.985
	XLNet+BiLSTM	0.955	0.955	0.955	0.955
	DeBERTa+BiLSTM	0.974	0.974	0.973	0.974
	GPTJ+BiLSTM	0.970	0.970	0.969	0.969
GRU	BERT+GRU	0.982	0.982	0.982	0.982
	XLNet+GRU	0.962	0.963	0.962	0.963
	DeBERTa+GRU	0.973	0.973	0.972	0.972
	GPTJ+GRU	0.973	0.973	0.973	0.973
BIGRU	BERT+BiGRU	0.983	0.983	0.983	0.984
	XLNet+BiGRU	0.955	0.956	0.955	0.956
	DeBERTa+BiGRU	0.962	0.963	0.962	0.962
	GPTJ+BiGRU	0.971	0.971	0.971	0.971
CONVNET	BERT+ConvNet	0.972	0.972	0.972	0.972
	XLNet+ConvNet	0.947	0.948	0.946	0.947
	DeBERTa+ConvNet	0.958	0.960	0.957	0.959
	GPTJ+ConvNet	0.959	0.959	0.959	0.959
AVERAGE		0.969	0.970	0.969	0.970

International Academy, Research, and Industry Association (IARIA)
412 Derby Way
Wilmington, DE 19810

ISBN 978-1-7138-6953-5

CURRAN ASSOCIATES INC.
proceedings.com

Tenth International Conference on Sensor Technologies and Applications (SENSORCOMM 2016)

Held at NetWare 2016

Nice, France
24 - 28 July 2016

IARIA